WTF?!

WTF?!

An Economic Tour of the Weird

Peter T. Leeson

STANFORD ECONOMICS AND FINANCE

An Imprint of Stanford University Press • Stanford, California

Stanford University Press
Stanford, California

Special discounts for bulk quantities of books in the Stanford Economics and Finance imprint are available to corporations, professional associations, and other organizations. For details and discount information, contact the special sales department of Stanford University Press. Tel: (650) 725-0820, Fax: (650) 725-3457

Printed in the United States of America on acid-free, archival-quality paper

Library of Congress Cataloging-in-Publication Data

Names: Leeson, Peter T., author.
Title: WTF?! : an economic tour of the weird / Peter T. Leeson.
Description: Stanford, California : Stanford Economics and Finance, an
    imprint of Stanford University Press, 2017. | Includes bibliographical
    references and index.
Identifiers: LCCN 2017015546 (print) | LCCN 2017017380 (ebook) |
    ISBN 9781503604490 (e-book) | ISBN 9781503600911 (cloth : alk. paper)
Subjects: LCSH: Manners and customs. | Economics. | Rational choice theory.
Classification: LCC GT95 (ebook) | LCC GT95 .L44 2017 (print) | DDC 390--dc23
LC record available at https://lccn.loc.gov/2017015546

Cover design by Christian Fuenfhausen
Typeset by Bruce Lundquist in 11/15 Adobe Garamond

For Stephanie, Mark, and Brenna

Precisely because the tyranny of opinion is such as to make eccentricity a reproach, it is desirable, in order to break through that tyranny, that people should be eccentric.

John Stuart Mill, On Liberty, *1859*

Tour Stops

Waiting in the Lobby

"Weird" is how we describe things that don't make sense to us—from Donald Trump's presidential victory to modern-day witch trials in Ghana to Kim Jong-un's haircut. Contemporary life is overflowing with weirdness. And yet historical life is weirder still. Consider human sacrifice among the Aztecs, self-immolation in eighteenth-century India, love magic in ancient Greece, cargo cults in midcentury Melanesia. On and on it goes.[1] It's easy to get the feeling that life might be an unwitting tour of one big odditorium, that "Ripley's Believe It or Not!" is everywhere you turn.

Confronted with life's weirdness, curious people wonder, "Why?" I developed the tour on which you're about to embark for just such people. "Don't you mean book?" you're wondering. No, I mean tour. You're sitting in a museum lobby, and I'm your guide. We'll get there in a minute. But first, let me speak to why we're gathered here.

To honor the grandest museum of oddities, our world, I decided some years ago that I wanted to showcase the weirdest practices that human history has to offer. What better way to share my exhibits than through an interactive tour? And thus began the construction of my museum of social oddities, bound up in the pages of this "book" but also reaching back into the depths of time and unfolding before you as you read.

The tour has eight stops. Just beyond the velvet rope, a few pages from here, is the first. That one isn't an exhibit; actually it's more of a preparatory station: you're going to encounter some strange shit in this museum, so I want to make sure that you have the tools to handle it. The other stops are par for the museum course.

First, we'll look at trial by fire and water in medieval Europe. Next, wife selling in Industrial Revolution England. At the following stop, Gypsy superstitions. Then a brief intermission about cursing monks in eleventh-century Francia. We'll look at oracular divination in twentieth-century Africa. Then on to the prosecution of insects and rodents in Renaissance France, Italy, and Switzerland. At our final stop, you'll hear about judicial combat in Norman England. Now please squeeze together and make room for the incoming patrons. I hope you weren't expecting a private tour (that would be much more expensive). You look like a lively bunch.

Turning to me, your guide: I'm an economist by training but a collector of *curiosa* by, well, curiosity. Upon encountering a weird social practice I wonder, "Why?" But behind my wonder lies an openness to the possibility—a presumption, even—that there's a good reason for whatever it is; there's sense in the seemingly senseless, I believe. And so I've found it to be in the decade I've been studying the specimens you're about to encounter—and so many more.

I've found that people—all of them, regardless of time or place, religion or culture, wealth, poverty, or anything else—are rational. To be rational, as I see it, means simply to pursue your goals as best you can given your limitations and the limitations of your environment. In this form at least, the claim that people are rational isn't one that most will find hard to accept. Yet the immediate and certain implication is that people don't do senseless things.

One of this tour's purposes is to show you that what seems like senseless behavior actually makes sense, and thus what seems like irrationality is actually *rational*. Weird social institutions strike you as weird because you're unfamiliar with the constraints that the people who developed them confront. But once you step into those people's shoes and look at their worlds through their eyes, it's easy to see that very unconventional practices reflect the canny pursuit of very conventional goals—ones with which perfectly rational folks like yourself can commune.

If people are rational and rational people don't do senseless things, it's not a step much further to conclude that the weird social practices people engage in are often good for their societies; they make them better off. Practices that make people worse off aren't likely to survive. Which brings me to this tour's second purpose: to show you how even seemingly senseless social practices can be, and often are, *socially productive*.

A particular approach to analyzing human behavior—the economic approach, or what's sometimes called rational choice theory— is the perfect tool for accomplishing these goals because it starts, as I do, from the presumption that people are rational. After we leave the lobby, I won't explicitly discuss rational choice theory again apart from brief mentions at the tour's first and last stops. I suspect most of you, quite reasonably, don't care about this theory per se. What you care about is finding compelling answers to the whys that accost your mind when you encounter weird behavior. Why can't you get full service at a gas station anywhere—except New Jersey and Oregon, where you're forced to get it? Why is it harder to find good oranges at a grocery store in Florida than in Michigan? Why do you have to take out a second mortgage on your house if you want to shave with a halfway decent razor? And that brings me to this tour's final purpose: to help you learn how to apply rational choice theory in your everyday life.

It can help you answer all of the questions I've just posed—and many more. In fact, if that theory were a physical device, it might be called the Incredible Answering Machine—not because it fields missed phone calls but because it can answer any "Why?" question about human behavior that life might throw at you. If rational choice theory were a physical device, it probably would've been hailed as one of humanity's greatest inventions—right along with your iPhone.

I stand before you a man transformed. I started my own journey into the world of social oddities wondering why it is that for centuries, criminal justice systems decided defendants' guilt or innocence by asking them to plunge their arms into boiling water. I ended it concluding that shaking a poisoned chicken to decide how to behave toward your neighbors can be very wise. I have the answers. So if you're wondering "Why?" follow me. If you're not, check your pulse.

1

Your Favorite Acronym

"WTF?!" in its fully articulated glory, is probably one of your favorite exclamations. You say it often and think it more often still.

"WTF?!" captures the combination of bewilderment, astonishment, and perplexity you feel when you experience something unexpected, disconcerting, and, well, weird.

You realize that sea-monkeys have no relation whatsoever to actual monkeys.

"WTF?!"

Mr. Peanut's doppelganger just stole your purse.

"WTF?!"

Marzipan.

"WTF?!"

Welcome, officially, to *WTF?!* the economic tour of the weird that will make you say "WTF?!" Our museum of social oddities is stocked with human practices certain to shock and amaze. Whether you're a gorehound or a romantic, antiquarian or modernist, saint, sinner, animal lover, or anything in between, we've got something just for you.

I hope you didn't come expecting ephemera, though. Our museum houses no fleeting fripperies or frivolous flashes in the pan. The bizarre practices you'll find exhibited here lasted for centuries—some are still in use—and were, or are, central to organizing humanity's most important social affairs.

Remember me from the lobby? I'm Pete, your tour guide, here to help you find your way literally and figuratively through the museum.

The museum itself is a bit of a maze; you can thank the zoning board for that. But I know every nook and cranny, so I'll get you where you need to go.

As to the social practices on exhibit: they're going to seem . . . bat-shit crazy. My goal is to help you see the sense in their seeming senselessness.

To that end, before we get started, let me give you this tool you're going to need.

[begins distributing tiny slips of paper to the crowd]

[*The patrons, looking at the slips, have puzzled looks on their faces; irritated, one of them interrupts.*]

"My card just says 'Rational choice theory' on it."

They all do. You may not have been paying attention as we gathered in the lobby. Or maybe some of you were late. But that's your tool. With it, and a bit of assistance from me, "WTF?!" will morph into, "That's reasonable," before your very eyes!

[*An exasperated patron blurts:*]

"WTF?!"

Your new tool is incredibly simple to use, so simple it's sometimes unkindly likened to a hammer by people who've been trained to operate unnecessarily complicated contraptions. Pay no mind to such trash talkers. They're just jealous, and like my hammer, this tool has always worked just fine for me.

Now, let's read the instruction manual. Please turn over your slips.

[*The crowd members turn over their pieces of paper. The irritated patron from before interjects:*]

"Mine just says, 'Think in terms of incentives.'"

I told you it was simple to use.

Incentives are the reason you go to work on days when you'd rather stay home or the reason you're playing hooky right now. Why you paid to get into this museum instead of sneaking in—right? And why the fine folks at the Department of Motor Vehicles take their sweet, sweet time: I'll just take my auto registration business elsewhere! Oh, wait.

Incentives are shorthand for the relationship between benefits and costs, which attend every choice you make. The benefit of a choice you make is the value you expect to get from it. The cost is the value you expect to give up by making that choice. The larger your benefit is of making some choice relative to your cost, the stronger your incentive is to make it, so the more likely you will, and vice versa. Incentives are the reason you're more likely to moon a stranger for $1,000 than for a nickel, forget to feed your goldfish as opposed to your son, or eat pie over poop—paleo dieters notwithstanding.

"Rules"—those pesky principles governing what's permissible and what's not, stipulating rewards or penalties for your compliance or noncompliance—affect your incentives. Rules can come from your government, employer, society, dominatrix. No matter their source, since they affect the benefits and costs of your choices, rules affect what you choose.

Suppose the government, in an effort to prevent this tour's subversive message from getting out, began enforcing a new rule: "Anyone who takes the *WTF?!* tour will be summarily executed by officers of the law." The incentives affecting your choice to be here would be very different than they are right now. Unless you're extremely enlightened, you'd see the new cost of taking this tour as larger than the benefit, so you wouldn't. But if, in an uncharacteristic moment of good judgment, the government announced that everyone who takes this tour will be exempt from paying taxes for the next decade, the museum would become much more crowded. Different rules, different incentives, hence different choices.

Rules have a cousin: "constraints." Whereas rules govern what's permissible, constraints govern what's possible. You'd like to buy a new

Ferrari, but your net worth is $5,000; your wealth is a constraint. You'd like to make a living as a carnival barker, but you're a mute; your physiology is a constraint. You'd like to be able to read people's minds, but the laws of physics won't allow it; physics, a constraint.

The benefit of these things may be enormous, but the cost is infinite. Thus, constraints also affect your choices—by placing certain ones out of your reach.

The rules we create to incentivize people to make certain choices are themselves choices. Suppose that instead of trying to prevent you from taking this tour using the rule that I mentioned before, the government tried to do so with this one: "Anyone who takes the *WTF?!* tour will be summarily executed by invisible fairies." How would this rule affect your choice to be here? It wouldn't. The reason: presumably you don't believe in invisible-fairy executioners.

The government might prefer to use this kind of rule to affect your incentives; it would certainly save the expense of hiring officers of the law to do the executing. Never mind the gore. But your belief or, rather, disbelief is a constraint that precludes the government from doing so.

What, then, can the government do? Choose an alternative kind of rule: one in which you'll believe. It's not as enticing as invisible fairies, but this kind of rule has the distinct advantage of actually deterring you from our delightful tour. Of course, any number of cases are possible: government may not exist (conspiracy theorists, hold on a minute), but people may believe that invisible fairies do. In such circumstances, the constraints are very different; hence, so too are the kinds of rules that are chosen to incentivize behavior. Get it?

The "WTF?!"-worthy practices you're going to encounter as we make our way through the museum work the same way. They create rules that affect the benefits and costs of choices for the people who live under them, their incentives. And those rules reflect the existence of particular constraints in particular contexts. If, like detectives, we can sniff out the incentives, rules, and constraints inherent in every social practice, my dear Watsons, we'll have seen the sense in it.

Once you get in the habit of thinking about things in this way, it's easy. With your new tool, the remarkable, alien, and insane become mundane, familiar, and reasonable. Your bewilderment, astonishment, and perplexity become clarity, common sense, even glee.

The lessons you'll learn dissecting the world's weirdest practices on this tour will serve you long after you've walked through the exit, back into the weirdness of your everyday life.

Why does the Forest Service enlist the assistance of a cartoon bear to prevent you from committing arson? Why does American currency presumptuously declare, "In God You Trust"? Why does your uncle toss a coin to settle arguments with your aunt? Why does your religion have a say in your diet? And Santa Claus, of all "people," why does he care whether you're naughty or nice?

The answers to such questions are right in front of you—you just have to know how to see them. The power to do so is in the palm of your hands, so put that slip of paper in your pocket and follow me. I think you're ready.

At the next stop, you'll find our first exhibit. Try to stay with the group, but in case you get lost, a few directions: if you see a cycloptic dachshund, you haven't gone far enough—turn the page again. If you see a bearded lady, you've gone too far—turn back a couple hundred.

You're so quiet. Don't be shy. Comments and questions are welcome. If you have something to say, just raise your hand. Oh, one more thing: if you're the sensitive type, you may want to plug your ears. "WTF?!" is flying around in here like bugs at a BBQ.

2

Burn, Baby, Burn

I'm not exactly what you'd call a churchgoing man, though I was forced to attend Catholic mass and Sunday school growing up. My great aunt was a nun, so a march through the sacraments was mandatory too.

Despite my resistance, I had some good times with the religious part of my upbringing. There was the time I gave up going to mass for Lent (not the crowd pleaser I anticipated). And there was the time I suggested to my priest that we spice up communion by "bobbing for the Body"—fishing communion wafers out of a barrel of communion wine as one would bob for apples at a Halloween party (my parents got a phone call).

Less sacrilegiously, I enjoyed some of the biblical stories I heard—among my favorites, that of King Solomon. I'm sure you know this story; it's one of the Bible's greatest hits.

Two women come before the king disputing the maternity to a baby. Neither woman has evidence to show for her claim, and they want Solomon to decide their dispute.

Solomon proposes the following: he'll cut the baby in half. Each woman will receive an equal share. This will be equitable, if a bit messy.

On the face of it, Solomon was a baby-hating madman. Or he was an idiot. Killing a baby and divvying up its corpse hardly seems like a reasonable response to a maternity dispute. The women who came to the king must've been shocked when he suggested his solution. The Bible doesn't mention it, but I'm pretty sure both of them uttered "WTF?!" when Solomon presented his proposal.

You and I, on the other hand, know perfectly well what Solomon had in mind: the baby's true mother would rather sacrifice her child's custody than her child. Thus, the king inferred, she would turn down his proposal, allowing him to award the baby—in its entirety—to her. Which is exactly what happened. They didn't call him "Solomon the Wise" for nothing.

We can learn a couple things from Solomon. First, judicial procedures that seem downright stupid may in fact be very wise. Second, when "ordinary" evidence is lacking, judicial officials may still be able to get to the bottom of things by creating clever rules—even ones that are based on a lie ("When maternity is in doubt, cut the child in half"). Clever rules manipulate people's incentives, leading them to publicly reveal otherwise private information—information only they have about the truth—through the choices they make.

If you come over this way, you'll see a metallic cauldron:

[*The crowd shuffles down a few steps into a dim, stone-walled cellar.*]

My goodness, it's dark in here. Let me just . . .

[lights a torch dangling precariously from the wall]

Much better. As I was saying, what you see here is an ordeal cauldron. Ordeals were medieval European judicial officials' way of deciding difficult criminal cases.

Those of you who've seen *Monty Python and the Holy Grail* might remember a scene involving ordeals. Some villagers are trying to decide if a woman is guilty of witchcraft. Their method is to compare her weight to that of a duck. In genuine ordeals, there was no duck, but there was a cauldron like this one.

The golden age of ordeals was the ninth through thirteenth centuries, when two types of them flourished: hot and cold.[1] The former included hot water and hot iron ordeals (for Latin snobs, that's *iudicium aquae fervantis* and *iudicium ferri*).[2] The latter, cold water ordeals (*probatio per aquam frigidam*).[3] In the hot water ordeal, a priest boiled a cauldron of water into which he threw a stone or ring.[4] The task of the "proband"—the ordeal taker—was, as Bishop Eberhard of Bamburg's twelfth-century breviary instructed, to "plunge his hand into the boiling water" and pluck it out.[5] "Afterwards let" his hand "be immediately sealed up." If he's innocent, he'll "bring forth his hand safe and unharmed from this water. But if he be guilty and presume to plunge in his hand," it will show burn injuries on inspection three days later.[6]

The hot iron ordeal was similar, but the proband carried a piece of burning iron nine paces instead.[7] The formula for deciding guilt was the same: burn = you did it; don't burn = you didn't.

The cold water ordeal dispensed with the hot stuff in favor of a tepid pool. Ninth-century theologian Hincmar of Rheims described it this way: "He who is to be examined by this judgment is cast into the water bound, and is drawn forth again bound." If he's guilty and "seeks to hide the truth by a lie, [he] cannot be submerged"; he'll float.[8] If he's innocent, he can be; he'll sink.

Medieval law reserved ordeals for certain kinds of cases—typically those involving accusations of serious crimes, such as homicide, robbery, or arson.[9] Punishments for failing them ranged from fines to mutilation to death.[10]

The law also reserved ordeals for cases that judges couldn't confidently decide without them.[11] "The ordeal of hot iron is not to be permitted except where the naked truth cannot otherwise be explored," twelfth-century English legislation decreed. Or as thirteenth-century German law put it, "It is not right to use the ordeal in any case, unless the truth may be known in no other way."[12]

If a defendant confessed or reliable witnesses testified against him, judges would convict him straightaway, without an ordeal.[13] This merely required criminals to spontaneously admit their guilt or to have attacked their victims in broad daylight in front of an audience.

In the unlikely event that this didn't happen, judges would exonerate the defendant if he and a court-determined number of "oath helpers" swore his innocence—provided that their oaths were "acceptable."[14] Oaths of unfree persons, who composed much of the medieval population, were not acceptable. Nor were those of foreigners or people who had perjured themselves, failed in a legal contest, or had less than sterling reputations. So, just a few.[15]

When such "ordinary" evidence was silent, judges unwilling to convict or exonerate accused criminals indiscriminately needed another way to determine their guilt or innocence.[16] That way was ordeals.[17]

I see a raised hand in the back . . . The guy with the unorthodox sideburns . . . Yep, you sir. Did you have a question?

"I do. WTF was the rationale the legal system gave for these ordeals?! Boiling people in cauldrons? Dunking them in pools? How did they justify it?"

Good question. And thank you for not pointing those chops at me.

Ordeals were justified on the grounds that they were *iudicia Dei*—judgments of God.[18] Where man couldn't correctly assign criminal status, he recruited the Lord. "Let doubtful cases be determined by the judgment of God," a Carolingian capitulary directed. "The judges may decide that which they clearly know, but that which they cannot know shall be reserved for Divine judgment."[19]

According to medieval Christian belief, if priests performed the appropriate rituals, God would reveal individuals' guilt by letting boiling water or burning iron harm them or making holy water reject their guilty bodies and reveal their innocence by miraculously saving their limbs from harm or accepting their guiltless bodies into his blessed pool.

[skeptical looks and murmurs from the crowd]

In addition to seeming strange, ordeals seem, well, stupid. But similar to King Solomon's baby-dicing idea, lurking below that facade was a good deal of wisdom. In fact, the basic logic behind the former may have been behind ordeals too.

There are two obvious alternatives to asking God to find fact in "doubtful cases": ask the accused if he's guilty, or torture him to encourage him to tell the truth.

The trouble with both approaches is that they produce lots of mistakes. Every accused person asked about his guilt proclaims his innocence. Torture has the opposite problem: if it's painful enough to prompt the guilty to confess, it's painful enough to prompt the innocent to confess too.

[The crowd is noisy; a slender hand goes up at the back of the room.]

Pipe down, please. The stunning eastern European lady is trying to ask a question. Miss?

"Ania."

Pardon me?

"My name is Ania. And yes, I have a question. You say that tor-
ture isn't a good way to decide accused criminals' guilt or innocence
because if it's effective, everyone who's tortured will profess their
guilt. I get that. But I'm surprised to hear you contrast ordeals
with torture. Listening to you describe them, ordeals sound a lot
like torture to me."

Ania. That's a lovely name. You ask an excellent question. But you might be surprised by the answer. You see, it seems that ordeals actually *exonerated* the majority of people who underwent them.

[*surprise and incredulity from the crowd*]

That's right: boiling water rarely boiled those who put their hands in it, and burning iron rarely burned those who carried it. "If we suppose, that few, or none escaped conviction who exposed themselves to these fiery trials," one historian warns, "we shall be very much mistaken. For the histories of those times contain innumerable examples of persons plunging their naked arms into boiling water, handling red-hot balls of iron, and walking upon burning ploughshares, without receiving the least injury."[20]

You can see this by examining historical records of ordeal outcomes. Our first source for such records is the *Regestrum Varadinense*, an ordeal register from Várad, Hungary (modern-day Oradea, Romania) during the reign of King Andrew II. The *Regestrum* records the outcomes of 208 hot iron ordeals administered by Hungarian clerics in the basilica of Nagyvárad between 1208 and 1235.[21] Their results? Probands passed in 130 cases, 62.5 percent of the time.[22] Unless nearly two-thirds of ordeal-officiating priests didn't understand how to heat iron, something funny must've been going on.

Our other source for ordeal outcomes is the English plea rolls, which were kept by the royal courts between 1194, the year of the first surviving roll, and 1219, when English courts stopped ordering ordeals. The rolls contain outcomes for far fewer probands than the

Regestrum—just nineteen—but they point to the same phenomenon.[23] Sixteen of these probands underwent cold water ordeals; fourteen passed. All three probands who underwent hot iron ordeals passed too. This means that in these records, ordeals exonerated their takers 89 percent of the time.[24]

If ordeals were really just torture—a way to compel the people who underwent them to confess to crimes—they were remarkably ineffective. Judges could've gotten better results by giving defendants noogies. I'm delighted that Ania is trying to find the sense in the seemingly senseless, but the torture story doesn't fit the facts.[25] We'll have to look elsewhere for the incentives behind ordeals.

To see what I have in mind, consider a medieval fellow named Frithogar. Suppose Frithogar's neighbor, a farmer, accuses him of stealing. Frithogar denies it. The farmer has no witnesses but is well respected. Frithogar isn't, so the court orders him to the hot water ordeal.

Frithogar believes in *iudicium Dei*—that priests, by performing the appropriate rituals, can get God to reveal the truth, performing a miracle that prevents the boiling water from burning him if he's innocent, letting him burn if he's not.

What will Frithogar do?

Put yourself in his shoes. Suppose Frithogar stole from the farmer. He knows he's guilty, but nobody else does. In this case, if Frithogar undergoes the ordeal, he expects to burn. Moreover, he expects to suffer the legal punishment for theft upon being convicted—a large fine.

Frithogar's other option is to decline the ordeal, confessing his crime or settling with the farmer instead.[26] Both of these alternatives punish Frithogar, but neither is as punishing as the fine for stealing and neither will burn him.[27] Thus, if he's guilty, Frithogar will choose to decline the ordeal.

Now suppose that Frithogar didn't steal from the farmer. He knows he's innocent but nobody else does. In this case, if Frithogar undergoes the ordeal, he expects to pull his arm from the boiling water unburned. Moreover, he expects to avoid legal punishment upon being exonerated. If Frithogar declines the ordeal and confesses or settles instead, he suffers punishment for a crime he didn't commit. Thus, if he's innocent, Frithogar will choose to undergo the ordeal.

In other words, the specter of the ordeal sorts Frithogar by his guilt or innocence. Leveraging his belief in *iudicium Dei* incentivizes him to choose one way if he hasn't stolen from the farmer, undergo the ordeal, and another way if he has, decline it, revealing his criminal status through how he chooses. This is similar to the way that King Solomon leveraged the specter of cutting the baby in half to incentivize the disputing women to reveal their maternal status.

The young man wearing what appears to be a pair of ladies' clam diggers has a question. Sir?

> *"These are men's board shorts—I guess it's still dark in here. Anyway, according to the logic you just described, guilty people never undergo ordeals but innocent ones always do. But in that case, the innocent will always be convicted. They stick their arms in the boiling water thinking it won't burn them, but of course it does. So they get burned and wrongly convicted. The innocent suffer more than the guilty!"*

Our capri pants–wearing friend raises an important point: ordeals work only if they exonerate those who undergo them. And as you already heard, that's exactly what they did in most cases. So, short of genuine *iudicia Dei*, how can boiling water be made innocuous to human flesh?

> [*The questioner shrugs.*]

By *iudicia cleri*. Because of the way that ordeals sorted the accused, the clerics who administered them went in knowing that willing probands were innocent. They could therefore fix ordeals to find the "correct" result.

Suppose Frithogar is innocent and thus chooses to undergo the ordeal. The cleric can lower the water's temperature so it doesn't burn him. Frithogar plunges his arm into the cauldron expecting to be unharmed, and his expectation is fulfilled—not by God but an informed priest.

[*the young man wearing capri pants*]

"*But how could the priest pull that off?*"

I was just about to tell you. To rig ordeals, priests required latitude. And plenty was given to them by ordeal instructions, prescribed by liturgical *ordines* (directions for religious services) and royal dooms (the laws of the land). Consider the instructions for conducting the hot iron ordeal from a tenth-century English doom:

> Concerning the ordeal we enjoin in the name of God and by the command of the archbishop and of all our bishops that no one enter the church after the fire has been brought in with which the ordeal is to be heated except the priest and him who is to undergo judgment. . . . Then let an equal number from both sides enter and stand on either side of the judgment place along the church. . . . And no one shall mend the fire any longer than the beginning of the hallowing, but let the iron lie on the coals until the last collect. . . . And let the accused drink of the holy water and then let the hand with which he is about to carry the iron be sprinkled, and so let him go [to the ordeal].[28]

Several features of these instructions seem fishy.[29] First, only the priest and proband are initially allowed in the church after the priest makes the ordeal fire. This gives the priest opportunity to manipulate the fire, hence the temperature of the iron. The doom indicates that before the proband begins the ordeal, "two men from each side go in and certify that [the iron] is as hot as we have directed it to be."[30] But the priest's isolation until this point allows him to defraud the certifiers—for example, providing them with a different iron for inspection than he provides the proband.

Second, the instructions forbid mending the fire after the communion consecration. The iron has to remain on dying coals until the priest makes his final prayer. This seems strange too—unless, of course, the goal is to give clerics a chance to let the ordeal iron cool before the proband handles it. If the priest fails to cool the fire or switch the iron, he can do just that by delaying and drawing out the final prayer (maybe that's why I recall the masses of my youth being so damn long).

Third, the ordeal instructions require observers to align along the church's walls for the ordeal's duration. In a reasonable-sized church, this puts them a considerable distance from the ordeal "stage," facilitating priestly chicanery.

Finally, the instructions direct the priest to sprinkle the proband's hand with holy water immediately before he carries the iron. It's easy to imagine how "sprinkling" could become dousing under a manipulative priest's control. The water helps offset any injurious heat remaining on the iron that fire fixing or iron tampering doesn't address.

Hot water ordeal instructions had the same features: only the priest and proband were initially allowed in the church after the fire for heating the water was made; observers lined the church walls to watch the ordeal; and the priest "sprinkled" holy water, in this case over the cauldron.[31]

Ordeal formulas also granted clerics discretion in deciding ordeal outcomes.[32] They directed that the proband's "hand be sealed up, and on the third day" for the priest to examine "whether it is clean or foul within the wrapper."[33] But they were silent about what it meant for a hand to be "clean or foul." That depended on the priest's judgment. A severely burned arm that when unwrapped three days later looked like Freddy Krueger's face would certainly qualify as "foul" to any disinterested onlooker.[34] But for the many degrees of foulness short of this state, the priest had leeway to declare the proband's innocence.

[*A patron interrupts.*]

"What about the cold ordeals? How did priests find people innocent with those? Wouldn't they have to make sure the defendant sank? I don't see how that would be poss . . ."

Cold water ordeal instructions gave priests opportunity for manipulation too. While priests couldn't manipulate the density of water (well, not easily anyway), they could control cold ordeal outcomes through other avenues, such as their authority to grade pass or fail.

A Carolingian capitulary describing cold water ordeals required a knot to be made in the rope attached to the proband at a prescribed length from his body, defining the depth to which he had to sink to prove his innocence.[35] It also required the proband to be lowered gently into the water to prevent splashing. Still, scope for priestly discretion remained. Whether a proband had indeed sunk to the "depth of innocence" could be ambiguous.[36] And cold water ordeal formulas didn't specify how long he had to spend at that depth to prove himself.

A priest could improve the chance that his proband would sink by directing him to exhale before entering the water. In fact, he could do better: order the proband to fast for several days in holy preparation for the ordeal—a sort of medieval Gas-X, which made him more likely to sink.

[*The previous questioner interjects.*]

"I guess I can see how that could work. But it still doesn't make a whole lot of sense. I mean, why, if the legal system was interested in finding the people who underwent ordeals innocent, would it ever resort to pool dunking, which was clearly harder to rig?"

Think about it: hot ordeals require a "miracle" to exonerate probands. Boiling water and burning iron really do boil and burn human flesh, so if the priest can't intervene—because his sleight of hand is poor, observers are too close to the stage, or any other reason—these ordeals can backfire. Cold water ordeals, however, can exonerate probands without priestly intervention. People can sink in water all by themselves. In fact, certain ones almost always do: lean men.

Men have a lower body fat percentage than women. Because of this, the average lean male has an 80 percent chance of sinking in water, while the average lean female's chance is only 40 percent. It was therefore possible to exonerate probands in cold water ordeals without the need to resort to any chicanery at all simply by sending men, but not women, to them.[37]

And according to the historical evidence, this seems to be exactly what medieval justice systems did. Between 1194 and 1208, ninety-one ordeals appear in England's eyre rolls—the records of traveling "circuit-court judges." In eighty-four of them, probands were men; in seven they were women. Judges sent seventy-nine of the men to cold water ordeals, one to the hot iron ordeal, and four to unspecified ordeals. In contrast, they sent all seven women to hot iron ordeals.[38] This means that men were ordered to cold water ordeals between 94 and 98.8 percent of the time, but women, 0 percent of the time.

Two cases that involve a man and woman jointly accused of the same crime are particularly telling. In one case, the defendants were accused of burglary, in the other of murder. In both cases, judges ordered the men to cold water ordeals but the women to hot iron ordeals.[39] In a third case, a woman was accused of murder, sent to the hot iron ordeal, and passed. A man was then accused of the same murder but sent to the cold water ordeal instead.[40]

I see another hand. The pious-looking fellow. Did you have a question, sir?

> *"I most certainly do! I happen to be a priest. And while I was willing to let your 'bobbing for the Body' sacrilege pass in silence, this I cannot! Are you suggesting that my holy predecessors knew they were tricking everyone—that they consciously rigged these ordeals to find the results they wanted?! You're a heathen! A heathen, I say, plain and simple!"*

Take a deep breath, Padre. I'm not necessarily suggesting that at all. Whether priests believed ordeals were *iudicia Dei* or instead understood that they were really *iudicia cleri* is an interesting historical question, but it's unimportant for the logic we've been considering. As long as priests manipulated ordeals to reflect the information they received about defendants' guilt or innocence after defendants chose to decline or undergo them, ordeals would work as I've described.

Such manipulation doesn't necessarily mean that priests didn't believe ordeals were genuine judgments of God. "Clergy," as you know, "were believed to possess special interpretive powers of God's law on earth"; they viewed themselves as worldly instruments of God's will.[41] This view was the basis of their role in confession. It underlay the developing doctrine of *in persona Christi*—the idea that priests act in the person of Christ when they administer sacraments. It's at least possible, then, that clerics also believed they were being guided by God when they manipulated ordeals.

Of course, it's also possible that priests appreciated that *their* intervention, not God's, determined probands' fate. The fact that priests said ordeals were *iudicia Dei*, perhaps even to one another behind closed doors, doesn't mean they really believed this. There are plenty of examples of medieval clerics behaving in ways that suggest they may not have taken all their professed beliefs totally seriously.

[*The priest shakes his head vehemently from side to side.*]

Sorry, Padre. But it's true.

The historical evidence is unclear about what priests truly believed. But even if they believed ordeals could be genuine *iudicia Dei*, that doesn't mean they believed every ordeal outcome reflected God's judgment. Just as a corrupt cleric could abuse his powers of reconciliation to sell absolution, he could abuse his powers of ordeal administration to sell a judicial verdict.

There was a check on priestly corruption, though. Priests worked for privately owned bishoprics whose revenues depended on judicial honesty. Bishopric owners exercised the rights of local governments, including collecting taxes connected directly to local productivity. If crime was higher, resident productivity would be lower and bishopric revenues would suffer. Bishopric owners therefore had an incentive to limit activities that undermined productivity, such as priestly corruption, where they could. Their ability to do so was imperfect. Still, by controlling the selection of clerical administrators in their territories and these individuals' finances, bishopric owners could exercise at least some oversight.

The burly fellow with the convincing piercings has a question. Go ahead there, Karnov.

"Ordeals only work—and what you say only makes sense—if defendants totally buy the idea that God will let boiling water or a hot iron burn them if they're guilty and spare them if they're innocent. Otherwise, they'd know they could game the system. But if ordeals exonerate everyone, people must have caught on. I'm calling bullshit!"

Let's not be rash. You raise a great point. Let me explain why you're right, but really, really wrong. Please don't hurt me . . .

[cowering]

It's true that if defendants aren't completely sure that ordeals are genuine judgments of God, things get a bit more complicated. And you're right that a 100 percent acquittal rate might seem suspicious to some.[42] In fact, people may have been skeptical about ordeals for other reasons too. The presence of observers at ordeals, for instance, suggests that some medieval citizens at least entertained the idea that ordeal outcomes could reflect worldly influences in addition to otherworldly ones.

Skeptics pose a potential problem. Innocent ones may decide they don't want to hazard ordeals because they fear the possibility that boiling water will boil them or burning iron will burn them. If everyone passes, this fear disappears. But then the problem Karnov mentioned emerges: guilty skeptics may decide they want to hazard ordeals instead. In both cases, the sorting I talked about earlier breaks down, destroying the ability of ordeals to distinguish the guilty from the innocent.

But surely people clever enough to come up with the idea of using ordeals to sort criminal defendants in the first place wouldn't let this get in the way of their ability to do so. Ordeal-administering priests had a simple solution to the problem of skeptics: condemn some probands.

I'll spare you the details, but it turns out that as long as defendants reposed even the faintest faith in the possibility that ordeals were genuine judgments of God, there existed some proportion of probands whom priests could condemn that would accomplish this goal. The more skeptical people were that ordeals were *iudicia Dei*, the more probands priests had to condemn to save the sorting feature of ordeals. The less skeptical people were, the fewer they could get away with condemning.

[*The burly, pierced fellow says something inaudible.*]

What's that, Karnov? You were saying?

"I said that I think I see what you're saying. But I still don't believe you."

I'll tell you what: since everyone else seems to be onboard, rather than wasting their time, when the tour is over I'll show you explicitly why what I'm saying is right. We'll meet to discuss in the appendix, just past the portrait of the bearded lady I mentioned when we started.

Now, I was telling you about how when people were sufficiently skeptical that ordeals were really judgments of God, priests had to condemn some probands to make them work.

The probands whom priests had to condemn in this case were, of course, innocent ones—the only people who are willing to undergo ordeals when they're sorting properly. This too posed a potential problem.

When priests don't have to condemn any innocent people to ensure that ordeals sort properly, the only evidence ordeals produce actually reinforces people's belief that they're legit. The guilty always decline ordeals, so their belief in *iudicium Dei* is never challenged; the innocent always undergo ordeals and are exonerated, so their belief is always fulfilled. But when priests have to condemn some innocent people, this is no longer true. Some probands now have experiences that contradict their belief that ordeals are *iudicia Dei* instead of confirm it. They know they're innocent, but the ordeals they undergo say otherwise.

This problem, however, was minor. After all, what could an innocent person condemned by an ordeal do? Proclaim his innocence and tell everyone that ordeals are a sham? Maybe. But this is the same thing a truly guilty person would do, so no one's belief is affected. Exploit his knowledge that ordeals are a sham by committing crimes and hoping to be sent to ordeals? I doubt it. But suppose he did: now he repeatedly confronts the priest, who becomes suspicious and condemns him, foiling his plan.[43]

The real potential danger for ordeals when priests had to condemn some innocent people wasn't that those people would tattle or become career criminals. It was that publicly observed events would contradict ordeal results, evidencing the illegitimacy of ordeals. One medieval defendant who was accused of murder, for instance, underwent an ordeal, failed, and was hanged. A few weeks later the man he murdered came home.[44]

Such incidents threatened to initiate a process that could destroy the operation of ordeals. An occasional contradictory incident could be explained away, but belief that ordeals were *iudicia Dei* would weaken considerably if they were frequent.

Fortunately for ordeals, they weren't, for two reasons.[45] First, the cases in which judges used ordeals militated against such situations. Those cases, recall, were when ordinary evidence was lacking. The prospect that evidence would come back later to contradict ordeal results was therefore slim. Second, medieval citizens' belief that ordeals were *iudicia Dei* was strong, so priests didn't have to condemn a high proportion of probands to ensure that ordeals sorted properly.

Why were the folks of the day believers? Well, they tended to be the religious sort. Ordeal ceremonies capitalized on this and were arranged to access and remind probands of their religious beliefs.

One way they did so was by rendering ordeals explicitly religious, nearly sacramental, rituals. "The Church," historian Henry Lea pointed out, "followed the policy of surrounding [ordeals] with all the solemnity which her most venerated rites could impart."[46] *Priests* administered ordeals in *churches* as part of ordeal *masses*. Consider the ceremonial instructions for the hot water ordeal prescribed in a medieval German liturgical:

> Let the priest go to the church with the prosecutors and with him who is about to be tried. And while the rest wait in the vestibule of the church let the priest enter and put on the sacred garments except the chasuble and, taking the Gospel and the chrismarium and the relics of the saints and the chalice, let him go to the altar and speak thus to all the people standing near: Behold brethren, the offices of Christian religion. Behold the law in which is hope and remission of sins, the holy oil of the chrisma, the consecration of the body and blood of our Lord. . . . Then he shall designate a spot in the vestibule where the fire is to be made for the water, and shall first sprinkle the place with holy water, and shall also sprinkle the kettle when it is ready to be hung and the water in it, to guard against illusions of the devil. Then, entering the church with the others, he shall celebrate the ordeal mass. After the celebration let the priest go with the people to the place of the ordeal, the Gospel in his left hand, the cross, censer and relics of the saints being carried ahead, and let him chant seven penitential psalms with a litany. . . . [And let the priest pray:] O God, Thou who within this substance of water hast hidden. Thy most solemn sacraments, be graciously present with us who invoke Thee, and upon this element made ready by much purification pour down the virtue of Thy benediction.[47]

Ordeal ceremonies also reminded the guilty of the painful condemnation they would suffer by undergoing the ordeal and the innocent of their miraculous, pain-free deliverance. Consider the priest's prayer over the cauldron of ordeal water:

> O holy water, O blessed water, water which washest the dust and sins of the world, I adjure thee by the living God that thou shalt show

thyself pure . . . to make manifest and reveal and bring to naught all falsehood, and to make manifest and bring light to all truth; so that he who shall place his hand in thee, if his cause be just and true, shall receive no hurt; but if he be perjured, let his hand be burned with fire, that all men may know the power of our Lord Jesus Christ.[48]

Ordeal ceremonies highlighted the supposed biblical foundations of ordeals too, emphasizing their divine precedent and successful track record. Consider the following hot water ordeal prayer:

> O God, just Judge, firm and patient, who are the Author of peace, and judgest truly, determine what is right, O Lord, and make known Thy righteous judgment. O Omnipotent God, Thou that lookest upon the earth and makest it to tremble, Thou that by the gift of Thy Son, our Lord Jesus Christ, didst save the world and by His most holy passion didst redeem the human race, sanctify, O Lord, this water being heated by fire. Thou that didst save the three youths, Sidrac, Misac, and Abednego, cast into the fiery furnace at the command of Nebuchadnezzar, and didst lead them forth unharmed by the hand of Thy angel . . . and, as Thou didst liberate the three youths from the fiery furnace and didst free Susanna from the false charge . . . so, O Lord, bring forth his hand safe and unharmed from this water [if he's innocent].[49]

The "three youths" referred to here are the righteous boys whom God saves from a fiery death ordered by King Nebuchadnezzar in the Book of Daniel. Susanna is the woman sentenced to death in the same book, whom the prophet Daniel exonerates in her last hour. His name means "judgment of God" in Hebrew.

Even the mechanics of *iudicia Dei* in ordeals were grounded in citizens' religious beliefs. In the hot water ordeal, Hincmar informs us, "The guilty are scalded and the innocent are unhurt, because Lot escaped unharmed from the fire of Sodom, and the future fire which will precede the terrible Judge will be harmless to the Saints, and will burn the wicked as in the Babylonian furnace of old."[50] And in the cold water ordeal, the guilty float because "whoever . . . seeks to hide the truth by a lie, cannot be submerged in the waters above which the voice of the Lord God has thundered; for the pure nature of the water recognizes as impure and therefore rejects as inconsistent with itself such human nature as has once been regenerated by the waters of baptism and is again infected by falsehood."[51]

Finally, ordeal ceremonies reminded probands of God's omniscience, omnipotence, and infallible power to exculpate the innocent and condemn the guilty through trials of fire and water. Consider the priest's benediction of the water in the hot water ordeal:

> I bless thee, O creature of water, boiling above the fire, in the name of the Father, and of the Son, and of the Holy Ghost, from whom all things proceed; I adjure thee by Him who ordered thee to water the whole earth from the four rivers, and who summoned thee forth from the rock, and who changed thee into wine, that no wiles of the devil or magic of men be able to separate thee from thy virtues as a medium of judgment; but mayest thou punish the vile and wicked, and purify the innocent. Through Him whom hidden things do not escape and who sent thee in the flood over the whole earth to destroy the wicked and who will yet come to judge the quick and the dead and the world by fire. Amen.[52]

The effect of all this religious rigmarole? Lea put it this way:

> In those ages of faith, the professing Christian, conscious of guilt, must indeed have been hardened who could undergo the most awful rites of his religion, pledging his salvation on his innocence, and knowing under such circumstances that the direct intervention of Heaven could alone save him from having his hand boiled to rags, after which he was to meet the full punishment of his crime, and perhaps in addition lose a member for the perjury committed.[53]

Given the importance of religious belief to the operation of ordeals, it should come as no surprise that when the Church's support for that belief ended, ordeals did too. That didn't happen until the thirteenth century, but the road to the demise of ordeals was already being paved a century earlier.

High-ranking ecclesiastics began to seriously question the relationship of ordeals to their religion in the twelfth century:[54] "The twelfth century was the great age of [canonical] sifting, and the credentials of the ordeal were among the things sifted."[55]

Ecclesiastic critics of ordeals argued that they lacked scriptural support. Despite their allusions to Daniel, Susanna, and the fiery furnace, the Bible contains but one instance of what might be construed as an actual judicial ordeal: in the Book of Numbers, an accused adulterer undergoes an ordeal of bitter waters—poison ingestion—to prove her fidelity.[56] And medieval judicial ordeals weren't ordeals of bitter waters.[57]

A still bigger problem, the critics charged, was that ordeals violated an important Christian proscription with plenty of scriptural support: "Thou shalt not tempt the Lord thy God."[58]

[*The priest shouts:*]

"That's right! No tempting!"

Trials of fire and water required priests to command God to perform miracles at their whim, which the Bible forbids.

[*The priest nods vigorously in agreement.*]

Together with the fact that there were more papal decretals questioning than supporting the religious status of ordeals, these factors led the Fourth Lateran Council to reject their legitimacy in 1215 and ban priests from participating in them.[59] "Let no ecclesiastic," the council decreed, "pronounce over the ordeal of hot or cold water or glowing iron any benediction or rite of consecration."[60]

Secular judicial systems quickly abandoned ordeals where their religious trappings evaporated. Denmark prohibited them in 1216, England in 1219, and Scotland in 1230. Italy ended ordeals in 1231, though some Italian towns had already abandoned them by then, and

Flanders' criminal justice system dispensed with them between 1208 and 1233.[61] Shortly after, Norway, Iceland, Sweden, and others followed suit. France never formally abolished ordeals, but the last mention of them that historians can find is in 1218, just after the Church's ban.[62]

Where priests defied the council's prohibition and continued to participate in ordeals—places such as Germany, Greece, Hungary, Poland, and Croatia—they lingered longer. But "with trifling exceptions, the ordeal could not continue without priests."[63] So it went extinct where clerics refused to officiate it. "Robbed . . . of all religious sanction," trials by fire and water became useless for sorting criminal defendants.[64]

[*The young man wearing capri pants interrupts.*]

"If these ordeals were so great, why don't we use them today?"

Actu . . .

[*The burly fellow with the piercings:*]

"Because modern trials are obviously much better, moron!"

One at a time, please. And that's not quite right. It's not that post-ordeal trial methods are inevitably superior. It doesn't make sense for *us* to use medieval-style ordeals because (1) technological advance has made fact finding infinitely cheaper than it once was and (2) we—with the possible exception of Scientologists—don't believe that trials of fire and water are *iudicia Dei*, which medieval-style ordeals require to work. But under less technologically advanced conditions, for people who did have such belief, medieval-style ordeals could be a sensible option even today.

In fact, where these conditions prevail, medieval-style ordeals *are* the sensible option. And people continue to rely on them.

[*skeptical murmuring from the crowd once again*]

Don't believe me? Google "sassywood" and see what comes up.

[*Nearly every patron pulls out an iPhone.*]

That's right, medieval-style ordeals are alive and well—in Liberia, to a lesser extent in Sierra Leone, and probably in a few other places in sub-Saharan Africa too.

You might know something about Liberia. If not, here are the Cliffs Notes: it's a political-economic basket case. Liberia's government is corrupt, its public judicial institutions are dysfunctional, its people are impoverished, and a large portion of them have strong superstitions supporting the effective use of judicial ordeals.

Sassywood is actually a kind of catchall term for a variety of medieval-style ordeals currently in use there, including hot water and hot iron ordeals like their European predecessors used. *The* sassywood ordeal, however, is trial by poison ingestion. It takes its name from the poisonous concoction that criminal defendants in Liberia are asked to drink, made from the toxic bark of the *Erythrophleum suaveolens*, or sasswood tree.[65]

Like medieval ordeals, sassywood is reserved for important crimes in difficult cases—where ordinary evidence is lacking and thus conventional fact finding has failed. Accused criminals can respond to the charges against them by confessing their guilt or proclaiming their innocence. In the latter case, they're invited to undergo sassywood.

A spiritual leader, analogous to the medieval priest, who wields authority in his community to perform socioreligious rituals, mixes the concoction, administers the ordeal, and acts as the trial's judge. The defendant's physiological reaction to imbibing the sassywood potion decides his guilt or innocence: "If the drinker by vomiting throws up all the [poison] . . . before the sunrise the following morning or much more if he does it during the very trial then he is innocent and publicly declared not guilty of the crime for which he was accused. But if he should die on the spot" or display signs of intoxication, "then he is believed and proclaimed Guilty."[66]

According to a widely held Liberian superstition, sassywood's power to correctly identify the drinker's criminal status resides in a spirit that "accompanies the draught, and searches the heart of the suspected individual for his guilt. If he be innocent, the spirit returns with the fluid in the act of ejection, but if guilty, it remains to do more surely the work of destruction."[67]

There should be no mystery for you now—no "WTF?!" moment—about Liberians' use of ordeals. Given the paucity of conventional evidence-gathering technologies, such as reliable police and government courts, there's little for Liberians in rural communities to go on when criminal accusations are made. But given their superstition, these communities *can* tap into defendants' private information about their guilt or innocence through ordeals. So that's exactly what they do.

[*A patron begins snickering loudly.*]

The gentleman in the camouflage hat and stylish American flag T-shirt finds something amusing. Sir, would you like to share?

[*swallows a wad of chewing tobacco*]

"*Wha? Sure. I was just a laughin' at them peoples in Liberia. Don't misunderstand or nothin', I'm glad they gots the superstitions needed fer ordeals to work 'n' all. Still, in this day 'n' age, it seems purty stupid how their legal systems gotta use hocus-pocus to gets some justice. Thank the good Lord we live in Amurica!*"

Finished?

[*The tobacco-chewing man smirks arrogantly and nods.*]

Good. Now wipe that smug grin off your face.

America's legal system leverages superstition to improve its judicial outcomes too, and in much the same way as ordeals. Our "ordeals" just have a fancier name: polygraph tests.

Better known as lie-detector tests, more than a dozen states permit polygraph results under certain circumstances as evidence in judicial proceedings. American law enforcement is especially fond of them. Police departments use lie detector tests, the FBI uses them, even the CIA.

Lie detector tests are bullshit. Like astrology, they have their supporters, but the scientific community overwhelmingly rejects their validity. There's about as much science supporting the idea that you can physiologically measure whether someone is lying or telling the truth by strapping them to one of those funny-looking machines as there is supporting the idea that God intervenes in trials of fire and water to reveal defendants' guilt or innocence.

Although lie detector tests can't really discover whether people are lying or telling the truth, if people believe they can, lie detectors can facilitate sorting in the same way as ordeals. The innocent believer has nothing to fear by taking a polygraph. He expects it to exonerate him, hence an incentive to take the exam. The guilty believer fears being outed by the polygraph. He expects it to condemn him, hence an incentive not to.

Polygraph administrators probably realize this. So they interpret the sophisticated-looking squiggly lines on the polygraph paper accordingly—similar to how medieval priests found the "correct" outcomes in hot water ordeals or Liberian spiritual leaders do in sassywood.

Also similar to "official" ordeals, this works only if people hold the appropriate belief—that lie detectors are really capable of discovering whether they're lying or telling the truth. But lots of people—modern people, in the United States, who pride themselves on their scientific approach to life—hold this superstition. So law enforcement officials keep on truckin'.

Superstitious elements in modern America's legal system don't stop at lie detectors. You can also find them in at least one other notable place: the courtroom.

Ever notice that movies depict people swearing an oath to tell the truth in God's name, even on the Bible, before testifying in court? That's not movie magic: until relatively recently, God swearing was, and in some cases still is, customary in American courtrooms.[68]

America's religious history may be part of the reason for this. But a more important part may be the logic I've been telling you about.

When testifying is voluntary and testifiers have to swear before God to tell the truth, who do you think is more likely to provide testimony: truth tellers or bullshit artists? If people believe that swearing before God has real meaning—that God might punish them if they lie—the answer is truth tellers.

In fact, God swearing may produce more reliable testimony even when testifying is mandatory. If you have to swear to tell the truth in God's name before you testify and you believe that God dislikes lying, you're going to think twice before committing perjury. God swearing helps the legal system weed out horse hockey.

I'm not claiming that most Americans think God will smite them if they lie after swearing to tell the truth in his name. But a few probably do. Given that God-swearing costs next to nothing to use, it's not hard, then, to see why it would have some role in the courtroom.

Superstition, it turns out, can provide a useful foundation for securing criminal justice. And even clever people, it turns out, can believe in superstition. Societies of superstitious but nevertheless clever people, past and present, have developed institutions that leverage their beliefs to incentivize fact finding and truth telling more generally. Beneath the strikingly senseless surface of medieval judicial ordeals, Liberian sassy-wood, even American polygraph tests and courtroom God swearing, there's actually a lot of sense.

You look like you could use some refreshment. Why don't we take a quick break before moving on to the next part of the tour. If you're thirsty, you can dip your cup into the ordeal cauldron. It's filled with Hawaiian Punch. Also, on the table behind the torch I lit when we first walked in, you'll find cookies in the shape of ordeal irons.

[*the crowd rushes toward the table*]

Careful! Unlike actual ordeal irons, the cookies are hot. Help yourself and follow me.

3

FSBO: Like-New, Preowned Wife

Looks can be deceiving. They can also be completely accurate. Take me, for example: at 5'7", 160 pounds, I don't exactly have what you'd call an athletic build, which is appropriate, since I also don't have anything resembling athletic ability. Speed, strength, the agility to walk up a flight of stairs—not me.

I was in denial about this fact for years. As an adolescent, I loved baseball and desperately wanted to play. The good folks who organized Little League in my town let anyone who was bipedal join a team, so I got to play . . . sort of.

I sucked and everyone knew it. My parents knew it. My Little League coach knew it. My teammates knew it painfully.

I mostly saw bench time. And on the rare occasion when, out of obligation, I was put into play, I did things like "catching" a fly ball with my left eye and flailing feverishly at pitches (which I feared).

I guess on some subconscious level, I too knew I sucked. But denial is a powerful force. So I continued to play . . . for years . . . many years. Eventually my Little League teammates weren't so little, and game watchers weren't so forgiving. Their amusement became embarrassment, even anger, when I unfailingly flubbed a play.

It was about this time that I realized I had to face the facts: I would probably never hit a ball, catch one, or even throw one in a helpful direction. To the great relief of everyone but me, I decided to "retire." You know how people say that if you want something bad enough you can achieve it? Well, that's horseshit. There's this constraint called Mother Nature—and she's a dream-smashing bitch.

I hardly pay attention to what's happening in Major League Baseball (MLB) anymore. But when something that holds my economic interest happens, I perk up. Enter Japanese pitching phenom Daisuke Matsuzaka.

Matsuzaka began his MLB career with the Boston Red Sox. Before that, he was a pitcher in Japan's Nippon Professional Baseball (NPB) league, where he was under contract with a team called the Seibu Lions. The Red Sox and several other MLB teams wanted to poach Matsuzaka from the Lions, and Matsuzaka wanted to leave the Lions to play for an MLB team. To accomplish this move, Matsuzaka needed to buy out of his existing contract. There was just one snag: he didn't have the money.

To deal with cases like Matsuzaka's, America's MLB and Japan's NPB developed what's called the "posting system." Under this system, MLB clubs seeking to hire contracted NPB talent bid against one another in a sealed auction for the right to negotiate with a Japanese player. Unlike the foreign players they seek to hire, MLB clubs have more than enough money to buy those players out of their current contracts. The Red Sox, for example, spent $51.1 million in their bid to negotiate with Matsuzaka. They won.

If the Japanese player and bid-winning MLB team can come to an agreement, the player gets released from his contract with his NPB team and enters a new one with the bid-winning MLB team, just like he wanted. The MLB team gets the Japanese player, whom it values more than the NPB team does. And the NPB team gets the sum of the winning bid, which it values more than the player it gives up. Everyone is better off.

In other words, the posting system aligns the incentives of Japanese talent, American baseball teams, and Japanese baseball teams so that they can realize gains from trade they couldn't realize otherwise. This system illustrates an incredibly simple, but incredibly important, fact of life: potential gains from trade don't remain potential forever. When some obstacle stands in the way of their capture, people find clever ways to overcome it. And so it was in the case of our next "WTF?!"-worthy practice, which you'll find just behind these curtains:

You'll note that I'm standing on an auctioneer's platform. The wedding picture you see behind me is of a nineteenth-century English wife sale. The woman with the rope around her neck was just sold by her husband at a public auction to the man holding the rope—her new husband.

[*A man raises his hand.*]

You have a question already?

"Is this one like the ordeals, where it's practiced some places today? Could I sell my wife?"

Say, you don't happen to be married to that lovely woman who asked the question about torture at our previous stop, do you? In that case, we might be able to find a way . . .

"No, no. My wife works for Greenpeace. She's . . ."

I see. I'll have to pass then.

Returning to the picture . . . The woman on the left was publicly auctioned as a wife in Industrial Revolution England. For over a hundred years, from the early eighteenth century through the end of the nineteenth, working-class English couples, such as the one this woman was part of, offered their better halves to the highest bidder.[1]

The procedures that wife sales followed were the same ones commonly used to sell livestock. Which is fitting, since wives were sold at the same public fairs and marketplaces as livestock, led there by their husbands with halter ropes tied around their necks, like cows.[2]

To ensure a good crowd for their auctions, and thus plenty of potential bidders, wife-selling husbands sometimes hired town criers who strolled the streets ringing bells, announcing the locations and times of impending sales.[3] The crier hired by one Moses Maggs to announce his wife's sale used this little ditty:

a woman—
     and her little baby—
will be offered—
     for sale—
in the Market Place—
     This afternoon—
at four o'clock—
     by her husband—
Moses Maggs.[4]

Other husbands advertised their wives' sales in local newspapers, using ads like this one, published in a late eighteenth-century paper:

To be sold for *Five Shillings*, my Wife, Jane Hebbard. She is stoutly built, stands firm on her posterns, and is sound wind and limb. She can sow and reap, hold a plough, and drive a team, and would answer any stout able man, that can hold a *tight rein*, for she is damned *hard mouthed* and headstrong; but if properly managed, would either lead or drive as tame as a rabbit. She now and then makes a *false* step. Her husband parts with her because she is too much for him.—Enquire of the Printer. N.B. All her body clothes will be given with her.[5]

Or they posted public notices, such as this one:

NOTICE

This here to be hinform the publick as how James Cole be disposed to sell his wife by Auction. Here be a dacent, clanely woman, and be of age twenty-five [y]ears. The sale be to take place in the New Inn, Thursday next at seven o'clock.[6]

These tactics worked. Wife sales attracted hundreds, sometimes thousands, of attendees.[7]

To participate in a public market, a wife-selling husband had to pay the market toll collected from everyone selling goods there and sometimes a turnpike toll to access the roadway leading to the market grounds. Once inside, he might walk his wife around the venue so potential buyers could get a closer look. Then she was auctioned off amid cattle and horses.

An auctioneer prefaced the bidding by extolling the virtues of the wife on the block. Professionals could be hired for this purpose, or the seller could act as his own auctioneer. "Henry Broom, of the parish of Buckerell," for example, "put his wife up at auction," but only "after enumerating her various qualifications in the language and style of a jockey."[8] Mr. Maggs acted as his own auctioneer too:

Laerdies an' gentlemin, I ax lafe to oppose yer notice . . . Her's a good creature . . . an' goos pretty well in harness, wi' a little flogging. . . .

Her can carry a hundred and a 'alf o' coals from the pit for three good miles; her can sell it well, and put it down her throat in less ner three minits. . . . Now my lads, roll up, and bid spirited. . . . I brought her through the turnpike and paid the mon the toll for her. I brought her wi' a halter and had her cried. . . . Now gentelmin, who bids? Gooin, gooin, gooin! I cawn't delay—as the octioneer sez, I cawn't dwell on this lot! . . . Come, say six shillins!⁹

Husbands surely erred on the side of emphasizing their wives' finer points in preauction priming. But some were shockingly honest in describing their lots to crowds of bidders. Consider how one fellow presented his wife, described by an observer as "a spruce, lively, buxom damsel":

Gentlemen,—I have to offer to your notice my wife . . . whom I mean to sell to the highest and fairest bidder. Gentlemen, it is her wish as well as mine to part for ever. She has been to me only a bosom serpent. I took her for my comfort, and the good of my house, but she became my tormentor, a domestic curse, a night invasion, and a daily devil. . . . Now I have shown you the dark side of my wife, and told you her faults and her failings; I will now introduce the bright and sunny side of her, and explain her qualifications and goodness. She can read novels and milk cows; she can laugh and weep with the same ease that you could take a glass of ale when thirsty. . . . She can make butter and scold the maid, she can sing Moore's melodies, and plait her frills and caps; she cannot make rum, gin, or whisky; but she is a good judge of the quality from long experience tasting them. I therefore offer her with all her perfections and imperfections, for the sum of 50s.¹⁰

Other husbands' honesty more likely reflected the fact that their wives' "idiosyncrasies" were readily observable. Thus, a husband in York was probably unable to avoid mentioning that, as one observer put it, his wife "appeared to be on the wrong side of 50; has lost one leg, and has a wooden substitute." The same reasoning probably motivated another seller to acknowledge that only one of his wife's eyes "looks straight at you, the other wanders up to the North."[11]

After describing the wife for sale, the auctioneer solicited bids from the crowd. The husband could set a reservation bid. The high bidder who met this reservation and satisfied another important requirement, which I'll discuss in a moment, won the preowned wife. All the seller's rights and obligations to her transferred to her buyer. In the eyes of participants and transaction observers, the sale terminated one marriage and began another.

Most wife sales were final. Returns weren't possible, but resale was, and a few preowned-wife buyers flipped their purchases. The occasional husband, however, sold his wife on a contingency basis. These gentlemen followed the policy used by all reputable purveyors of electronics and fine furniture. One allowed his wife's purchaser to try her out for three days, after which, if the buyer was unhappy, he could bring her back for 50 percent of her purchase price.[12] Another gave his wife's buyer a full month to decide if he was happy with his purchase.[13]

To formalize their transactions, wife buyers and sellers sometimes procured the services of a lawyer who created a receipt recording their exchange's terms, such as this:

Oct. 24, 1766

Memorandum.

It is this day agreed on between John Parsons, of the parish of Midsummer, Norton, in the county of Somerset, cloth-worker, and John Tooker, of the same place, gentleman, that the said John Parsons, for and in consideration of the sum of six pounds and six shillings in hand paid to the said John Parsons, doth sell, assign, and set over unto John Tooker; with all right, property, claim, services, and demands whatsoever, that he, the said John Parsons, shall have in or to the said Ann Parsons, for and during the term of natural life of her, the said Ann

Parsons. In witness whereof I, the said John Parsons, have set my hand
the day and year first above written.[14]

In other cases, parties formalized their transactions with receipts from
market toll collectors, like this one:

> Aug. 31, 1773. Samuel Whitehouse, of the parish of Willenhall, in
> the county of Stafford, this day sold his wife Mary Whitehouse, in
> open Market, to Thomas Griffiths of Birmingham *value, one shilling.*
> To take her with all faults.[15]

Or they drew up their own memoranda certifying the exchange.[16]

> [*The man who earlier offered to sell his wife interrupts after listen-
> ing with intense curiosity.*]

> "*What did these preowned wives go for? I'm willing to let mine go
> to any interested member of our group for the low price of just . . .*"

Some friends and I were curious about that too. So we went through
eighteenth- and nineteenth-century English newspapers and collected
information on 222 wife sales in England and Wales.[17] The cases we
found spanned 165 years, from 1735 to 1899.[18]

In 209 of them, the newspapers said something about the wife's
price. But it wasn't always monetary: alcohol was a popular supplement
to cash compensation. We also found payments by lottery ticket, din-
ner, and a donkey.

After we excluded the sales whose prices were expressed only in
terms of goods and converted the money prices to common units (the
value of money changed over the 165 years our cases covered, so we
had to account for that), we found that the average preowned wife in
our collection sold for £5.72 (in 1800 British pounds sterling). Prices
were much higher in some decades than others, though. In the 1860s,
the average wife we came across sold for £25.27, whereas in the 1770s,
she sold for just £0.93.

I spot someone in the back who looks desperate to ask a question. You, madam. Yes, the woman who looks like Janeane Garofalo. How can I help y . . .

"I can't belieeeve this! You're standing here telling us about the sale of women like slaves—for pennies on the dollar—and you're doing it so matter-of-factly! This practice is an abomination! An insult to women everywhere! You have some nerve including this practice on your 'WTF?! tour.' More like a misogynist tour for members of the oppressive, capitalist patriarchy! Including my heckling husband!"

[The man who has twice tried to sell this woman, his wife, now blushes and shrinks from the crowd.]

Please calm down, madam. You're frightening the other patrons. Have I commented on that dashing hemp choker you're wearing? Surely the envy of everyone back at Greenpeace. Now if you just let me . . .

"Don't patronize me, you misogynist pig!"

I'm not patronizing you. I'm trying to . . .

"I said don't patronize me!"

It appears as though the "WTF?!" in English wife selling has struck quite a . . .

"Women of the world unite!"

What? Miss, if you'll just let me . . .

"Women of the world unite!!!!"

Miss, I'm just trying to say that . . .

"Uniiiiite!!!!"

[The woman pauses momentarily to take a breath.]

Wives had veto power over their sales! Wives had a choice!! Their sales were voluntary!!! To be sold to other men, their "consent was essential."[19] And "in many instances the wife appears to have been retained because she did not like her purchaser."[20]

"Huh. So these auctions were more like, 'I am woman, hear me roar' than glorified slave sales?"

[The woman's husband visibly relaxes.]

As I was saying, when a wife vetoed a transaction, the auction would end or, if she was willing, her husband could put her up again to the remaining bidders.[21] "After several biddings," a wife in Manchester, for instance, "was knocked down for 5s; but not liking the purchaser, she was put up again for 3s and a quart of ale."[22]

Of course, as in any market, there were a handful of fraudulent sellers—husbands who tried to sell their unconsenting wives to purchasers as consenting ones. But, these sales typically failed. Historian E. P. Thompson collected information on 218 wife sales covering the years from 1760 to 1880. Among them he found only four instances in which a wife whose husband offered her for sale didn't consent to the transaction.[23] Only one of these sales actually transpired, and even this case of alleged coercion is suspect. After her sale, the supposedly unwilling wife wrote a letter to the magistrate—not to complain that she had been sold against her will, rather, to complain that her former husband wasn't honoring the terms of her sale agreement. He was pestering her new husband for more money!

"The strangest thing about these sales," a nineteenth-century periodical puzzled, "is, that the women sold seem to have rejoiced in the change more than they lamented the degradation."[24] Indeed. A woman sold at Smithfield market, for example, "declared it was the happiest moment of her life."[25] One in Whitechapel "went off, in high spirits, with her new master."[26] Another "appeared overjoyed at the change."[27] This isn't puzzling at all once one recognizes that wives were sold to other men only when they wanted to be.[28]

These wives wanted out of their existing marriages, and they weren't exactly shy about the fact. A wife sold at Tunbridge Market, for instance, "declared her husband was such a good-for-nothing rascal she could not live with him."[29] Another was happy to be sold by her husband because she had "had enough of him."[30] Yet another remarked "that her first husband was such a brute that she was glad to get rid of him."[31]

The descriptions we have of wife-selling husbands provide some clues as to their wives' enthusiasm about being sold. "Few of the husbands involved in these dealings are described as beauties." But "common are the 'drunkard, non-communicant, [and] contemner of the ministrie,' the 'ill-looking diminutive fellow, of apparently low and profligate habits,' the laboring man 'of idle and dissolute habits' and the 'wretched-looking fellow' or 'burly rascal.'"[32]

Wife buyers were considerably more desirable—men of greater means and social status. "In almost all examples there was a tendency for the wife to be upwardly mobile," and "in no case was the woman left with a partner who was demonstrably socially inferior to the man who sold her."[33] In other words, sold wives traded up.

[*The tobacco-chewing man raises his hand.*]

Captain America has a question.

"*What's all this gotta do wit Kristi Yamaguchi? That baseball-playin' feller you was talkin' bout afore.*"

You mean Daisuke Matsuzaka! Right. To understand that, you need to appreciate why sold wives were willing to be sold. Since their sales required their consent, they must've wanted something.

[*A patron shouts.*]

What's that? The acoustics in here are terrible, and that damn tapping noise . . .

[searching for the source of the noise and spotting a man with a glass eye]

Sir, would you please stop tapping your eye with your pen?!

[*The patron who shouted a moment ago does so again.*]

*"I said: Better husbands! You already told us what the wives got
when you told us about how their previous husbands were ugly,
mean, and poor—and how the new husbands they were getting
were richer, fancier—more like George Clooney."*

That's right. I did tell you that. But why, if sold wives wanted new
husbands, didn't they just divorce their existing ones and marry anew?
Why submit to sales at public auctions?

To answer *that* question, you need to know a little about marriage
and divorce in Industrial Revolution England—and how English law
relates to Captain America's question about the posting system. There,
the law called an unmarried woman a *feme sole*—a "single woman."
Such a woman could own property, enter contracts, and enjoy freedom
of her person. In these respects, legally, she was like a man.

When she got married, she became a *feme covert*—a "protected
woman." But that protection didn't come cheap. For the typical wife,
all the property she owned before marriage and all that would have
come into her possession as a single woman, such as inheritance, her
wages from working, and the revenues generated by real estate she formerly owned, became her husband's exclusive property.[34] A married
woman also lost the right to enter contracts—most of her legal person-
ality, in fact. Those rights and attendant obligations, such as responsibility for debts she incurred on her husband's behalf, accrued to her
husband too.

In many ways, *a woman* became her husband's property when she
got married. Her husband could beat her "within reason," have sexual
relations with her on demand, and "restrain a wife of her liberty"—
imprison her in his home—"in case of any gross misbehavior."[35]

Wives did retain some important rights in their persons. Their
husbands couldn't murder or mutilate them, sell them into slavery, or

compel them to service others sexually. Still, legally, husbands' property rights to their wives were extensive.

In return for surrendering her property rights, a woman who married received a legal claim to her and, if she had any, her children's maintenance from her husband. The law required him to provide them support consonant with his means.

[Ania raises her hand.]

Ania?

> *"That's it?? Women sacrificed their property rights and personal freedom, and all they got was food and shelter? Why did any of them do it? I mean, why get married?"*

Well, back then, women's employment prospects were slim, and their wages were low compared to men's. Many working-class women couldn't earn enough to support themselves, especially if they had children.[36] That required men's higher wages, which marriage offered them.

[A woman in the front of the crowd interrupts.]

> *"What about love? Did people ever marry for love?"*

Sure they did. And among the working-class sort who resorted to wife sales, marriage for love was common.[37]

Even when people married for love, though, their marriages could break down—just like marriages can today. A marriage partner might prove less materially productive, sexually satisfying, fertile, or loving than their spouse anticipated. If life outside the marriage—alone or with a new partner—looks better to the unhappy spouse than continuing life inside it, they'll want to dissolve the marriage—a divorce.

In theory, the law in Industrial Revolution England granted husbands and wives the right to exit marriage, with or without their spouse's consent, under only two circumstances: adultery and life-threatening cruelty. In practice, however, husbands tended to be able to leave their marriages when they wanted without their wives' consent, while wives tended to be able to leave only if they had their husbands' permission.

One option that spouses had for separating from each other was a private Act of Parliament—the only means of divorce that permitted remarriage.[38]

[*The woman in the front of the crowd interrupts again.*]

"Are you telling us that the only way to get a divorce back in those days was to get the government to pass a special law granting you one?!"

That's what I'm telling you.

"WTF?!"

If an unhappy husband could prove his wife was an adulterer and could afford to undertake the necessary legal steps, he could secure a divorce through such an act. The first step was to seek a judicial separation from "bed and board," which, until 1857, only an ecclesiastic court could grant. Judicial separation permitted spouses to live apart. The court awarded the wife alimony because it was her husband's obligation to maintain her; their marriage technically remained intact. However, if she committed adultery, she forfeited her husband's support.

After obtaining a judicial separation, the typical husband seeking a private Act of Parliament sued his spouse's lover for "criminal conversation"—a legal euphemism for sleeping with another man's wife.[39] Victory here was helpful for proving that his wife was an adulterer. Having satisfied Parliament of as much, the legislation-seeking husband secured a divorce from his wife that freed him of all financial obligations to her and allowed both spouses to remarry.

The cost of this process was enormous. It could run into the thousands of pounds. A successful late nineteenth-century unskilled laborer, however, earned a mere 75 pence a week.[40] The only official means of divorce was therefore unavailable to working-class people.

An unhappy wife could also seek divorce through a private Act of Parliament, but her obstacles were far greater. Since she lacked legal personage, she needed to initiate legal action through a legal agent. And she couldn't do so simply because her husband was an adulterer; she also had to prove he was guilty of aggravating acts, such as incest or bigamy.

Demonstrating aggravation was difficult. Parliamentary members laughed in one wife's face for claiming aggravation based on repeated beatings. Of the 338 people who attempted to divorce their spouses using a private Act of Parliament in the 157 years from this instrument's inception in 1700 to its termination in 1857, only 8 were wives. Three-hundred eighteen husbands petitioned successfully, but only four wives did so. [41]

While a private Act of Parliament was the only official means of divorce in Industrial Revolution England, several forms of de facto divorce existed—legal and illegal spousal separations that could accomplish the same unofficially.

I just mentioned the first: judicial separation. If an unhappy husband could prove that his wife had committed adultery, the court would award him an alimony-free separation. Even if he couldn't prove it, he might still work the system to obtain a judicial separation by kicking his wife out of his house.

Under the law, remember, husbands were required to supply their wives housing. So, if a husband exiled his wife, she could, through an agent, sue him for restitution of conjugal rights—her right to live with her husband.

The court would then order the husband to let her back into his home. If he refused, the court would award a separation and alimony for the wife. If the husband was unsatisfied with paying his wife alimony, he could wait for her to slip into the arms of another man and *then* sue her for adultery, freeing himself from future alimony payments.

For an unhappy wife, separating from her husband judicially was much harder. In principle, the law allowed wives to sue for judicial separation on the grounds of adultery or life-threatening cruelty.[42] But in practice, judges vindicated wives seeking separation on the grounds of adultery only when they could prove their husbands guilty of cheating and, much more difficult to prove, aggravating acts, such as infecting them with venereal disease. Furthermore, unlike an unhappy husband, an unhappy wife had no legal back door—no way to kick him out—to secure a separation.

That wasn't all: even if an unhappy wife managed to get a judicial separation, legally she remained in a state of *feme covert*. As Lord Lynd-hurst complained to the House of Lords in 1856, this put her "almost in a state of outlawry. She may not enter into a contract, or, if she does, she has no means of enforcing it. The law, so far from protecting, op-presses her. She is homeless, helpless, hopeless, and almost destitute of civil rights. She is liable of all manner of injustice, whether by plot or by violence. She may be wronged in all possible ways, and her character may be mercilessly defamed; yet she has no redress. She is at the mercy of her enemies."[43]

If judicial separation put a wife almost in a state of outlawry, the second means of de facto divorce in Industrial Revolution England made her an outlaw: desertion.

To desert his wife, an unhappy husband simply packed up his be-longings and moved to another county or enlisted in the services over-seas. When his wife returned home one day, he was gone.

Desertion was illegal: it violated the law requiring husbands to maintain their wives. If the law caught up with a deserting husband, an ecclesiastic court could order him to pay alimony. Unfortunately for wives, it was tough to bring deserting husbands to justice. Ecclesiastic courts had but one means of enforcing alimony payment directly: ex-communication. And by the eighteenth century, this sanction carried little weight in the minds of most.[44]

An unhappy wife, in contrast, couldn't just pack up and leave. She often had no property and no property rights, and it was hard for her to find employment. "Although it was possible in some cases for the single wife to support herself, the additional burden of children often placed an unfair weight on her shoulders. The result . . . was usually impoverishment."[45]

Perhaps most important, it was much more likely that a deserting wife would be caught. Religious officials called "overseers of the poor" administered relief to unfortunate souls in English counties. They kept a watchful eye on newcomers to their communities with the aim of discovering and booting people they thought they would have to support. Normally that meant keeping an eye out for single women, since their slim employment opportunities and low wage-earning potential made them likely future recipients of aid.

The third means of de facto divorce was closely related to desertion: elopement. Eloping with an unmarried woman was as easy a way for an unhappy husband to informally dissolve his marriage as desertion. For an unhappy wife, however, things were again much harder. Eloping allowed unhappy wives to overcome one of the problems that desertion posed: in running away with other men, they had a ready means of financial support. But it posed another: How could they run away with their lovers in secret?

Husbands exercised close oversight over their wives. If their wives had lovers, they were likely to know or, at the very least, suspect that their wives might be cultivating relationships with other men. And if their suspicion was aroused, husbands who wanted to prevent their wives from eloping had plenty of control over their "property" to do so.

The final means of de facto divorce in Industrial Revolution England was private separation agreements: contracts between spouses relieving them of some of marriage's obligations. Typically in such agreements, husbands agreed to pay their wives some amount of support and return to them some of their legal rights.

In exchange, wives, through contracting agents, agreed to live apart from their husbands and absolve them from obligations for future debts. In some private separation agreements, the parties agreed not to legally harass the other for potential violations of marital law. Implicitly, such clauses were intended to secure husbands' promise not to sue their wives' current or future lovers for criminal conversation.

Private separation agreements permitted some unhappy wives to leverage the one bargaining chip that English law gave women at marriage: the right to maintenance. In return for her husband's permission to live separately, an unhappy wife could agree in a private contract to reduced support.

But even then, she faced difficulties. Until the 1840s, separation agreements weren't reliably enforceable in English courts, which, officially at least, didn't permit spouses to privately dissolve marital obligations.[46] This meant, for example, that a husband who had agreed to separate from his wife under a private contract but later changed his mind might forcibly seize her to reestablish cohabitation or, similarly, sue for the restitution of his conjugal rights and do so successfully. In this case, an unhappy wife remained separated from her husband only as long as he desired it.

Enforcement problems aside, unhappy wives could play their potential bargaining chip only if their husbands could be persuaded to privately separate in exchange for a lower maintenance fee. According to the law, maintenance was to be consonant with a husband's means. For a wealthy husband, then, the reduction could be considerable. But for the poorer sort, it would be small—perhaps too small to trade for a wife he wanted to keep.

[*A patron interrupts.*]

"So, because of the way marriage and divorce worked in Industrial Revolution England, unhappy husbands could leave their wives whenever they wanted and unhappy wives could never do so without their husbands' permission?"

You've the gist of it. But the way you put it is a little too strong. Some husbands who wanted to leave their wives couldn't because the law prevented them. And some unhappy wives managed to exit their marriages, even without their husbands' permission, through one of the channels I was just telling you about. Still, many unhappy wives, in particular the working-class sort, weren't able to do so.

I see some hands. You sir, the socially awkward fellow with robotic mannerisms. What would you like to ask?

"I'm an economist."

Me too. I'm sure your parents are very proud. Did you have a question?

"I see where you're going with this. You want us to believe that English wife selling reflected unhappy wives' means of exiting their existing marriages in an environment where the law basically required them to get their husbands' consent. The sale was like a bribe to secure his consent."

Very good, sir. That's exactly where I was going, I . . .

"But there's a problem with your analysis."

What's that?

"You've forgotten the Coase theorem."

I'm afraid you and I might be the only ones on this tour who know what the Coase theorem is.[47] Would you be so kind as to enlighten the group?

"The Coase theorem says it doesn't matter to whom the law assigns a property right. As long as it isn't too expensive to trade rights, trade will reshuffle the property into the hands of the person who values it most. In this case, English law is, for all intents and purposes, assigning a property right to wives' marital status to their husbands. So if wives value that right more than their husbands do, say, because wives want out of their existing marriages more than their husbands want to remain in those marriages, wives will just buy it from them."

Right. The Coase theorem is just another way of saying that people trade, and that their trading doesn't stop until the thing being traded ends up in the hands of person who values it most. However, in order . . .

"But that's why you're wrong."

What's why I'm wrong?

"The Coase theorem. It's the reason why the story you want us to believe can't be correct. If English divorce law required wives to get their husbands' permission to exit marriage, wives would've just paid their husbands to let them do so. There would be no need to subject themselves to humiliating public auctions."

Yes, but you're forgetting a crucial assumption behind the Coase theorem. In order for unhappy wives to purchase the right to exit marriage from their husbands, they must have something—property rights to income, land, *something*—with which they can pay their husbands for that right.

"Well, of course. For anyone to buy anything, they must have something with which they can pay the seller. But that's always . . ."

No, it's not.

"What's not?"

It's not always true that a potential buyer has property rights with which he, or rather she, can buy things.[48] You must not have been paying attention to what I was saying earlier when I was talking about marriage law in Industrial Revolution England.

"I tune out all descriptive nonsense. I'm still waiting for the equations."

Who can inform Dr. Spock here what I was telling you about wives' property rights in Industrial Revolution England?

[*A woman raises her hand.*]

Please, miss . . .

"*They didn't have any!*"

That's right. Most wives didn't have any property rights. When they got married, all their property rights transferred to their husbands. Thus, under the law, most wives' wages, real property, and anything else they might've used to purchase the right to exit marriage from their husbands *was* their husbands'.

[*The economist:*]

"*Ohhhh. I get it now!*"

Go ahead . . .

"*Unhappy wives who wanted out of their existing marriages needed permission from their husbands because the law effectively gave husbands property rights over their wives' marital status. Wives would've just bought their permission when they wanted out of marriage more than their husbands wanted to stay in, but they didn't have any property rights with which to do so. So married couples sought out people who* did *have the property rights needed for this—men who valued the unhappy wives more than their existing husbands did* and *who the unhappy wives valued as husbands more than they valued their current husbands—and sold the unhappy wives to them! That's how this is related to that Japanese baseball player and the posting thingy you were talking about.*"

You got it. And I guess you were paying some attention after all. You remembered what I said about Matsuzaka.

Wife sales reflected indirect divorce bargains between husbands who wanted to remain married to their wives and wives who didn't want to remain married to their husbands even more. They allowed

unhappy wives to buy the right to exit marriage from their husbands
when the law prevented them from buying it directly.

In this sense, wife sales were like the posting system, which leverages the buying power of MLB teams to facilitate bargains between
Japanese baseball teams and their contracted players when players can't
buy themselves out. Just as the posting system aligns the incentives of
Japanese teams, contracted Japanese talent, and American teams to enable player trades that benefit all involved, wife sales aligned the incentives of husbands, unhappy wives, and men seeking spouses to enable
divorce trades that made all of their participants better off.

[*The woman who spoke a moment ago raises her hand.*]

Miss, you wanted to say something?

"I don't get it."

An example might help. Consider an eighteenth-century English couple, Hattie and Horace. Horace likes Hattie. His valuation of Hattie-
as-wife is £5. But Hattie detests Horace. She values Horace-as-husband
at –£7.

Hattie wants to exit the marriage. To do so, she requires Horace's
consent. Horace is willing to sell Hattie his consent for anything more
than £5, and Hattie would be happy to pay him that much. But since
she's married, she has no property rights with which to do so. All that
Hattie might use to pay Horace is already his. A direct trade that would
enable Hattie to exit the marriage is impossible.

An indirect trade, however, isn't. Consider Harland, an English bach-
elor. Harland is Horace and Hattie's neighbor. He likes Hattie more than
Horace does. His valuation of Hattie-as-wife is £6. Furthermore, Hattie likes Harland more than she likes Horace. She values Harland-as-
husband at £1.

Horace knows this, so he proposes the following: if Harland will
agree to pay him £5.5, he'll sell Hattie to him. Unlike Hattie, Harland
has property that isn't Horace's, so this trade is possible. Horace would

benefit £0.5 from the trade. Harland would benefit £0.5. And Hattie would benefit £8. So, Hattie and Harland agree to Horace's deal.

[*The woman raises her hand again.*]

Miss?

"I get it now! But I have another question. How could it be that forced sales were so uncommon, as you told us before? I mean, you say that Hattie's consent is needed for the sale, but you also said that English law basically deprived wives of rights. So I don't see why husbands couldn't just sell their wives against their will."

Remember, although Industrial Revolution English law deprived most wives of the right to own property and granted their husbands considerable property rights over them as spouses, it did not, as I mentioned earlier, permit husbands to enslave their wives, nor did it permit them to sell their wives as slaves to others. So, if a husband sold his wife to another man without her consent and that man somehow managed to take possession of her against her will, such a woman could've, and presumably would've, run away at her first opportunity and sought the protection of the local justice of the peace—if a family member, or even a concerned citizen, hadn't brought the matter to the authorities' attention first. Potential legal repercussions for a coerced-wife seller aside, the possibility of such repercussions for a coerced-wife purchaser, together with the fact that he probably would've lost possession of his purchase soon after making it, made a coerced wife a poor bargain. Thus, as a simple practical matter, wives' consent really was necessary for these sales to be profitable for their husbands and buyers.

[*The woman nods in agreement. As she does, the economist interrupts.*]

"Wait a minute!"

What now, Dr. Spock?

*"I heard numbers when you were giving your childish Hattie-
and-Horace example to explain indirect Coasean bargaining, so
I started listening again."*

How kind of you. But that was like ten minutes ago. You must've . . .

"But you still have a problem."

What's that?

*"Your explanation demonstrates why some English married couples
used wife sales. But it doesn't explain why they sold wives* at public
auctions. *Harland is Horace and Hattie's neighbor. What's the
point of using a public auction there?"*

As Dr. Spock points out, in the example I gave you it's convenient
that Harland, a higher-valuing user of Hattie-as-wife, lives next door to
the troubled couple. What if he didn't?

In that case, he might not know he could purchase Hattie. Furthermore, Horace and Hattie might not know that Harland—their means
of realizing a mutually beneficial marital dissolution—exists. Gains
from trade would go unrealized. Most important, Hattie would remain
unable to secure the right to exit her marriage.

How can Horace and Hattie identify an appropriate suitor—a higher-
valuing user of Hattie-as-wife whom Hattie values as husband more than
she values Horace—when he isn't living right under their noses?

[*The economist shrugs.*]

By selling Hattie at a public auction. A public auction identifies
potential suitors who bid on Hattie-as-wife. Horace sets a reservation
bid at his valuation of Hattie-as-wife and solicits offers. Hattie agrees to
the auction provided that she may veto her sale to the highest bidder,
marriage to whom she may value less highly than marriage to Horace.

From Horace's perspective, a public auction accomplishes another
purpose: it permits him to realize the maximum price for selling Hattie's

right to exit by identifying the highest-valuing user of Hattie-as-wife whom Hattie is willing to take as her new husband. It also ensures that Hattie becomes the wife of the suitor who values her highest whom she prefers to Horace.

[*The woman who looks like Janeane Garofalo appears angry and has her hand up.*]

I'm going to call on you, Janeane, but only if you promise not to explode like last time.

"*This is all well and good for the men involved. But what about the women?! The men's exploitation of unhappy wives is despicable and . . .*"

Remember, wives had to consent to be sold, so . . .

"*Yes, they had to consent. But what does that mean when, as you described, wives could be beaten, imprisoned, and generally treated like dirt by their husbands?!*"

Right. But given that lamentable state of affairs, wife sales still . . .

"*Given nothing! I say, down with wife sales! Down with the capitalist patriarchy! Down with the . . .*"

Here we go again. Look, English *law* is what gave husbands such power over their wives! In the presence of that law, wife sales *improved* wives' welfare. Without wife sales, unhappy wives would've remained in marriages they didn't want to be in when alternative marriages they preferred to be in were available. Would you rather that unhappy wives be stuck in marriages they preferred less?

"*Well, when you put it that way . . .*"

You can get a good sense of the fact that many sold wives saw greener marriage pastures outside their existing unions by considering the identity of their purchasers, which "seems to have been . . . the lover on most occasions."[49] These wives valued marriage to other men more highly than marriage to their current husbands.[50] One couple, for example, decided it should resort to a wife sale "hav[ing] lately lived together on unpleasant terms, in consequence of the wife having a strong 'affinity' for a man on the opposite side of the street."[51] Similarly, for another, "The alleged ground of the separation was the incontinence of the wife, whose affections were stated to have been alienated by an old delver, who had occasionally got his dinners at their house."[52]

The frequent existence of a ready and likely high bidder—a wife's lover—explains why some wife sales were transacted without public auctions and why, even in some cases when they were, "the affair was a pre-arranged one between the buyer, the seller, and the sold."[53] If a wife-selling husband was fairly certain that his wife's lover was her highest-valuing user, a public auction was unnecessary to identify the appropriate suitor. Alternatively, if he thought that an unknown suitor might value his wife more highly still, he might want to put her up for auction if only to see whether he could motivate her lover to raise his bid. At a wife sale in London, for instance, although the couple had prearranged a buyer, "and he offered the price demanded, the husband still repeated his cries to try to draw some bidders, but none appearing, he pocketed the money."[54]

[*Someone shouts:*]

"*I have a question!*"

Go ahead, sir.

"*I get why some wives wanted to be sold and why their husbands were happy to sell them for the right price. What I don't get is the wife buyers. Why would anybody want to get a wife by buying her?*"

Since many wife buyers were wives' lovers, buying them was often the only way they could get the wives they wanted. For other desiring husbands, it was cheaper to buy a preowned wife at auction than to "buy" a new one, who they would have to spend time and money wooing. Some buyers didn't even want to spend the time to go to an auction: they hired purchasing agents to buy wives for them instead. In still other cases, wives' buyers weren't men seeking new mates at all. They were other people with the property rights required to buy wives' right to exit, such as wives' family members.[55] Regardless of who purchased a wife, though, since the sale required the husband's, the wife's, and the buyer's consent, the husband, the wife, and the buyer benefited.

I think the young man in the back has a question.

"Was this wife-selling business legal? I mean, how could English law do everything short of banning marital dissolution and yet allow this wife-selling business to go on?"

The legal status of wife sales was peculiar. While wife sales weren't legally sanctioned, they "were popularly believed to be a legal and valid form of divorce."[56] In large part, this was due to the ambivalent, and sometimes confused, attitude of public officials toward the practice.[57]

Public officials were aware of wife sales, but most turned a blind eye to them.[58] Some did more than that: they participated in wife sales as toll collectors and marketplace constables where wives were sold. Technically, wife sales constituted bigamy, which was illegal. But several jurists expressed confusion about whether wife selling itself was prohibited, as did the parties to wife sales and the lawyers who sometimes codified them.

"As to the action of the sale itself," one judge remarked, "I do not believe in the right to prevent it, even to put an obstacle in its way, because it was founded on a custom preserved by the people, a custom, perhaps, that it would even be dangerous to pass a law which abolished it."[59] Authorities rarely prosecuted wife selling and, when they did, typically punished it lightly.[60]

Public officials' laissez-faire attitude helps explain why, though wife sales lacked official legal sanction and in some cases clearly flouted it, they were often conducted in the open, in the most public of marketplaces, before throngs of spectators, and commonly reported in newspapers for all to see.

[*The previous questioner has his hand raised.*]

You have a follow-up question, sir?

"So did wife selling stop when public officials decided to crack down on the practice? Is that why wife sales ended?? They did end. Right?"

The heyday of wife selling is long past. But wife sales didn't end because authorities stepped up enforcement against the practice. Rather, it seems they ended because eventually they stopped being useful.

Wife sales were needed to enable unhappy wives to exit their marriages when most wives didn't have the legal property rights required to buy permission to exit marriage from their husbands directly. But when wives finally got those rights, Dr. Spock's intuition about the Coase theorem kicked in. At that point, unhappy wives could buy the right to exit marriage from their husbands without an intermediary.

The first major step in English law that granted wives some property rights was the Matrimonial Causes Act of 1857. It declared that a wife "who obtained a decree of judicial separation . . . should henceforth be treated as a feme sole with respect to her property and contracts" and permitted deserted wives to own property they earned or received after their desertion.[61] The 1857 act also made it easier to obtain a de jure divorce—one enabling remarriage—by replacing the costly process of obtaining a private Act of Parliament with a cheaper one through the secular courts.[62]

Next came the Married Women's Property Act of 1870, which was much more significant. This act endowed married women who earned income separately from their husbands with property rights in such income earned after the act's passage, as well as income from investments they made based on those earnings. Furthermore, the act endowed wives married after its passage with rights to revenues from real property inheritances; to personal property inheritances from their next of kin, including cash up to £200; and to maintain legal action in their own names for the recovery of such property.[63]

In 1882 the Married Women's Property Act was modified to include still more sweeping changes. In addition to clarifying and expanding the property wives could own, this legislation extended property rights to women regardless of when they married and covered property regardless of when it was earned or received. It gave all English wives complete and unfettered property rights, as well as rights to bring legal action pertaining to them, consonant with those they were entitled to as unmarried women.

This new legal environment greatly diminished the need for wife sales by diminishing the need for unhappy wives to purchase the right to exit their marriages from their husbands indirectly. In consequence, wife sales declined precipitously. More than 75 percent of the 222 wife-sale cases my friends and I collected occurred before the first important English legal change that granted some wives some property rights in 1857. More than 80 percent occurred before the next significant legal change, which extended wives' property rights in 1870. And more than 90 percent occurred before the final important English legal change, which granted all wives total property rights in 1882.

In the cases we looked at, there were seventeen wife sales between 1870 and 1879. Between 1880 and 1889, there were sixteen. And between 1890 and 1899, there were ten wife sales. One scholar reports finding nine cases between 1900 and 1909, and rare reports pop up after that—one as late as 1972.[64] But by the turn of the twentieth century, English wife sales were exceptional.

It's unsurprising that wife sales took some time to disappear following England's 1870 and 1882 legislation. Important provisions in the 1870 act applied only to women who married after its passage, others only to property that wives received after this date. Even after 1882, when these limitations were lifted, a shortage of funds, confronted in particular by poorer wives, likely prevented direct divorce bargaining between some spouses. The 1882 act made it possible for all wives to own the property required to purchase marital exit from their husbands, but it didn't give them any property.

Although wife sales didn't end until the turn of the twentieth century, their usage may have started declining some seventeen years before the first English legal change granting wives property rights—around 1840.[65] In the 1830s, the newspapers my friends and I looked at reported thirty-five cases of wife sales. In the 1840s, they reported only about half that number.

This decline may simply be an artifact of data availability or newspaper reporting. Alternatively, it may be related to England's Custody of Infants Act, which Parliament introduced in 1839.

Under that act, wives who were judicially separated from their husbands received the right to custody of their children under age seven and access to their older children if the court deemed fit. Prior to that, wives' children, like everything else they had, was their husbands' exclusive property. Wives had no right to custody, and not even the right to see their children.

The fall in wife sales that appears around 1840 is consistent with the logic we've been considering if you think about the Custody of Infants Act as granting wives new property rights in their children.[66] Presumably some husbands valued their children's custody and didn't want to lose it. This act, then, may have given some unhappy wives seeking to remarry a new and significant bargaining chip for negotiating with their husbands. After 1839, they could agree not to seek custody in exchange for their husbands' consent to let them be.

Since these property rights applied only to wives who were judicially separated, I don't want to push this argument too far. The drop in wife sales seems too steep to be the result of that law alone. Still, it provides a potential contributing explanation.

Another possible contributor was a contemporaneous improvement in the legal enforceability of private separation agreements between spouses. In 1835, Parliament clarified the confused, and confusing, legal status of the financial terms contained in such contracts by declaring that secular courts should enforce them. Over the next thirteen years, legislators extended the variety of provisions in private separation agreements that should be considered enforceable, which by 1848 included nearly all of them.

At least in principle, private separation agreements, remember, permitted some unhappy wives to leverage the one property right that English law granted them at marriage—the right to their husbands' maintenance—to secure their husbands' consent to leave their marriages. By reducing one of the impediments to such agreements—enforceability—these legal changes improved the odds for some wives to exit through private contracts, reducing their reliance on wife sales.

To look at it, the practice of publicly auctioning wives to the highest bidder was misogynistic madness run amok, which is why just "looking at it" is a bad way of evaluating wife sales and other seemingly senseless social practices. A much better means of assessment is to look at them through the lens of incentives. Everyone has that piece of paper from the start of the tour, right?

Where the law erected obstacles to husbands and unhappy wives dissolving their marriages for mutual benefit, spouses didn't just sit on their laurels. They developed an informal work-around that provided the right incentives to the right parties to realize bargains that—given the prevailing constraints—made wife-selling husbands, wife buyers, and sold wives better off. To look at it *through the lens of incentives*, the practice of publicly auctioning wives to the highest bidder was an aid to many unhappily married women, an exceptionally clever answer to a regulatory roadblock.

That concludes the wife-selling segment of the tour. Use the restroom. Get the glass-eye-tapping out of your system. Do what you need to do. Then step this way and I'll show you to our next "WTF?!"-worthy social practice. There are more unexpectedly witty solutions to social problems on the stop ahead. This one has—how do I put it?—a more feculent flavor.

4

Public Uses for Private Parts

Once upon a time there was a little girl named Petra. Petra was a delightful young lady. But she was a biter. If things went wrong at playgroup, she snapped—quite literally—at the offending playmate.

Petra wasn't hostile, mind you. Most of the time she got along well with others. But occasionally a malicious or stupid child would provoke her.

[*Several members of the crowd show disdain.*]

I see the contempt on your faces. But what would you've had Petra do? She certainly wasn't going to sit idly by while her toys were run roughshod over by some lout whose parents hadn't bothered to teach him playgroup manners. So Petra bit. She bit hard.

Petra's defense worked a little too well. She soon discovered that the threat of her powerful jaws was enough to get almost any other child to do what she wanted. She went from defense to offense.

A coalition of "concerned parents"—the progenitors of Petra's delinquent playmates—brought this to her parents' attention. They were mortified. At first, Petra's parents tried talking to her. "You can't bite others, no matter how much they might deserve it," they instructed her. But Petra was drunk with biting power. Reason couldn't stop her.

So Petra's parents tried another approach. "When boys and girls bite other boys and girls, they make Santa unhappy," they told her. "And if Santa is unhappy with a boy or girl, he might not bring them any presents for Christmas."

Petra was shocked. She had always thought of Santa as an understanding, if somewhat pompous, fellow. Surely he could appreciate that she bit only those who had it coming—playmates who had done something to her first, or perhaps hadn't just yet but she strongly suspected were considering it.

"No," Petra's parents informed her. "Santa abhors and punishes all biting."

After much thought, Petra decided it was probably best if she forewent displays of her chomping prowess henceforward. She would cease biting to ensure an appropriate Christmas haul.

Many years later, when Petra was in college, one of her friends relayed a story to her in which two other students got into a fight. In an act of desperation, one of the students, her friend described with some amusement, bit the other. Upon hearing this, in an uncharacteristic moment of emotional Tourette's, Petra blurted, "No! It's not worth it! Santa will punish you!!"

Petra's friend looked at her in astonishment.

"WTF?!" he said a moment later. "Oh, nothing," Petra uttered nervously. "Did you just say that Thomas shouldn't bite because Santa would punish him?!" her friend asked.

Petra was outed. She had internalized her parents' warning from back when she was in playgroup. And to that day, she had abstained from biting for fear of Santa's wrath.

Petra's friend proceeded to inform her that Santa wasn't real and that, if he were, he certainly wouldn't care about biting. Petra played it off. She knew that! Geez, nobody believes in Santa, let alone that he cares about biting.

But secretly, inside, Petra was crushed. Of course, as a woman nearing twenty years old, she knew that Santa was fictional. Yet only then was it driven home that her parents had lied to her all those years ago.

After a few minutes, Petra's embarrassment and anger turned to an inner smirk. She realized *why* her parents had lied to her: to prevent her from growing into the worst kind of biter—the adult kind. Petra's parents couldn't be with her all the time to make sure she behaved. But they could incentivize to her to do so even when they weren't around by convincing her that Santa disapproved of biting. So that's what they did.

When I think back to that time, I still . . .

[A patron shouts:]

"Are you Petra?!"

What!?! Of course not! Do you think *I* would believe something so ridiculous?! Petra was a little *girl*.

"It's just that you got really emotional there. And then you said 'I.'"

Enough stories. You get the point. Now, does anyone have a tissue I could use? I seem to have something in my eye.

[sniffling]

If you come this way, you'll see a bar of soap:

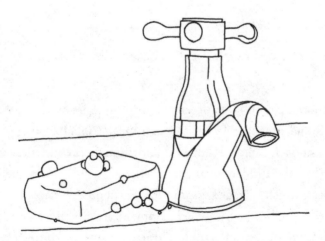

You probably have a similar one at home next to your kitchen sink where you wash your dishes, your hands . . . well, except for Janeane, who "keeps it organic." Or if you're a Gypsy.

[A patron speaks:]

"Gypsies don't bathe?"

No. Gypsies are very clean. But a Gypsy would never use a bar of soap he used to wash his hands to do his dishes. That would be *defiling*.

[The crowd looks puzzled.]

It's part of how Gypsies use beliefs about their private parts to create public order.

[blank stares]

Let me explain.

"Gypsy" is an ethnoreligious designation. It refers to the Romani people, or Roma.[1] These people descended from India.[2] Gypsiologists are unsure about the precise reasons for their exodus, but they believe Gypsies' migration began in the High Middle Ages.[3]

There are several Gypsy subgroups. The largest and most prominent one in the United States is the Vlax Roma.[4]

[The previous questioner interjects:]

"There are Gypsies in the United States? Like, the modern United States??"

Yup, more than 100,000 of 'em.[5] I'm going to focus on the American Vlax Roma from the 1920s through the 1970s. That's a pretty long period, and a lot surely changed in American Gypsy societies over those years. But the fundamental characteristics of Vlax Roma beliefs and practices, which is what I want to tell you about, didn't.

The most basic unit of Roma organization is the extended family, or *familia*. Multiple families, often with some kin relation, compose a Gypsy clan, or *vista*. Multiple clans compose a Gypsy "nation," or *natsia*. There are four Vlax Roma nations: the Kalderash, Lovara, Machvaya, and Churara. Economic partnerships between Gypsies currently living and working together in an area compose another organizational unit: the *kumpania*.

Gypsies have two kinds of leaders, *bare* (or *shaturia*) and *pure*. *Bare* are administrative leaders—the first among elders in their communities. A *baro* oversees community members' everyday interactions, in particular economic ones, in each *vista* or *kumpania*. He's also his *kumpania*'s interface with non-Gypsy authorities, such as police and social workers. *Pure* are spiritual leaders—old, well-respected heads of large Gypsy families and clans.[6]

Gypsies are superstitious—very superstitious. Their superstitions are embodied in a code of sorts called *Romaniya*. This code, customary and oral, defines the rules Gypsies must follow according to their belief system.[7]

The core of *Romaniya* is a concept of ritual pollution, or *marime*, and ritual purity, or *vujo*. A person or object may be dirty, what Gypsies call *melyardo*, without being *marime*. What's *marime* is "spiritually soiled," not physically soiled like Janeane.[8]

Gypsies divide the human body's ritual cleanliness at the waistline. Below the waist, the body is *marime*, made so by the genitals and anus. The lower body's polluting power is contagious; unguarded contact with it can contaminate the individual and people he has contact with. Above the waist, the body is *vujo*. The head, which is physically farthest from the ritually contaminated nether regions, is most pure.

Nearly all Gypsies' other beliefs, and the attendant *Romaniya* rules that govern them, stem from this division. I'm going to describe some of these beliefs to you now, but my description isn't exhaustive.[9] It can't be: *Romaniya*'s customary nature makes for ever-evolving particulars, and particulars vary among Gypsy families, clans, and nations. Still, the basic principles are common.[10] They largely define what it means to be a Gypsy.[11]

According to Gypsy superstition, menstruation makes women's lower bodies more polluted than men's. Even women's skirts are *marime* since they directly contact their lower bodies, and simply brushing a man with them when passing him may be enough to pollute him.

If a Gypsy woman wants to assault a male Gypsy, she doesn't use her fists; she tosses her skirt at him, exposing her genitals, which makes him *marime*. Walking in front of a man seated on the floor, such that a woman's genitals pass in front of his face, or over him on the floor above, such that they pass over his head, has the same effect. Both must be avoided.

When preparing food, women must wear aprons to block their skirts from contaminating the food. When menstruating, they must refrain from preparing food altogether; an apron can't block a pollutant so strong. Women must also eat alone during that time of the month; the risk of polluting others is too high.

Naturally sex is a delicate affair since it involves physical contact between bodies' lower halves. In fact, nudity itself is problematic. Since women's genitals are exposed, they're likely to pollute the men they're facing. To avoid this, when undressing, women must turn their backs to them.

Separating laundry is crucial—not by color but gender—to prevent women's contaminated undergarments from polluting men's clothing and ultimately their wearers. On similar grounds, men mustn't walk under clotheslines on which women's clothing is hanging.

The hands are tricky since they negotiate the body's upper and lower halves. Careful cleaning can prevent hands that have touched the lower half from contaminating the upper half, but Gypsies must take other precautions to avoid making themselves or objects they handle *marime*.

They mustn't wash their hands in the same sink as dishes or eating utensils. Pollution on the hands from contact with the lower body would spread to the water. From the water, it would spread to the sink. From the sink, to the dishes and utensils. And from there, to the food, infecting the eaters.

Similarly, as one Gypsy described, "You never take a sponge or a wash rag that you use to clean out the bathtub in the kitchen sink. It doesn't matter if you washed it out a million times. It would be *marime* because it touched the tub where your lower body was."[12] As I mentioned earlier, even soap can be polluting if someone has washed his hands with it.[13]

The lower body's pollution is so powerful that directly referencing its sources or the functions associated with them is taboo. A Gypsy must pretend to be leaving the room for another purpose when he leaves to relieve himself. Even yawning is frowned on because it suggests sleepiness, which in turn suggests a bed, which has *marime* connotations.

Cats and dogs are *marime*: they clean their genital and anal areas with their tongues.[14] Gypsies should avoid physical contact with them, and thorough cleaning is important if contact occurs.

Any person who doesn't follow *Romaniya*'s rules for ensuring ritual purity is also *marime*. Thus, non-Gypsies, who by definition don't follow these rules, are in a constant and full-blown state of defilement. A Gypsy must scrupulously avoid unnecessary contact with them to avoid becoming defiled.

With a few exceptions, such contact is limited to economic necessity. Here, too, however, Gypsies must carefully guard interaction. In *ofisi*—Gypsy fortunetelling businesses—for example, Gypsies cover the seats with protective slips to Scotchgard them against non-Gypsy contamination.

Gypsies won't allow non-Gypsies into private living spaces in their home. They might permit one into the front rooms, but they'll provide the guest with a special seat reserved for non-Gypsies. Similarly, if a Gypsy offers a non-Gypsy visitor food or drink, it will be in special cups or dishes, along with special utensils, reserved for *marime* persons. This way he avoids polluting himself and his belongings.

I see a hand. Did you want to say something, ma'am?

"WTF?! This Romaniya *business is crazy! Can you imagine what a pain in the neck it must be to follow all those rules?! There's no reason . . ."*

[*Ania interrupts:*]

"*There must be a good reason Gypsies believe that weird stuff. That's the point of this tour, right? We need to think about incentives.*"

Beautiful and intelligent! That's right, Ania. So, what do you think?

"*Well, you started this part of the tour with that story about how your parents told you—I mean, Petra's parents told her—that Santa wouldn't bring her any presents if she bit other kids. So maybe Gypsies' beliefs do something similar? Prevent them from hurting each other?*"

Bingo!

[*Someone grumbles unintelligibly.*]

You sir, with the misshapen head. Did you have a question?

"*I think your flirtation with Ania is clouding your judgment. What she said doesn't make sense; Gypsies already have a system of governance to keep them from hurting each other: the government of these here United States. America isn't like Liberia or those other places you were talking about earlier.*"

You raise a good point. But Ania is correct. Also, thanks for awkwardly drawing attention to my fondness for her.

Gypsies are self-employed. They abhor wage labor and, with rare exceptions, such as performing occasional seasonal work in the fields for others, eschew it. Gypsy men often work as metalworkers and tinkerers, tarmacers and roofers, used auto traders and repairers (in the old days, horse traders). Gypsy women are usually fortunetellers.[15]

In non-Gypsies' eyes, Gypsies are thieves, a stereotype some Gypsies have contributed to by stealing from and defrauding *gaje*—their term for non-Gypsies.

Gypsies look on *gaje* with contempt; the word, loosely translated, means "barbarians."[16] Using cleverness to relieve a *gajo* of his money or property is a virtue, not a vice.[17] Thus, Gypsies don't scruple at defrauding fortunetelling customers or engaging *gaje* in other confidence games.[18]

To engage in these economic activities, Gypsies commonly forge partnerships involving Gypsies from other families, clans, and Gypsy nations, creating the *kumpania* I mentioned before. They pool resources to start and operate fortunetelling businesses. They work together in teams, tarmacing, tinning, and roofing. And to restrict competition in their fields of work, they collude—carve up geographic territories, each *kumpania* receiving the exclusive right to operate in a given area.

These economic relationships, of course, can sour. Someone doesn't pull his weight on the job; one business partner cheats another; there's disagreement about the scope of exclusive territories. Such conflicts threaten to undermine Gypsies' ability to cooperate for mutual gain.

Gypsy marriages also have an economic element. Gypsies tend to marry at much younger ages than we non-Gypsies do, and when a boy is betrothed to a girl, his family pays her's for the privilege—a bride-price. Gypsy marriages can also sour. And when they do, they too create conflicts—clashes not only over the division of children and assets but also over the division of bride-prices—which similarly threaten Gypsies' ability to cooperate.

In non-Gypsy societies, preventing and resolving economic and divorce-related conflicts is the government's job. But in Gypsy societies, it can't be. The reason is that Gypsies' economic activities and marriages are often illegal.

Government won't enforce the terms of agreements aimed at theft or fraud, nor will they enforce collusive agreements.[19] Many municipalities prohibit fortunetelling, and Gypsies rarely seek or obtain the licenses and permits that local governments require of independent contractors and business owners to operate.

Nor will government oversee divorces involving people who were never legally married in the first place. Gypsies don't seek marriage licenses. Even if they did, they wouldn't be able to get them in many cases, since they often marry before the legal age of consent. It's also questionable whether government would be willing to recognize Gypsy brideprices. Besides, Gypsies' understanding of marital fault, and thus how resources should be divided in the event of divorce, probably wouldn't comport with *gajikano* understanding.

[*The gentleman with the misshapen head interrupts.*]

"Okay, Gypsies can't use government to deal with their conflict. I still don't see why they need all this marime *business, though. Why don't Gypsies just kick people out of their communities when they do something bad—you know, ostracize 'em? I'm pretty sure that other groups do stuff like that."*

Other groups do do stuff like that. And the threat of ostracism plays a crucial role in governing Gypsy societies too. But in Gypsies' situation, boycott alone isn't enough.

Social ostracism requires several things to work well as a form of governance. To start with, social rules—"laws"—need to specify what counts as acceptable behavior and what doesn't. Ostracism doesn't provide those rules; it's just a way to enforce them.

Second, members of society need to know who has broken a rule and thus should be ostracized. They could find this out by observing a rule breaker firsthand, or they could find out by hearing about a rule breaker from someone else who observed that person firsthand. One way or another, though, they need to find out—because rule breakers can't be ostracized if the people who need to do the ostracizing don't know about transgressions.

Which brings me to the third thing a society needs for social ostracism to be effective: a way to ensure that *everyone* in it boycotts rule breakers. Suppose that you and I live on the same street, along with a few others. Several years ago, we all agreed on a rule against urinating on neighbors' lawns. I'm walking in front in your house one day when the urge to go hits me. I'm too lazy to walk back to my place, so I drop trou and relieve myself on your flowerbed. Everybody on the street is looking out their windows when this happens, so everybody knows what I did.

Now, you, obviously, would be perfectly happy to boycott me in this situation and surely will. But I'm besties with everybody else on the street; they really like me. Plus, they know that my cat just died and they don't want to make me feel any worse, so they can't bring themselves to boycott me. I know this, which is precisely why I was willing to pee in your yard. The threat of ostracism has failed to prevent me from breaking our rule because our neighbors found it too costly to carry out the prescribed punishment. To avoid this, and to make ostracism maximally effective, everyone—even the people who don't want to—must have an incentive to boycott those who break rules.[20]

Finally, for ostracism to be effective, the value you attach to remaining in your society's good graces needs to be high relative to the value available to you outside your society. If it's not, the threat of being booted from your community will be too weak to deter you from breaking social rules: Why should you care about being expelled if there are plenty of opportunities available to you in some other community that you can move to?

Each of these conditions poses a problem for Gypsy societies. Take the first one: the need for laws against antisocial behavior. Since Gypsies can't rely on government—the usual creator of laws—no external set of rules regulating economic or marital relationships is available to them.

Or the second one: the need for everyone to know a rule breaker's identity. Gypsies are nomads, so they're often separated from one another.[21] This means that firsthand knowledge of a rule breaker's identity is possible for only a few. And "as most of these Roms" are "constantly travelling about, . . . the problem of communication with one another [was] a serious one" prior to the advent of cell phones.[22] Which means that, until relatively recently, learning a rule breaker's identity if one didn't have firsthand knowledge required some serious work.[23]

Or the third condition: the need for everyone to have an incentive to boycott a rule breaker. In Gypsy society, such a person could very well be a family member or close friend, so some members won't want to boycott people who are supposed to be boycotted.

Or the final one: the need for value obtainable within one's community to be high relative to the value obtainable outside it. The Gypsy population is tiny compared to the *gajikano* one. The economic opportunities available to a Gypsy inside his society are therefore small compared to the ones available to him outside it, making the economic punishment of even a perfectly effective Gypsy boycott modest at best.

[*The gentleman with the misshapen head speaks up:*]

"So, basically, Gypsies can't just kick bad apples out of their communities because of particular features of their groups."

Precisely. Ostracism can work for them only if they can figure out some way to satisfy the conditions I mentioned despite their groups' features.

"Oh. Okay. So I guess that lady you're flirting with was right."

She was. And thanks again for . . .

[*A patron interrupts:*]

"But how do superstitions about defiled soap and skirts help Gypsies make ostracism work? Still seems like a lot of baloney to me."

In the words of one scholar, "it is only a short step from the concept of the antisocial to that of the unclean," or in Gypsies' case, a short step from the concept of the unclean to that of the antisocial.[24]

By hitching rules that govern antisocial behavior to the rules that govern what's ritually unclean under *Romaniya*, Gypsies use the superstitions that govern their invisible world to help govern their visible one. These superstitions fill the gaps left unfilled by simple boycott in Gypsies' context; they ensure that the conditions necessary for ostracism to work are satisfied in Gypsy societies.

To create rules against antisocial behavior, Gypsies leverage their concept of *marime*. What's *marime* is polluting, hence forbidden—like washing a fork in the same sink as hands. So Gypsies classify theft, fraud, and violence against other Gypsies as *marime*, rendering these behaviors polluting and thus forbidding them too.[25]

This is exceptionally clever, for it not only creates "laws" in Gypsy societies; it creates laws that are largely self-enforcing. Punishment unleashes "automatically" on a Gypsy when he misbehaves because misbehavior is *marime*. In this way, Gypsies' "unwritten law . . . is its own defence against violation."[26]

That defense, however, isn't perfect. If it were, no Gypsy would ever break any rules, and ostracism would be unnecessary. Suppose a Gypsy defaults on an agreement with his business partner but believes he has a good reason for doing so—that his breach is justified. In this case, punishment won't self-execute, since the lawbreaker doesn't believe his *Romaniya* violation is genuine. As far as he's concerned, he remains pure.

To prevent situations like this, the threat of a stronger, slightly different kind of punishment is needed. Bringing us to the *kris Romani*—Gypsy court.

If one Gypsy accuses another of violating *Romaniya*, the accused stands trial before a *kris*. Often persons related to the parties will first attempt to reconcile their conflict through an informal arbitration procedure called a *divano*, overseen by one or more *bare*. If either party remains unsatisfied, the dispute escalates to the *kris*.

A panel of judges called *krisnitorya* presides at the *kris*. Gypsies select *krisnitorya* from the ranks of the *pure*, the spiritual leaders I mentioned before. At the *kris*, both sides present testimony and evidence for their position. All adult Gypsy males are invited to participate in the proceedings; they provide their own testimony, weigh in with their opinions, and attempt to influence the court's decision.[27] When everyone has had his say and the *krisnitorya* are ready to offer judgment, the court declares its verdict.[28]

For non-Gypsies, "criminal law is secular, and consequently we . . .

differentiate between 'crime' and 'sin.'" But "for [Gypsies,] sins . . . are crimes and are subject to the kris"; they don't distinguish.[29] Thus, the *kris* "uniformly applies the same standards of and methods of proof, without concern for the type of case," be it one where the defendant stands accused of a spiritual crime, such as intimate interaction with a *gajo*, or one where he stands accused of a worldly crime, such as breaking his agreement with his business partner.[30]

If the *kris* finds someone guilty of violating *Romaniya*, it may order him to pay a fine. Alternatively, or if he refuses to pay, it may declare him *marime*. A *marime* sentence goes beyond publicly declaring the lawbreaker polluted, though it does that too. The sentence banishes him from the community—temporarily or, for the most serious transgressions, permanently. Whether he believes himself polluted or not, the lawbreaker now knows that everyone else does, as well as the disgust and shame with which they view pollution, hence him. Moreover, he faces a society-wide boycott.

Boycott is effective, recall, only if everyone takes part in it—even those who don't want to. And even if everyone is willing to take part, the lawbreaker can be boycotted only if everyone knows who he is. To address these problems, Gypsies again leverage their superstitions.

The belief that pollution is contagious incentivizes everyone who knows about the lawbreaker to avoid him, lest they become polluted themselves. As one Gypsy described it:

> Nobody in the world, neither his wife, nor his mother, nor his children will speak to [a Gypsy declared *marime* by a *kris*] any more. Nobody will have him at their table. If he touches an object, even one of great value, the sacred law insists that this object be destroyed or burned. For everybody, the person is worse than if he were a leper. Nobody will even have the courage to kill him in order to cut short his misfortune, for merely to go near him would risk making *marime* whoever has tried to do so. When he has ceased living, nobody will accompany him to his last resting place.[31]

The same superstition incentivizes everyone to find out who has broken the law. Gypsies who lack firsthand knowledge of a lawbreaker, such as those living in other communities, are willing to bear the cost of finding out whether a newcomer who shows up in their area has been banished from another one, since failure to do so could result in contracting his pollution. Thus, a lawbreaker banished by one Gypsy community won't be able to find refuge in another.

Nor will he be able to find refuge in the non-Gypsy world. The reason, again: Gypsies' superstition. In addition to offering many more economic opportunities, there's little chance that anyone in the non-Gypsy world would know, or care, about the lawbreaker's pollution. Unfortunately for the lawbreaker, that world is glowing with spiritual toxicity. According to Gypsy belief, recall, *gaje* are in a permanent state of contamination. Since "disdain for the non-Gypsy world, acquired in early infancy, maintains its hold over most Roma even after their expulsion from the community," there's nowhere for the lawbreaker to run.[32] It's not a pretty picture, and some Gypsies who've found themselves in it decided that death was preferable and committed suicide.[33]

Precisely to avoid such a fate, the vast majority of Gypsies follow the law. As Jan Yoors, who spent much of his youth growing up with Gypsies, remarked, "theft from a fellow Rom was unheard of."[34] Gypsiologist Irving Brown observed the same degree of cooperation in Gypsy society. "As for the morals of the Nomads in their relations among themselves," he noted, "they are probably higher than the average for the country at large."[35] Violence occasionally breaks out, but "cheating and robbing among themselves occur but very rarely."[36] "Each group," another writer observed, "functions like clockwork."[37]

Gypsies' "legal system . . . derives its coercive force from magic."[38] Yet that system works because, not in spite, of this fact.

[*The economist raises his hand.*]

Dr. Spock. You have a question? I still haven't presented any equations, so I'm surprised you're listening.

"Against my better judgment. You can spin a good yarn. But real scientists like me demand a test of our theories."

What would persuade you that my "yarn" is a plausible one?

"I'd like to see some Gypsy group that doesn't confront the problems of social cooperation you say these Vlax do and see if they believe in the same superstitions as the Vlax Gypsies. Your 'theory' says they shouldn't, but I'd bet you can't find . . ."

Like the Finnish Kaale Gypsies?

"Huh?"

The Finnish Kaale Gypsies. They have neither the economic- nor the marriage-cooperation problems that the Vlax Roma do. So by looking at them, I should be able to address your concern at least partly.

"You mean to tell me that there's a Gypsy group that doesn't confront the economic problems your other Gypsies do and that doesn't have marriage?! I highly doubt that. Marriage, as you should know, is universal."

Actually, it's not. If you can tolerate my lack of rigor a moment longer, hear me out.

In contrast to Vlax Gypsies, Kaale Gypsies are notable for what Kaale Rom scholar Martti Grönfors calls their "institution of non-marriage." As Grönfors describes it, "the Finnish Roma ignore the institution of marriage altogether."[39] They forbid it and "have no accepted way in which two individuals can legitimately form a marriage-type relation."[40] This precludes the main source of marriage-related conflict among the American Vlax: divorce.[41]

Also unlike the Vlax, who commonly forge economic partnerships with the members of other Vlax families and clans, the Kaale mostly partner economically within their kin groups; partnerships between kin groups are rare.[42]

In these respects, Kaale Gypsies' organization is peculiarly asocial. Compared to the Vlax, the Kaale confront few potential problems of social cooperation. According to Dr. Spock's prediction, the Kaale, then, shouldn't have developed the key superstitions of the Vlax.

And they haven't. Like all other Gypsies, the Kaale have a *marime* concept and ritual taboos associated with pollution and purity. But *marime* isn't physically contagious according to their beliefs, as it is for the Vlax, who rely on this superstition to facilitate the boycott of lawbreakers. Furthermore, the *gajikano* world isn't dangerously defiled according to Kaale beliefs, as it is for the Vlax, who rely on this superstition to augment the boycott of lawbreakers: "The Finnish Roma considered the non-Roma to have no power to pollute the Roma or anything belonging exclusively to that community." According to their beliefs, "there [is] no need to fear contamination from the outside."[43]

Male Kaale Gypsies have sexual liaisons with *gaje*, openly acknowledge this in front of other Kaale men and women, and suffer no social approbation for doing so. This contrasts sharply with Vlax Gypsies, for whom, "with the exception of . . . making money or by reason of economic necessity, the *gaje* are forbidden to Rom contact and association."[44]

Nor do the Kaale have an institution like the Vlax's *kris*. Since Kaale interactions are kin focused, most of their conflicts occur and can be handled within the family. The Kaale have no need for a more formal or encompassing judicial body to enforce laws against antisocial behavior, so they don't have one.

Of course, this doesn't mean that there's *no* potential for social conflict among Kaale Gypsies. Even when interkin-group relations are limited, conflict between kin groups can emerge, and the Kaale require some way of addressing it. Instead of the *kris*, their way is blood feuding.[45]

[*A woman interrupts.*]

"*Blood feuding???*"

Think Hatfields and McCoys.[46] The basic idea is simple: if you know that if you kill me, you and your entire family will remain locked in a state of war with my family for many generations to come, you're going to think twice about doing so. A protracted, lineage-encompassing feud is a much more severe punishment for killing me than if you expose only yourself to retribution. So blood feuding can actually prevent misbehavior known to trigger feuds, such as killing, and promote social cooperation—even though if someone is stupid enough to trigger one, lots of killing results, promoting social conflict instead.

Blood feuding is more costly to society than the *kris after* conflict has emerged and a feud has been triggered. Violence destroys more resources than peaceful conflict resolution in a Gypsy court. But blood feuding is cheaper than the *kris before* conflict emerges, when the threat of a feud is doing its job by preventing social conflict. Unlike Gypsies who rely on the *kris*, those who rely on blood feuding don't need to identify spiritual leaders, convene judicial bodies, or develop and maintain beliefs that make certain kinds of social interactions dangerous.

This makes blood feuding a sensible practice for promoting public order in a Gypsy society where there are relatively few opportunities to lock horns, such as the Kaale's, and makes the *kris* and its associated mechanisms for enforcing public order sensible in a Gypsy society that expects relatively more opportunities for social conflict, such as the Vlax's.

[*The economist looks eager to speak.*]

Dr. Spock?

"*That's all very interesting. But I doubt you can survive another test.*"

What did you have in mind?

"*If you're right that Vlax Gypsies use their superstitions to prevent antisocial behavior, then members of society who almost certainly*"

won't misbehave—old people and children—shouldn't be bound
by the same absurd rules. Having the rules apply to these people is
all cost and no benefit."

Why do you think that old Gypsies and Gypsy children are unlikely to
cheat other Gypsies?

"Because they're not integrated into the economic world. Children
don't have the same opportunities to take advantage of others that
adults do. Physically, children are less capable of inflicting seri-
ous violence on others than adults, and children's mental abilities
are less advanced and sophisticated. Only 1.3 percent of persons
arrested for violent crimes in the US in 2004 were under the age
of thirteen. And only 2.7 percent of persons arrested for prop-
erty crimes were that young. Barely any children are committing
crimes. The same reasoning holds for the elderly.[47] Only 2.7 percent
of persons arrested for violent crimes in the US in 2004 were over
age fifty-five. And only 2.1 percent of persons arrested for property
crimes were that old."[48]

You know those figures off the top of your head?

"My dissertation was on crime in America."

I see. So, what can I tell you about *Romaniya* and Gypsy children and
seniors?

Under *Romaniya*, the power to ritually pollute others and to become polluted by failing to abide its proscriptions follows the life cycle.
"Children are believed to be blameless to sin, including defilement,
because they are new and innocent, and not yet fully aware of the consequences of their deeds."[49] They therefore "enjoy a privileged status in
society until puberty, when they become subject to *marime* taboos."[50]
Then, in old age, Gypsies regain part of their immunity against pollution. "Old people are highly respected and are regarded as intrinsically
moral and clean."[51]

Pollution's contagiousness also follows the life cycle. Children can't become *marime*; thus, they can't transmit pollution if they do something that would be *marime* for an adult. Likewise, children are less prone to *gajikano* contamination than adults. They can eat *gaje*-prepared food and interact more freely with *gaje* without becoming polluted.[52] The elderly are less contagious too. Postmenopausal Gypsies, for instance, can't pollute men by tossing their skirts at them.

Just like you predicted, Dr. Spock. Any other tests?

"Hrumph. I guess that's all for now."

[Ania raises her hand.]

Ania?

"I have another test. If Gypsies use the superstitions that underpin Romaniya *to govern their societies, then their ability to use the practices grounded in those superstitions, like the Gypsy court, should wane when Gypsies' belief in those superstitions wanes, right? Didn't you show us something like that with ordeals?"*

I did. And you're right. Historically, *Romaniya* itself has largely ensured strong belief in its superstitions. It's a pain to avoid common situations and everyday occurrences proscribed by *Romaniya*'s ritual rules, like brushing against the wrong person's clothing or washing up in the kitchen sink. So only people who really believe in ritual pollution stick around to follow them. In this way, *Romaniya* filters out non- or weak believers, leaving the strong behind.

Several decades ago, however, this filter began to fail. According to Gypsy, and Gypsiologist, Ronald Lee, Gypsies' belief in the *marime* concept—*Romaniya*'s cornerstone—has weakened considerably since perhaps the 1970s. The idea of spiritual pollution still exists, but "the younger generation of Rom in the United States" has "difficulty in defining just what a *marimé* offense is."[53] Indeed, "more and more younger Rom refuse to take the old customs seriously."[54] As they do, Gypsy society becomes increasingly populated by weaker believers.

This, in turn, weakens *Romaniya*'s solutions to Gypsies' social problems. The fear of becoming *marime* is less effective in discouraging lawbreaking. The specter of contracting a lawbreaker's pollution is less effective in facilitating social ostracism. The non-Gypsy world is less ominous, weakening the fear of expulsion from Gypsy society.

And this has led to exactly what Ania suggested. In 1986, two hundred Gypsies from twenty-six American states convened a meeting "because Rom leaders felt that the overall effectiveness and structure of the *kris* was being eroded and weakened and that consolidation and reaffirmation of its strength were needed."[55] Also over the past several decades, some Gypsies have attempted to move away from *Romaniya* toward government to support their cooperation—at least when they can. Already in the late 1980s, Gypsies in southern California, for instance, attempted to integrate the *kris* and California's state court system to improve the former's power.[56]

Increased reliance on government contributes to a cycle that slowly undermines *Romaniya* and thus Gypsies' ability to use it to promote cooperation. The more that Gypsies rely on government, the less need they have for strong belief in the superstitions that underlie *Romaniya*. And the weaker is Gypsies' belief in these superstitions, the more they need to rely on government. Perhaps because of this dynamic, "the *kris-Romani* is not what it used to be in terms of its ability to administer problems that arise in the Rom-Vlach community."[57]

For all but perhaps adolescents struggling with hormonal impulses, structuring one's life around unguarded contact with the lower half of the human body at first seems insane. Building a legal system around that idea—in a class of its own. Not only can using beliefs about private parts to create public order be sensible, however; for some societies, it can be their saving grace.

Incentivizing social cooperation requires rules that proscribe antisocial behavior and ways of enforcing them. But not every society can rely on government to create and enforce such rules. Here, they must be gotten elsewhere—such as the superstitions embodied in *Romaniya*.

These superstitions provide a basis for rules proscribing antisocial behavior and have mechanisms that facilitate their enforcement built right in. When leveraged through institutions such as the *kris*, they powerfully incentivize good conduct. We can learn a thing or two from Gypsies—not only about good hygiene but also about how seemingly senseless social practices can be used to create alternative institutions of social order.

There's much more to tell you about superstition, but we need to move on. So please follow me to our next stop. Oh, and do me a favor: wash your hands in the sink reserved for that purpose near the exit. A few of you look like you may have defiled yourselves today.

5

God Damn

This marks the halfway point of our tour. Those of you who need a break or are hankering for some alone time, feel free to wander about. Those who are capable of digesting more than an episode of *The Real Housewives* in one sitting should come this way. I have a brief intermission planned for you.

Shortly after I realized my chances of baseball stardom were looking faint, I decided to direct my swing downward. I took up golf. The fact that men in their eighties—men of approximately my athletic ability—seemed to be able to make a go of it suggested that golf would be more my speed. Plus, I figured a stationary ball couldn't hurt me, which meant less flinching.

My dad had taken me to a course, and we were somewhere on the front nine, staring down our second shots of a par five—one of the longer holes. I hit a solid three wood . . . directly off the face of my club and into my father's thigh.

I'd seen my dad get angry plenty of times before, and I was no stranger to his temper or its physical manifestations about my head and neck. I'd also heard my dad curse before—often, in fact. But when my Titleist No. 2 went zinging off that three wood, I witnessed anger and heard expletives the likes of which I'd never heard before and haven't since.

He began with a guttural "God damn you, son!" That was followed by thirty seconds of incontinence-inspiring and vaguely pornographic execrations. My dad's pain eventually subsided, and he began to calm down, but he has a golf ball–sized welt in his thigh to this day. And though I doubt he'd admit it, I'm pretty sure he loves me a little less because of it.

Years later, I still remember that fateful outing vividly. People "God damn" other people, even objects, all the time. But my dad made dreadfully clear to me what people are really doing when they say that: they're asking God to damn—to curse—the object of their ire. That request is typically figurative. What struck me in his case was that I'm pretty sure the request was literal. He was asking the good Lord to curse his bad, bad son.

It turns out that literal requests for God to damn troublesome people have a long history. And the historical requesters are even more unexpected than my father: they're monks. If you follow me upstairs to the museum library, you'll see a genuine tenth-century monastic malediction formula:

[*Someone blurts:*]

"*A mala-who?*"

A malediction. It's like a benediction—you know, a divine blessing. Only the opposite. Today monks are known for turning the other cheek, honoring saints, and blessing humanity with brotherly love. But for centuries, they were known equally for fulminating their foes, humiliating saints, and casting calamitous curses on those who crossed them.

The monastic communities that specialized in maledictions were located in tenth- through twelfth-century Francia, a territory that on a contemporary map most closely corresponds to France.[1] Cursing monks used multiple kinds of maledictions. Historian Lester Little has translated and compiled many of these, so we have a good idea about what they were like.[2] And they were scary . . . very scary.

Liturgical benedictions are divine blessings following prescribed forms, bestowed on people that clerics want to venerate at times of community worship, such as mass. Benedictionals are the books containing clerical formulas for these blessings.

Medieval clerics had no "maledictionals." But they did have liturgical maledictions—divine curses following prescribed forms, leveled at people they wanted to damn at times of community worship. Consider this one, hurled by monks of the Abbey of Féfchamp at their enemies circa the late tenth century:

> We curse them and we separate them from the company of the holy
> mother church and of all faithful Christians. . . . May they be cursed
> in the head and the brain. May they be cursed in their eyes and their
> foreheads. May they be cursed in their ears and their noses. May they
> be cursed in fields and in pastures. . . . May they be cursed when
> sleeping and when awake, when going out and returning, when eating
> and drinking, when speaking and being silent. May they be cursed in
> all places at all times.[3]

The second kind of malediction that clerics used was called a "clamor."[4] To clamor is to make a vigorous appeal, which is precisely what monks did when they used clamors to curse. They publicly appealed to God and other holy figures—apostles, confessors, and, most frequently, saints—and sometimes they publicly humiliated them. Clerics would move holy figures' remains (relics) or related corporeal extensions (crucifixes and holy texts) from their traditional places of exaltation to the ground, covering them with brush or thorns. They might also humiliate themselves—God's servants—by lying prostrate on the floor.

Monks' idea was that humiliating holy figures (or themselves) would, in the eyes of those they sought to imprecate, agitate such figures, who expected to be venerated rather than denigrated. So provoked, supernatural overseers would turn their displeasure on the persons prompting clerics' rude call. Consider the clamor instructions from the Abbey of Farfa, copied circa 1020:

> An ecclesiastical clamor to God should be made in this way. At the principal mass, after the Lord's Prayer, the ministers of the church cover the pavement before the altar with a coarse cloth, and on this they place the crucifix, the text of the Gospels, and the bodies of the saints. And each cleric lies prostrate on the floor singing silently Psalm 73. Meanwhile two bells are rung by the church's custodians. The priest alone stands before the newly consecrated body and blood of the Lord and in front of the aforementioned relics of the saints, and in a loud voice he begins to say this clamor.[5]

If clerics combined their clamor and humiliation with a proper malediction, next came the cursing, such as: "May their lot and inheritance be perpetual flames with Dathan and Abiron, Judas and Pilate, Simon and Niro."[6] No doubt, this was a fiery affair that struck fear in the hearts of all who witnessed it.

The third kind of malediction that clerics used is probably more familiar to you churchgoers: excommunication and anathema.[7] Although these tools of fulmination were predominantly the privilege of popes and bishops, higher-ranking ecclesiastics sometimes "licensed" lower-level ones to excommunicate and anathematize people too.

Excommunication came in varying degrees, ranging from cutting one off from the holy sacraments to cutting him off from the Holy Church altogether. Anathema was excommunication with gusto— a more dramatic affair reserved for contumacious excommunicants, which often involved a ceremony of snuffing out candles or stomping them on the floor to symbolize the anathema's effect on a targeted soul.

Though curses weren't the proper province of an excommunication, clerics weren't averse to throwing some in against major offenders to punch things up. Consider the excommunication that Pope Benedict VIII launched against some people troubling the clerics of the Abbey of Saint-Gilles in 1014:

> May they be cursed in the four corners of the earth. May they be cursed in the East, disinherited in the West, interdicted in the North, and excommunicated in the South. May they be cursed in the day and excommunicated at night. May they be cursed at home and excommunicated while away, cursed in standing and excommunicated in sitting, cursed in eating, drinking, and sleeping, excommunicated in waking, cursed when they work and excommunicated when they rest. May they be cursed in the spring and excommunicated in the summer, cursed in the autumn and excommunicated in the winter.[8]

[The priest, distressed, shouts:]

"It can't be true!!!"

Oh, yes, it can, Padre. And it is. Your medieval forefathers cursed others with terrible illnesses, plagues, starvation, and dehydration. They cursed their wives and children, their animals and homes, their souls to spend eternity in the bowels of hell.

"No! We bless people! We bless their bodies and souls, their sisters and brothers. We bless them all with the goodness of God's grace."

And don't forget the cursing.

[Rage comes over the priest's face.]

"God damn you!"

There you go again. Curse, curse, curse.

[*Another patron interjects:*]

"*Why then? Why did clerics curse???*"

To understand that, you need to know who they were cursing: people who violated their property rights.

Some of these people were knights or powerful lords who coveted and aimed to plunder what neighboring monastic communities had: land and wealth. Others sought to violate monks' property contracts—break agreements clerics had with laypersons whereby the latter gifted land to the former.

To defend against such encroachments on their rights, monks threatened people who might plunder them with divine curses—maledictions like the ones I've been telling you about—unleashing them on anyone who dared to steal from the Church.

[*The priest pipes up again:*]

"*That doesn't make sense! Monks wouldn't have cursed thieves! They wouldn't have needed to. They could just ask the government to protect their property.*"

You're right: Monks would've turned to the government to protect their property if they could have. But they couldn't: public justice in tenth-through twelfth-century Francia was almost nowhere to be found.

Under the Carolingian dynasty, the line of royals who governed this territory until the middle of the ninth century, a system of royal justice—king-appointed counts and, failing them, the king himself—protected monks' property rights. However, beginning with the reign of the last Carolingian king, Louis the Pious, that system began to degrade.

Aided by the Viking incursions of the ninth century, which did much to disrupt the previous pattern of governance, the Carolingian system of royal justice wasn't holding up in the tenth. First, comital authority became hereditary instead of dependent on royal discretion.

This rendered counts largely independent of the central government's control. Not long after, counts too lost their public authority. Local strongmen fortified in castles, or "castellans," replaced them as the basic unit of governance. The result was a system of petty fiefdoms headed by strongmen accountable to no one but stronger men than themselves.[9]

This system has been dubbed "feudal anarchy." Many scholars of medieval history now eschew the term, but it provides a good sense of the decrepit state that public institutions of property protection were in between the tenth and twelfth centuries in this part of Europe.

The situation might not have been so dire for monastic communities if they had wielded the physical strength—military means—for self-protection. But the typical "monastery did not directly command the physical or military means to defend its own properties."[10] Monks surrendered arms, horses, and the like when they gave up their lives as laypersons and took up the cloth. Their communities' extensive properties thus sat there like ducks for unscrupulous strongmen who, as a group, more or less monopolized the means of physical force.

Unable to rely on government or physical self-help to protect their property against such people's plunder, monks resorted to spiritual self-help. "Maledictions were part of the stock-in-trade of monastic defense programs."[11]

The logic was simple: if would-be property violators believed in God and the ability of God's servants—clerics—to invoke his divine intervention, then the threat of supernatural punishments through divine curses could incentivize the strongmen to leave the monks and their possessions alone. God was, after all, the strongest strongman of all.

The malediction I recounted to you earlier from monks of the Abbey of Féfchamp, for example, stated that its goal was to make the abbey's depredators "change their ways and give back what they unjustly took away."[12] The one leveled by monks of the Abbey of Saint Martial of Limoges in the late tenth century began this way: "We hereby inform you, brothers, that certain evil men are devastating the land of our lord Martial" (the monastic community's patron saint).[13] Or as some clamoring clerics explained:

> To you, Lord Jesus, we come; to you, prostrate, we clamor, because iniquitous and proud men, emboldened by their own followers, invade, plunder, and lay waste to the lands of this your sanctuary and of other churches subject to it. . . . And our belongings as well, by which we are supposed to live and which blessed souls bequeathed to this place for their own salvation, they seize and violently take away from us.[14]

The same property-protecting purpose motivated the "curse clauses" that clerics included in their land charters with laypersons. A common way that clerical communities came to possess property was by gift from a lay benefactor. Unfortunately, the benefactor's lord, heirs, or his lord's heirs might want the gifted land for themselves, leading them to challenge the community's right to it down the road. To make this less likely, the benefactor's lord, heirs, or both were required to explicitly consent to his gift. I'm going to tell you more about the effects of this requirement in the final segment of our tour. . . . For now, bear in mind that these persons' consent was then recorded in a charter remembering the gift, held by the receiving clerics.

To strengthen the enforcement of such charters, clerics in tenth-through twelfth-century Francia often inserted imprecations in them, cursing anyone who might try to transgress their rights in the future. Consider this example from a twelfth-century charter:

> And if any wish to destroy this charter, may God strike their names from the book of life and toss their flesh to the birds of the air and the beasts of the earth. May the Lord send them to an abominable death and banish them quickly from this world. May they have the curses of the three patriarchs, Abraham, Isaac, and Jacob; and of the four evangelists, Mark and Matthew, Luke and John; and of the twelve apostles and of the sixteen prophets and of the twenty-four elders and of the 318 holy fathers who deliberated on the canons at Nicea; and may

they have the curse of the 144,000 martyrs who died for the Lord; and may they have the curse of the cherubim and the seraphim, who hold the throne of God, and of all the saints of God. Amen, amen. So be it, so be it.[15]

Excluding the entire army of saints, which is undoubtedly large, this charter invokes the curses of no fewer than 144,380 holy figures to be brought down on the head of anyone who might try to violate it.

[*The economist, double-checking my math and overflowing with excitement at the opportunity to use arithmetic, sputters:*]

"3 and 32 . . . carry the 7 . . . 144,380! That's a lot of curses!"

Sounds like that technical training is really paying off.

As I was about to say, you might wonder why the targets of clerical curses believed in them—why they thought that clerics' ability to call on supernatural power was real. The thing is, the curses of liturgical maledictions, clamors, and the rest were grounded in a centrally important book: the Bible.[16]

[*A patron shouts:*]

"Cursing in the Bible?!"

Yup. Like medieval clerics' holy practice, the Bible itself is a curious mix of brotherly love and frightful wrath. Consider this sampling from Deuteronomy 28:

If you do not obey the Lord your God and do not carefully follow all his commands and decrees I am giving you today, all these curses will come on you and overtake you:

You will be cursed in the city and cursed in the country. . . .

You will be cursed when you come in and cursed when you go out. . . .

The Lord will plague you with diseases until he has destroyed you from the land you are entering to possess. The Lord will strike

you with wasting disease, with fever and inflammation, with scorch-
ing heat and drought, with blight and mildew, which will plague
you until you perish. The sky over your head will be bronze, the
ground beneath you iron. . . .

You will be pledged to be married to a woman, but another will
take her and rape her. You will build a house, but you will not live
in it. You will plant a vineyard, but you will not even begin to enjoy
its fruit. Your ox will be slaughtered before your eyes, but you will
eat none of it. . . . The Lord will afflict your knees and legs with
painful boils that cannot be cured, spreading from the soles of your
feet to the top of your head. . . .

All these curses will come on you.[17]

These curses should sound familiar: they're the same ones that
graced liturgical maledictions, clamors, excommunications, and charters. Compare the curses elaborated in Deuteronomy 28 with a liturgical malediction from the Abbey of Saint-Martial circa the late tenth
century:

May the curse of all the saints of God come upon them. . . . May
they be cursed in town. May they be cursed in the fields. May they
be cursed inside their houses and outside their houses. May they be
cursed standing and sitting. May they be cursed lying down and walking. May they be cursed when asleep and when awake. May they be
cursed while eating and while drinking. May they be cursed in castles
and villages. May they be cursed in forests and in waters. May their
wives and their children and all who associate with them be cursed.
May their cellars be cursed, as well as their casks and all the vessels
from which they drink and eat. May their vineyards and their crops
and their forests be cursed. . . . May all their cattle and their work
animals, both inside and outside the stables, be cursed. May the Lord
send over them hunger and thirst, pestilence and death, until they are
wiped off the earth. May the Lord strike them with heat and cold.
May the sky above them be brass and the earth they walk on iron.

May the Lord toss their bodies as bait to the birds of the sky and beasts of the land. May the Lord strike them from the bottoms of their feet to the tops of their heads. May their homes be deserted and may no one inhabit them. May they lose what they have, and may they not acquire what they do not have. May the sword devastate them on the outside and fear on the inside. If they sow seeds in the earth may they reap little, and if they plant vines may they not drink wine from them. May the Lord send great plagues upon them, and the worst, most relentless illnesses, unless they change their ways. But if they are not willing to change, then let them accept from God and Saint Martial damnation with the devil and his angels in hell, and may they burn in eternal fires, with Dathan and Abrion. Amen, Amen. Thus may all memory of them be extinguished for ever and ever.[18]

Medieval clerics didn't pull their maledictions out of thin air. They anchored them firmly in their targets' existing beliefs.[19] Sly fellows.

[*Ania raises her hand.*]

Ania?

"Okay, but wouldn't people lose faith in priests' curses when priests cursed them and the curses didn't come true?"

An excellent question. You're right: clerics' targets would lose faith if they saw that clerics' curses didn't come true. But that would've required clerics to curse in ways that allowed their targets to tell if their curses came true. Clerics didn't curse that way. They used unfalsifiable curses instead. An unfalsifiable curse is one whose genuineness can be reconciled with all states of the world. In other words, it doesn't produce evidence that speaks to its truth or falsity, so it can't be disproved.

Suppose our friend Padre curses you with the following fulmination: "May hyenas eat you alive tomorrow at noon!" If tomorrow at noon comes and you're indeed eaten alive by hyenas, you, if you survive, and others if you don't, will upgrade the probability assigned to the possibility that Padre's curses are genuine. But if tomorrow at noon passes and you haven't been devoured by hyenas, you, and others who learn of this outcome, will downgrade the probability assigned to the possibility that Padre's curses are genuine.

Unfortunately for Padre, his curses are bogus, so there's no way for him to produce the effects his imprecations threaten. If he curses you with devouring hyenas, odds are that the hyenas won't show.

This poses a problem. Even if your or others' initial belief that Padre's curses are genuine is strong, it won't take many contradictory events to erode it. The trouble with the man-eating-hyena-at-noon curse is that it's readily falsifiable. Its specificity of harm and time, circumscribed effects, and worldliness make it easy for you to establish that it's false.

An unfalsifiable curse, in contrast, doesn't suffer from this problem. Suppose that instead of cursing you with devouring hyenas, Padre cursed you with this fulmination: "May you be miserable and die!" At some point in your life afterward, you'll be miserable, and you'll die. The curse's vagueness means that when these events happen, there's no way to know whether they happened because of Padre's curse or because they were bound to happen anyway.

A closely related way to make a curse unfalsifiable is to make it comprehensive: "May you suffer pain when you're waking or when you're sleeping!" The vagueness of suffering pain, which is sure to be the case at some point, coupled with the fact that this curse covers all possible times in which you may suffer pain—when you're awake and when you're not—renders it unfalsifiable too.

Still another way to make a curse unfalsifiable is to curse a target with unobservable afflictions, for example afflictions in another world, such as the afterlife: "May vicious goblins saw your limbs with rusty tree-trimmers in the Underworld!" There's no way for the living to tell whether such a curse has come true, no matter how specific it may be. So this kind of curse is impervious to being disproved as well.

Medieval clerics used each of these methods to make their maledictions unfalsifiable. Consider the curse clause in a clerical charter from Conques circa 910:

> If anyone presume to contradict this charter, let him be excommunicated and cursed as well as damned forever with Judas the traitor and with the devil.[20]

This one combines two methods for making curses unfalsifiable: vagueness and other-worldly affliction.[21]

Other maledictions, like the ones I described earlier, favored comprehensiveness for this purpose. The one that the monks of the Abbey of Féfchamp used cursed people literally "in all places at all times." Spelling out ominous particulars—physical afflictions and spiritual ones, torments of one's parents and children, misfortunes in the winter and the summer—lent the appearance of specificity, but this appearance was no more than that.

Did any of these curses come true? We'll never know—at least not while we're still breathing. And neither did the people on their receiving end, preventing them from being falsified.

[*The priest, bristling with frustration, interjects defensively.*]

"Well, if what you say is true, why don't my brethren and I use cursing to protect our property now? I can assure you that we don't, which means your comments on this part of the tour are inspired by the tongues of demons and . . ."

Because you don't need divine curses to protect your property, Padre.

When, in the thirteenth century, royal institutions of justice in Francia reemerged under King Philip II from their decrepit state in the previous two centuries, monks put their malediction formulas away. The liturgical malediction came to a close, and the curse clauses that graced clerical land charters began to disappear, seemingly as miraculously as they were invoked.

The reason for their disappearance, however, is no more miraculous than the reason they appeared in the first place. When royal institutions of property rights reemerged, monks no longer needed the threat of "God damns" to protect their communities. They could secure their property rights the old-fashioned way, though government—just like clerics can do today.

You may have noticed that in addition to seeming senseless, ordeals, Gypsy law, and maledictions share several things in common. Each is based on the superstitions of the people who lived under them. Each produced socially desirable outcomes—criminal justice in the case of ordeals, public order in the case of Gypsy law, clerical property protection in the case of maledictions—because of this fact, not in spite of it. And each achieved these outcomes by institutionalizing people's superstitions to incentivize desired behavior.

Gypsy law and maledictions share something else in common: they incentivized desired behavior in situations where government couldn't. Both, in other words, used institutionalized superstition to substitute for the state.

As you saw with Gypsies, however, such substitution is effective only if people believe firmly in the appropriate superstitions, another reason why Padre and his friends don't rely on "God damns" to protect their property rights: at least where they live, today, not many people believe in them.

[*A patron interrupts:*]

"*What happens when people's faith in clerics' power fades* and *clerics can't use government to protect their property?*"

You'll have to wait until we get to a later stop on the tour to find out. First, I want to show everyone a different "WTF?!"-worthy social practice. It, too, involves institutionalized superstition and an inability to rely on government. Step right this . . .

[stubs toe on door frame]

God damn it!

6

Chicken, Please; Hold the Poison

When my brother, Mark, and I were still in elementary school, but old enough to smell like preteens . . .

[winks at the woman who looks like Janeane Garofalo]

my mom, quite reasonably, began insisting that we wear deodorant. Mark and I resisted. The sensation of applying antiperspirant was strange. Moreover, we couldn't see the point in smattering our underarms with what we likened to "men's perfume."

To remedy our funk, my mom devised a plan that would make hygiene "fun." My brother and I liked playing with spray paint, she reasoned. Why not turn us on to the joys of "spray painting" our underarms with aerosol antiperspirant?

It was a clever ploy and a successful one—at least initially. For days, Mark and I used our new spray for its intended purpose. Soon, however, the novelty wore off. In search of new ways to amuse ourselves with deodorant, my brother and I went with the obvious: use it to coat a hockey puck.

Several times a day, we each spent some seconds frosting the puck with the aerosol can. Our jubilant anticipation of what it would look like after several weeks of diligent application was hard to contain. At the same time, we were well aware that should our amusement be discovered, my parents would be angry. So we hid the deodorant-caked puck in the back of a drawer in a dresser in our closet, where my mom rarely went.

One of us, it pains me to recall, accidentally left the puck exposed one day. My mom discovered it and took it to my dad, who was doubly disappointed. Not only were my brother and I clearly eschewing the use of deodorant, we were wasting money—a cardinal sin.

When my parents approached us, Mark and I adamantly denied responsibility. Clearly one of our sisters had coated the puck in deodorant, possibly both. Despite our impenetrable logic and much to our surprise, my parents placed blame squarely on Mark and me. What's worse, while they guessed correctly that we both had conspired in the effort, they suspected that one of us was the ringleader—and they wanted to know who it was. My mom and dad left our room, closed the door, and announced that neither of us was to come downstairs until the mastermind was willing to come forward.

Over the next few hours, Mark and I vigorously debated whose idiotic idea the puck's was. This mostly involved wrestling and occasionally threatening to destroy the other's favorite toy unless he admitted to having hatched the notion. At some point during this conflict, Mark grabbed my Magic 8 Ball.

Most of you have probably seen this toy gracing the shelf of some novelty shop, but for those who haven't, the Magic 8 Ball is nothing but a black, softball-sized plastic ball, styled to look like its billiard counterpart. Inside it is a die suspended in blue fluid, one side of which can be seen from a clear plastic window on the ball's bottom. The way you operate the 8 ball is simple: ask it a yes-or-no question, shake it, then turn it upside down to see what the ball has answered.

Reposing much faith in the 8 ball's divinatory powers, my brother and I had resorted to it to answer questions for us on previous occasions. But this day we resorted to it for a different reason: to resolve our conflict.

Shaking the ball and speaking in a voice I think he must've heard in *Indiana Jones and the Temple of Doom*, my brother conjured: "Oh, Magic 8 Ball, why is Pete such a liar? I know he remembers coming up with the puck idea even if I don't. Tell us, oh 8 ball, did Pete come up with the idea? Huy-yuy, yuy-yuy, huy-yuy, yuy-yuy . . ."

As he chanted and shook the ball, Mark began to laugh. "Do it already!" I cried impatiently. Just then he stopped, turned the ball upside down, and we both read the ball's response in near unison:

"Yes, it is certain."

"Giddy-up!" Mark said gleefully, tossing the ball on my bed. I sat stricken with fear and grief. "The 8 ball doesn't lie!" he shouted as he ran downstairs to relay my guilt to our parents.

Despite my disappointing result with the 8 ball in this case, it wasn't the last time I suggested to Mark that we consult it when we disagreed about something, and vice versa. All told, my Magic 8 Ball probably arbitrated more brotherly disputes than my parents, from the urgently important: "Are the Legends of Valhalla based loosely on Mark's feats of greatness?" to the routine: "Does Pete's bone structure compare favorably to a sherpa's?"

Sadly, my Magic 8 Ball met an inauspicious fate—and an undeserved one, I might add, given the dependability it showed in resolving arguments between my brother and me. It was slammed carelessly one day on a Micro Machines track and, while the ball didn't break open, the die became lodged in a single position—halfway between "Yes, it is certain" and "Ask again later"—rendering it useless. Although Mark and I were both fiddling with the ball and the track when it happened, I'm pretty sure he was responsible for breaking it. But of course he blamed me.

Unfortunately, the 8 ball was no longer available to resolve our disagreement, so we threw candles at one another for 45 minutes instead.

Why was I telling you all this, you ask? Follow me this way . . . Ladies and gentlemen, I give you *benge*:

[*The entire group now looks thoroughly confused, and a frustrated spokesman interjects.*]

"What are you talking about? Deodorant, hockey pucks, some toy you had when you were a kid, now a chicken?"

Benge is an oracle.

[Someone else shouts:]

"You already told us about those! They identified the guilty and the innocent."

No, I told you about *ordeals*. An oracle is a different kind of medium for divining answers to difficult questions—like my Magic 8 Ball. Except *benge* wasn't used by a couple of head-butting brothers to answer occasional queries. This oracle was consulted by an entire society of adults to answer, well, nearly every important decision in their lives, especially how to handle interpersonal conflict.

This society is that of the Azande, a people who inhabit north-central Africa. Today there are at least a million Azande; according to some estimates there may be as many as 4 million. A famous anthropologist named E. E. Evans-Pritchard lived among and observed the Azande firsthand in the late 1920s.[1] His observations provide the basis for what I want to tell you about these people and their oracles.

They are far from the only ones who've relied on Magic 8 Ball–like devices to make important decisions, though.[2] In the Ndogo tribes of Sudan, the Balovale tribes of Zimbabwe, the Nzakara and Apagibeti tribes of the Central African Republic, the Ngbandi tribe of the Democratic Republic of Congo, the Yoruba tribe of West Africa, societies in Ghana, Cameroon, and elsewhere people have routinely relied on oracles too.[3] The Azande, however, were particularly fond of them.[4]

At the core of the Zande belief system is *mangu*, a belief in witchcraft. According to Zande thinking, witchhood is a physiological condition. In the intestine of some people resides a substance that enables them to use witchcraft against their enemies. Witchhood is heritable: fathers pass it down to their sons, mothers to their daughters.

Most people are witches and don't even know it. Their witch-selves operate when they're sleeping or otherwise unaware, engaging in all manner of nefarious business. They ruin Zande crops, disrupt Zande hunts, cause Zande dwellings to collapse, inflict injury and illness, and are responsible for nearly all naturally unaccountable Zande deaths.

The geographic scope of witches' malefaction is narrowly circumscribed. A person's witchcraft may injure his neighbors—the people with whom he's in petty conflict—but not people outside his community, whom he doesn't interact with, and thus for whom the feelings that generate such conflict are unlikely to arise.

Since most, if not virtually all, commoner Zande families have witches in them, and many are unaware of it, people accused of witchcraft are neither maligned nor even looked on with askance for being witches per se.[5] Zande witches thus occupy a very different status than witches did in early modern Europe (you'll hear about them on the next stop of the tour), who were both exceptional and hunted for persecution on the grounds of being witches alone. For the Azande, what matters are particularized instances of witchcraft—whether a witch is, in a specific instance, doing injury to them. A "person who has bewitched a man is not viewed by him ever afterwards as a witch but only at the time of the misfortune that has caused and in relation to these special conditions."[6]

A Zande suffers some misfortune: his crops fail; his hunt is fruitless; he or one of his family members becomes ill. This is when he becomes concerned with witches who are undoubtedly responsible for his difficulty. And it's at these times that he seeks to identify the offending witch so that he can command him to cease his injuries, which the unwitting witch will ordinarily do. Once this is accomplished, the Zande's interest in witches, including the particular witch he's requested to cease injuring him or his family members, abates and normal relations with the witch resume.

To identify the witch offending him in a particular case, a Zande consults the oracle I mentioned a few minutes ago—*benge*—which works as follows: Poison harvested from a special vine is fed to a fowl. The oracle consulter treats *benge* to "a speech of five or ten minutes" in which he "puts before the oracle every detail of the situation on which it is being consulted, in much the same way as a case would be stated in the court of a chief."[7]

The consulter then asks the oracle a yes-or-no question about whether some neighbor is bewitching him in whatever manner befits his recent misfortune. He shakes the fowl to ensure it has swallowed the poison, similar to how you would shake a Magic 8 Ball to elicit a response. The fowl's reaction to consuming the poison—living or dying—is the oracle's means of replying to the question posed to it.

As he shakes the fowl, the consulter queries the oracle like this: "If [a neighbor's name] is guilty of bewitching my [hunt, person, etc.], poison oracle kill the fowl. If [neighbor's name] is innocent, poison oracle spare the fowl." Or in the reverse way, like this: "If [a neighbor's name] is guilty of bewitching my [hunt, person, etc.], poison oracle spare the fowl. If [neighbor's name] is innocent, poison oracle kill the fowl."

Any male who respects certain ritual taboos, such as abstention from sex and eating meat for a specified period, and either owns or can borrow the requisite poison and fowl may operate *benge* and do so whenever he wants.

However, "one does not place names of people before the oracle in a haphazard manner. One selects only the names of those with whom one is on bad terms"—people with whom he's in petty conflict.[8] According to Zande belief, witchcraft is motivated by personal animus. "A witch attacks a man when motivated by hatred, envy, jealousy, and greed. . . . Therefore a Zande in misfortune at once considers who is likely to hate him."[9]

The Azande consult their oracles with the assistance, or at least observance, of one or several trusted people. These people can verify that the oracle was indeed consulted in a particular case, and properly.

If the poison oracle "exonerates" the neighbor whose name the consulter has put before it, clearing him of the particular witchcraft, the consulter is satisfied that this man isn't bewitching him and resumes friendly relations with his neighbor, whereas before, he may have remained cold, distant, even passively hostile toward the suspected witch. The consulter, in other words, apologizes to his neighbor implicitly, quashing the conflict between them.

If the poison oracle "convicts" the person whose name the consulter has put before it, the consulter is satisfied that his suspicion was correct. In this case, the consulter informs his neighbor that the oracle has declared that he's bewitching him. The consulter takes the wing of the fowl that affirmed his neighbor's witchcraft, fans its feathers, and impales it on a pointed stick. He then finds a respected man, in many cases one of his community's deputies, to deliver the stick with the wing on it, or he delivers it to his neighbor himself.

The messenger lays the stick on the ground before the neighbor and states that the consulter's oracle has declared him guilty of witchcraft.

The neighbor's response to this message is ritualistic: "When he is informed that the oracles have declared that he has bewitched a certain man he says that he is very sorry and is totally ignorant of having done so, blows some water from his mouth in a sign of goodwill," recalling or "cooling" his unwitting witchcraft, "and the matter is closed."[10] The neighbor, in other words, apologizes to the consulter explicitly, again quashing the conflict between them.

> [*The burly, pierced fellow's cell phone rings; the tone is a Celine Dion song.*]

Karnov! We didn't know you were a Celine fan! That's very impressive. You're a soft, delicate flower with a sensati . . .

> [*The burly fellow, fumbling to silence his phone and turning bright red, tries to change the subject.*]

> *"I stole this phone. But, anyway, what I was going to say was that your explanation of oracles seems pretty obvious. Like you and your brother, when people in this society were pissed at each other and needed a way out, they used their 8-ball device."*

Of course the Azande used *benge* to resolve interpersonal conflict, Karnov! I told you that when we started. The puzzle is this: Why would shaking a poisoned chicken be a sensible means of doing that?

To see why, it's useful to think in terms of traffic lights. Traffic lights coordinate traffic, of course. They direct drivers' behavior so the drivers don't crash into one another. Imagine an intersection without a traffic light. Two drivers unavoidably approach the intersection at the same time every day on the way to their mutual workplace. Both drivers are in a hurry and want to get to work as fast as possible. Moreover, they're competitive. Each imagines that he's racing the other and wants to beat the other driver to work.

If both cars simply blow through the intersection without yielding, the drivers will collide. But if one or both of them yields, both drivers will make it to their destination safely. If a driver yields, however, he makes it to work with some delay. Worse yet from the yielder's perspective, if only he yields and the other driver doesn't, he's more likely to lose the "race" to work.

It's clear what each driver wants: his most-preferred situation is for the other driver to yield so that he can go through. His second-most preferred situation is for both drivers to yield. In this case he avoids an accident, and while he's delayed in getting to work, so is the other driver since that driver yields too, so he's not any more likely to lose the race. His third-most preferred situation is to yield himself when the other driver goes through. Here he's delayed and likely to lose the race, but at least he avoids an accident. And his least-preferred situation is when neither he nor the other driver yields: both go straight through the intersection and crash.

Without a traffic light to coordinate them, what will the drivers do? It turns out that three outcomes are possible. The first is for one of the drivers to go through the intersection and the other driver to yield. The second, just the reverse: the latter driver goes through the intersection while the other driver yields. The logic behind these outcomes is straightforward. If one driver expects the other to go through the intersection, he achieves the most-preferred outcome that's available to him by yielding, and vice versa. The problem, of course, is that both drivers want to be the one who gets to go through the intersection and neither knows what the other is going to do.

In situations like this, a third possible outcome is likely. Here, each driver mixes his behavior—sometimes he goes through the intersection and at other times yields—instead of going through the intersection or yielding all the time. (For those interested in the details of why, meet me in the appendix after the tour.) The problem when the drivers do this is that sometimes both of them end up going through the intersection without yielding, causing them to crash.

As I mentioned a minute ago, introducing a traffic light at the intersection solves this problem. The traffic light instructs the drivers whether to go through the intersection or to yield, and it tells only one of them to do the former when it tells the other to do the latter. If one driver gets a green light, the other gets red, and vice versa. So they never crash.

As long as the traffic light is equally likely to give each driver the green light first, on average both will make it to work without delay an equal proportion of the time, both will beat the other to work an equal proportion of the time, and the drivers will never collide. Both are better off than without the traffic light. The light mixes the drivers' behavior, just as the drivers do themselves when the traffic light isn't there to coordinate them. But the light does so in a way that ensures that one driver's mixture is always consistent with the other's.

Oracles such as the Azande's *benge* work like traffic lights, but instead of coordinating cars, they coordinate bickering neighbors.

[*Several patrons at once:*]

"*Huh???*"

Let me try another example. Consider two neighbors, Myrtle and Mabel. They're constantly stepping on each other's toes, and each frequently feels that her neighbor has wronged her.

The same occasions that lead Myrtle to feel wronged by Mabel lead Mabel to feel wronged by Myrtle—the wronging is reciprocal. Myrtle is an insecure braggart. She boasts her every accomplishment, no matter how small, and when others don't flatter her, she feels disrespected.

Mabel is stingy with compliments. She rarely acknowledges others' accomplishments, and when others brag to her, she feels disrespected. Mabel's praise-stinginess often leads her to offend Myrtle's sensibilities, and Myrtle's incessant boasting often leads her to offend Mabel's.

Mabel and Myrtle interact closely and frequently, so situations generating reciprocal wrongs are common. As a result, so is petty conflict—antagonism and resentment—between them.

Myrtle and Mabel each have two choices for coping with their conflict. Each woman can "back down" by apologizing to her neighbor—explicitly through words or implicitly through her behavior. Or she can "stand tall" by refusing to apologize to her neighbor and insisting that her neighbor apologize to her.[11]

Each neighbor's most-preferred situation is if she stands tall while her neighbor backs down. Since she doesn't apologize, she preserves her pride completely. And because her neighbor apologizes, the conflict between them is quashed.

Each neighbor's second-most-preferred situation is if both she and her neighbor back down. Since each neighbor apologizes to the other, each swallows an equal, incomplete part of her pride. And because apologies are made, the conflict between them is quashed.

Each neighbor's third-most-preferred situation is if she backs down while her neighbor stands tall. Since she apologizes and her neighbor doesn't, she swallows her pride completely. But because an apology is made, at least the conflict between the neighbors is quashed.

Finally, each neighbor's least-preferred situation is if they both stand tall. Since neither neighbor apologizes to the other, neither swallows any part of her pride, but the neighbors' animus toward one another grows. Eventually their tensions erupt into a violent, or at least verbal, clash. Neither neighbor wins the clash, and no apology is made, so the conflict remains unresolved.

As in the case of the drivers, there are three possible outcomes for Myrtle and Mabel. Myrtle stands tall while Mabel backs down. Mabel stands tall while Myrtle backs down. Or what we might suspect is the most likely outcome given each woman's desire to be the one who gets to stand tall and her uncertainty about what her neighbor will do, both Myrtle and Mabel mix their behavior—standing tall sometimes and backing down at others. Also as in the case of the drivers, when Myrtle and Mabel mix their behavior, a problem results: sometimes both end up standing tall at the same time, yielding the worst scenario from both neighbors' perspective—a clash of words or, worse, fists.

Now suppose that, like my brother and me, Myrtle and Mabel decide to cope with their conflict by consulting a Magic 8 Ball instead. To use this oracle, Myrtle and Mabel ask it the following question:

"Tell us, Magic 8 Ball, great one and infallible teller of eternal truths, is Myrtle's [or Mabel's] animus toward Mabel [or Myrtle] justified?"

The die inside the 8 ball has three sides. One of them reads, "Yes, it is certainly true." Another reads, "No, it is certainly untrue." The third reads, "Ask again later."

The neighbors put their hands on the oracle and shake it together. They then turn it upside down to see what the oracle has divined. The women repose complete faith in the 8 ball's infallibility and agree to condition their behavior toward one another on whatever its answers.

If the 8 ball answers "Yes," the neighbors agree that Myrtle's animus is justified, which means that Mabel's animus is unjustified. In this case, Myrtle stands tall by insisting on Mabel's apology, and Mabel backs down by giving it to her, quashing the conflict between them. If the 8 ball answers "No," the neighbors agree that Myrtle's animus is unjustified, which means that Mabel's animus is justified. In this case, Mabel stands tall by insisting on Myrtle's apology, and Myrtle backs down by giving it to her, quashing the conflict between them. If the 8 ball answers, "Ask again later," the neighbors repeat the question, shake the 8 ball again, and see what the oracle divines. They repeat this procedure until the 8 ball answers their question definitively.

Like the traffic light, the Magic 8 Ball coordinates Myrtle's and Mabel's behavior in the face of their petty conflict. When it tells one neighbor to stand tall (don't apologize), it tells the other neighbor to back down (apologize), and vice versa. As a result, Myrtle and Mabel's conflict is always quashed and both of them are better off than if they didn't use the 8 ball.

[A man wearing Crocs, a fanny pack, and a cell phone holster on his hip interrupts.]

"Wait a minute! I can understand why one of these ladies would follow the oracle's decision when it tells her that she gets to demand an apology. But why on earth would the other lady—the one who is told to apologize—do what the 8 ball says?"

First, nice phone holster. I'm sure the swivel action on that is second to none.

[*The man blushes.*]

Now, to your question. Suppose the 8 ball answers "No" to the question about whether Myrtle's animus is justified, which means that she needs to back down and Mabel gets to stand tall. As you point out, we know that Mabel will stand tall in this case. Thus, if Myrtle follows the 8 ball's directive too and backs down, she'll get her third-most-preferred outcome. In contrast, if Myrtle refuses the 8 ball's directive and stands tall anyway, she'll get her least-preferred outcome—that in which both she and Mabel stand tall, causing them to clash—since Mabel, who's following the 8 ball, will be standing tall. Myrtle therefore has an incentive to do what the oracle says regardless of what it divines, and the same goes for Mabel.

[*The man with the cell phone holster:*]

"I get it! Since the losing lady knows the winning lady will follow the 8 ball, it behooves her to follow the 8 ball too."

Exactly.

[*A young man in the back interjects:*]

"I still don't see how poisoning chickens works like an 8 ball, though. The yes and no answers on the 8 ball come up randomly. About half the time you're going to get a yes, the other half a no. You can't control which answer you get. But with chickens, it seems like the oracle consulter could manipulate whether the chicken dies."

And why would that be a problem?

"Well, if I can dictate what the chicken says to me, I can always make it come out in my favor. And if it always comes out in my favor, the person I'm feuding with will lose faith in the fairness

of benge. *In fact, even if he doesn't, if he knows the chicken gives
answers that are biased against him, he won't be willing to go on
what the oracle says."*

Very good. You're quite right. In fact, you've hit on two of the three
conditions required for oracles to be effective conflict resolvers: they
need to be "fair"—produce outcomes that favor each party to the conflict about equally often, and, closely related, people need to repose
faith in their legitimacy—an oracle's ability to divine "correct" answers
to the questions posed to it. Only then will both parties have an incentive to follow the oracle and thus be able to escape their conflict.

[*The young man:*]

"What's the third condition?"

Oracles need to remove the parties' least-preferred outcome—that in
which both of them stand tall and thus clash. Why don't I start by explaining how *benge* satisfies the first condition; then I'll explain how it
satisfies the other two.

The way *benge* ensures fairness in its outcomes is wickedly clever.
When a Zande consults *benge* regarding a particular person, he does so
not once but twice. The first oracular consultation is called *bambata
sima*, the second, *gingo*. "To obtain a conclusive answer the result of
the first test has to be confirmed by feeding the poison to a second
fowl. The alternatives of the question are reversed and the effect of
the poison must be the opposite to the first test to be accepted as final
evidence."[12]

In other words, "the oracle must slay one fowl and spare another
if it is to deliver a valid verdict."[13] For example, if in *bambata sima,*
the consulter inquires of the oracle this way: "If [a neighbor's name]
is guilty of bewitching my [hunt, person, etc.], poison oracle *kill the
fowl*," in *gingo* he must inquire of it this way: "If [neighbor's name] is
guilty of bewitching my [hunt, person, etc.], poison oracle *spare the
fowl*." Only when both oracular tests agree by the poison acting on

the fowls oppositely has the oracle declared a definitive answer. If they disagree, the consulter must "ask again later."

The genius of this dual opposing test is that it tends to permit a definitive oracular declaration only when the poison fed to the fowl is of such strength that it has an equal chance of killing and sparing the fowl. Since the strength of the poison used in *benge* varies naturally and may be affected by exposure to certain elements, age, or (in principle) manipulation of the consulter, the dual opposing test throws out oracular declarations that have been influenced by such features and would produce biased results.[14]

Overly strong poison will kill both fowls, throwing out that result. Overly weak poison will spare both fowls, throwing out that one too. Only declarations based on poison whose strength gives the fowl a roughly equal chance of living and dying will be valid.

Other Zande rituals surrounding *benge* preparation and usage also promote definitive declarations of one kind or the other with 50 percent probability. There are rules, for instance, about how many doses of poison should be administered to fowls depending on their size. Larger fowls receive more doses, smaller ones fewer. Given variation in fowl size and thus potential susceptibility to oracular poison, this ritual promotes equal chances of fowl reaction to the poison across birds.[15]

Similarly, recall that the *benge* "operator performs in public. His audience, all parties interested in the dispute or inquiry, sit a few feet away and can see what he does, and they largely direct his actions."[16] It's just the opposite of the judicial ordeals we discussed earlier, where audiences were purposely kept at a distance. Audience proximity prevents funny business in oracular administration, such as killing the chicken by shaking it violently or using only one test instead of the required two—hence, Evans-Pritchard's observation: "I witnessed cases when it has been to the interests of the operator that the fowls shall live and they have died, and vice versa."[17]

The Azande also test newly procured *benge* poison before using it in a proper oracular consultation: "As soon as the poison is brought back from its forest home it is tested to discover whether some fowls will live and others die under its influence."[18] If it "kills fowls without discrimination, slaying one fowl after the other without sparing a single one, they say that it is 'foolish' poison" and throw it away. Alternatively, "If some four medium-sized fowls are in succession unaffected by the poison they stop the séance, and later th[at] poison will be thrown away" too.[19]

Benge results support the argument that it tends to produce opposing results with 50 percent probability. Evans-Pritchard observed forty-nine oracular tests firsthand in Zandeland. Fowls died in twenty-two of them, or 45 percent of the time, and survived in twenty-seven of them, or 55 percent of the time.[20] Given the sample size, the closeness of these rates to equal randomization is impressive.

The second thing oracles must do to be effective in resolving conflict is eliminate the possibility of assigning conflicting neighbors the worst pair of their behaviors—that in which they both stand tall. *Benge* does this by "vindicating one and condemning the other rival"—declaring one party's animus unjustified every time it declares the other party's animus justified, and vice versa.[21] Its method: requiring a yes-or-no question from the consulter about whether his neighbor is bewitching him, which doesn't include the possibility that the consulter is bewitching his neighbor.

If *benge* answers "yes," this means the same thing for both the consulter and his neighbor: the consulter is justified in demanding an apology and recall of witchcraft from his neighbor, and his neighbor must apologize to the consulter and recall his witchcraft. If *benge* answers "no," this means the same thing for both the consulter and his neighbor: the consulter's suspicion is mistaken, so he "apologizes" by resuming friendly relations with his neighbor. His neighbor, who hasn't been instructed to apologize to the consulter, needn't; he stands tall.

In the former case, when one neighbor apologizes to the other explicitly, *benge* ritual requires the apologizer to display genuineness in asking forgiveness: "It is not only laid down by custom that he must blow out water, but the phrases in which he is expected to express his regret are more or less stereotyped, and even the earnest and apologetic tone of voice in which he utters them is determined by tradition."[22] This ritual helps ensure that the conflict is indeed quashed.

There is one situation in which it's possible for *benge* to assign stand tall to both neighbors, though. *Benge*, recall, may be consulted by any man who has respected the requisite taboos at any time. In principle, then, two neighbors in conflict could consult their oracles simultaneously, and each of their oracles could vindicate their animus toward their neighbor by declaring that the other is bewitching him.

In practice, however, this is unlikely. Even if two neighbors consult their oracles simultaneously, the probability that both of their oracles will vindicate their animus toward the other is low. Approximately half the time *benge* is consulted, a fowl dies. And to render a definitive verdict, the oracle must produce the "correct" result twice. The probability that one party's oracle will vindicate his animus is 25 percent. So the probability that *both* parties' oracles will vindicate their animus is only 6.25 percent.

Among oracular consultations that deliver definitive verdicts, the probability that one or the other party's animus will be vindicated is 50 percent. But there's a 75 percent chance that at least one party's oracle will answer "ask again later." And at the moment he does so, he's likely to be the only one.

Also: recall that the Azande consult *benge* about witchcraft only in particular cases, such as when their crop fails, their hunt is fruitless, or they become ill. These misfortunes are likely to be distributed randomly among neighbors. Situations in which two neighbors in conflict may simultaneously desire to consult their oracles about the other are therefore rare.[23]

Finally, to effectively resolve conflict, an oracle must be trusted as accurate by its users. *Benge* is this—and then some: the Azande "consider the poison" administered to fowls under *benge*, the oracle's ostensible source of divinatory power, "an objective and infallible agent."[24]

Because of this, "the Zande puts his full trust in *benge*" and "the judgements of *benge* are always accepted as final."[25] For the same reason, "no Zande would state the declaration of an oracle other than it was given."[26] Besides the fact that observers who can confirm the oracle's declarations are present at oracular consultations, false oracular reports don't occur because respect for *benge*'s verdicts is too strong.

"The great authority of the poison oracle" renders it "useless to protest against its declarations."[27] Neither party would contemplate behaving in a manner other than that directed by *benge*. And since *benge*'s directions coordinate their behavior, the parties' conflict is resolved.

[*The young man in the back raises his hand again.*]

Another question?

> "Yeah. I understand now how poisoning chickens worked. What I don't get is why the Azande didn't just use the legal system to resolve their conflicts. I mean, they had courts, right? Seems like that would be a lot simpler. Plus, courts might actually be able to deliver genuinely just decisions rather than the fake decisions the oracles gave."

Glad you asked! I nearly forgot an important part of the story.

Raise your hand if you've ever been in a fight with a friend where each of you blamed the other for your disagreement and you remained on the outs for a while because neither of you wanted to be the first to admit his fault and apologize to the other.

[*Everyone but the economist raises a hand.*]

The conflicts that those of us *who have friends* have with our friends, like the conflicts we have with our neighbors, tend to be the low-grade variety—the petty, passive, everyday sort that arise out of feelings of jealousy, envy, rivalry, offense. These kinds of conflicts don't usually have a "right" person and a "wrong" one. Rather, they depend on the perceptions and sensibilities of the people who experience them. What one person interprets as a veiled gibe against him will appear totally innocent to a less sensitive sort.

Courts that tried to address such tiffs would be perpetually inundated with work. Moreover, given the nature of low-grade conflicts, it's unclear how they could do so effectively. Our legal system doesn't recognize petty, passive, interpersonal frictions as legal offenses. And neither did the Azande's.

In the years in which Evans-Pritchard lived among them—1926 through 1930 to be exact—Zande society was organized politically on the basis of a chief and several governors, typically the chief's sons.[28] Within each of the chiefdom's provinces, local communities selected trusted members to act as deputies in assisting governors to oversee their areas. And Zande political rulers administered native and colonial-created laws (the British colonized Zandeland in 1905), operating native courts alongside courts operated by colonial officials.

These formal political institutions could be used to address major conflicts, such as those involving murder and theft, but they couldn't be used to address low-grade conflict, opportunities for which abounded:

> There may have been quarrels about cultivations and hunting areas.
> There may have been suspicions about designs on a wife. There may
> have been rivalry at dances. One may have uttered unguarded words
> which have been repeated by another. A man may have thought that a
> song referred to himself. . . . All unkind words and malicious actions
> and innuendoes are stored in the memory for retaliation.[29]

Indeed, "in all [Zande] economic and social pursuits there is opportunity for offence to be given and offence to be taken where none is meant."[30] The Azande, as Evans-Pritchard describes them, are "extremely, almost morbidly, sensitive" people—sort of like our Celine Dion–loving friend Karnov.[31]

To cope with this "underground stream of" perceived "malice and backbiting, envy and hatred, greed and jealousy, which runs with ceaseless turmoil beneath the calm surface of native life," the Azande therefore had to look beyond government.[32] Oracles are what they found when they did so.

"Only in those areas of society which were left unstructured by the political system did men accuse each other of witchcraft."[33] And witchcraft suspicions, recall, investigated by consulting *benge*, were directed at neighbors with whom one was in low-grade conflict. In other words, witchcraft suspicions were the way the Azande expressed conflicts that couldn't be addressed through formal courts, and oracles were the way they addressed them instead.

Benge shares a crucial feature in common with *Romaniya* and monastic maledictions: the use of outwardly inane practices to promote social order *privately*. And another feature, which it shares with ordeals too: the institutionalization of superstition to facilitate desired, and socially desirable, ends. In fact, when you get down to it, oracles are similar to every "WTF?!"-worthy practice you've learned about so far—from sassywood to wife sales. Like these other seemingly senseless practices, oracles incentivize people to behave in ways that allow the societies they live in to function better. The bizarre, it turns out, can be beneficent.

I see some of you have your hands up, but if we don't move on, we're not going to make it through the full tour and I want to make sure we do. So please follow me to our next stop where I'll expose you to perhaps the most "WTF?!"-worthy social practice of them all.

[*A frustrated patron shouts:*]

"*But what about our questions?!*"

You can direct them to the Magic 8 Ball we'll pass on the way.

7

Jiminy Cricket's Journey to Hell

Perhaps I had a sheltered upbringing, but my freshman year of college was one unexpected eyeful after the next. I saw a guy smoke cigarettes with his feet (that would be my roommate). A classmate wet himself in front of the student union for $20 (not a lot to do for fun in a college of twelve hundred students). But one bizarre event I witnessed stands out as especially memorable. It involved a handicapped squirrel.

On our way to lunch one afternoon, a friend and I passed by the stairwell outside our dorm. When we looked down we saw an odd-looking fellow, clad in all black and sporting an unkempt ponytail, crouching near what appeared to be an injured rodent.

I shouted down to him, "What you doing there?"

"Nursing this squirrel back to health," he replied matter-of-factly.

"I'm sorry," I said. "Did you say that you're nursing an injured squirrel??"

"Are you deaf?!" he shot back.

My friend interjected: "What the hell is wrong with you? That thing probably has rabies."

The squirrel-nurser silently continued his triage.

A few other people on the way to lunch saw us peering down the stairwell and came over to see what we were doing. Then some more people stopped by to see what they were doing. Soon a small crowd had formed.

We watched, confused, for a few more minutes, after which time it became apparent to me that the fellow in the stairwell was trying to prop the squirrel up in a sitting position—as you might a doll or stuffed animal. The poor thing was barely alive.

I inquired further: "Are its legs broken or something?"

"I'm making a wheelchair for him," the fellow replied, clearly agitated by the crowd of spectators and motioning to the corner of the stairwell.

When I looked to where he was pointing, I saw a torn-open bag of large marshmallows and a half-empty bag of pretzel sticks. Next to that lay a few marshmallows on the ground with pretzel sticks jutting out of them.

"Holy shit," I uttered. "He's making a wheelchair for it out of marshmallows and pretzels." This precipitated a round of gasps and laughter.

"Can't you see he can't walk?!" the fellow in the stairwell shouted angrily.

Captivated, but hungry, my friend and I left the scene of the squirrelly sick bay for lunch. Others stayed behind to watch Dr. Doolittle finish his handiwork.

Now, besides the fact that (a) there's no way in hell to fashion a wheelchair from marshmallows and pretzels capable of fitting a full-grown squirrel, half dead or not, (b) even if it were possible, the resulting "wheelchair" wouldn't be functional, (c) even if it were functional, the squirrel wouldn't be able to operate it, and (d) even if the squirrel could operate it, the campus wasn't ADA compliant, so I don't know how he would've gotten around, I was astonished that in the stairwell outside my dorm, there was a creepy guy trying to create a wheelchair for a paralyzed rodent as though it were human.

I like animals and all, but I draw the line at manufacturing prosthetic devices for them that require human dexterity, intelligence, and volition to operate. Maybe that makes me a bad person, but there it is.

The squirrel-nurser, who later that evening I dubbed Lord of the Squirrels (it stuck), transferred at the end of the semester—I hope to a school of veterinary medicine. I'll never forget him though. WTF?!

I'll return to the Lord of the Squirrels in a moment. But first, I want to tell you about another episode from my youth. Just indulge me a bit further.

I attended elementary school in the early days of the D.A.R.E indoctrination campaign. For those of you who don't know, D.A.R.E. is the federally funded Drug Abuse Resistance Education program administered to kids before their teenage years.

In my school at least, it involved a policeman visiting our class once every few weeks, a stuffed and filthy-looking "D.A.R.E. Bear" that was supposed to be the mascot of the program, and lots of antidrug, antialcohol, and antitobacco propaganda. The propaganda included lectures from the policeman about the harmful effects of various substances; some booklets and worksheets containing the same; a scary video of a kid smoking a cigarette and then, in a nicotine-induced rage, slaughtering his family; and so on.

At the end of the D.A.R.E. program there was a "graduation," which was supposed to certify our newly acquired knowledge of the dangers of drugs, alcohol, and tobacco; our commitment to keeping our friends from trying them; and a song eerily reminiscent of the Communist Youth tunes that children were required to sing in the Soviet Union.

I must say, though, that for all of the D.A.R.E. program's silliness, in my case, it worked. I didn't become a chain-smoking drunkard until college. Given that the D.A.R.E. program has been run nationally for years now, I suspect that I'm not the only one for whom this is true.

You might wonder why the government goes to such lengths to indoctrinate kids about the dangers of illegal drugs. After all, they're illegal. There are laws on the books about purchasing and possessing them and potentially stiff penalties for people who break those laws. That would seem to be sufficient to align your incentives with the government's desire that you forgo illicit substances. But it's not.

One reason it's not is that enforcing laws against illegal drug use is incredibly difficult. Enforcement requires detection, and the chances of a government official detecting personal drug use are very low. One of you is probably flying high right now, and nobody knows but you.

In principle, the government could dramatically increase its detection efforts against drug use. It could, for instance, put cops on every corner. But that would be very expensive, and even then, a good number of people would still get away with using illegal drugs.

Enter D.A.R.E. If you're trained from the time you're eight years old that smoking one joint will cause your head to explode, render you destitute and homeless, and possibly result in the destruction of your entire network of family and friends, the odds that you'll be willing to use drugs, even when you know Big Brother isn't looking, go down. Indoctrination creates internal costs of drug use, no government detection required. This way, what's too expensive or difficult to accomplish through legal enforcement, government can accomplish through "education"—a combination of instilling fear, shame, and guilt.

Government's reliance on "moral suasion" of this kind is hardly unique to discouraging drug use. People don't like paying their taxes, at least not all of them, so many people evade what they owe. Auditing tax returns helps reduce evasion. But by manufacturing internal costs of tax evasion, government can reduce the amount of their taxes that people evade further still.

In 1943 the US Treasury Department commissioned the Walt Disney Corporation to create a special edition of the Donald Duck cartoon. The full video is available on YouTube.[1] You should check it out for yourself, but here's the gist: tax day is approaching and Donald has to make a decision—save his money and pay his taxes, which were especially high in 1943 because of World War II, or spend his money and evade part of his tax burden.

The cartoon depicts Donald struggling with his conscience. An "angelic Donald" appears over one of his shoulders encouraging him to give the government what it demands. A "demonic Donald" appears over his other shoulder telling him to spend his money however he wants. The two "spirit Donalds" engage in a tug-of-war over the corporeal Donald, and the cartoon launches into a prolonged, albeit entertaining, entreaty of the need for everyone to "pay their taxes to defeat the Axis."

The "WTF?!"-worthy practice you're about to encounter is a curious combination of my Lord of the Squirrels story and what I've just told you about moral suasion. Having trouble seeing how they could be connected? Come this way . . .

BARON BALDESMERE, Esq.

The taxidermied rat you're looking at here isn't just any rat. This bugger was tried for the crime of consuming some farmers' crops in late seventeenth-century France. He was convicted of stealing the farmers' wheat and duly punished for his skullduggery along with . . .

[a cacophony of disbelief and befuddlement from the crowd; someone exclaims]

"Wait! Rewind! Did you say that this stuffed rat was tried for a crime . . . and convicted?!"

What?! Oh, God no!

[*sighs of relief and laughter from the crowd*]

I'm sorry. I didn't explain that well. He wasn't stuffed *at the time of his trial*. He was alive for his trial and conviction! The stuffing is something we did to him after he died.

[*The impromptu crowd spokesman:*]

"Wait a minute! So the rat was tried in a court of law? That's unimaginable!"

Don't worry. Baron Baldesmere here—that's his name—enjoyed due process and the counsel of an excellent court-appointed defense attorney. But we're getting ahead of ourselves. Let me start at the beginning.

For 250 years, French, Italian, and Swiss ecclesiastic courts tried insects and rodents for property crimes as legal persons under the same laws and according to the same procedures they used to try actual persons. These courts summonsed snails to answer charges of trespass, appointed legal counselors to locusts, and considered defenses for grasshoppers on the grounds that they were God's creatures. They convicted cockchafers of cozening crops, fulminated against field mice for filching farmers, and exiled weevils under pain of excommunication and anathema.

Vermin trials weren't the province of Dark Age ignorance or impoverished primitivism. They were a much later, more enlightened vintage—a Renaissance one. Furthermore, they occurred in what were then the wealthiest countries in the world.

One interpretation of vermin trials is that the judicial officials who conducted them were lunatics. Examining these trials' records, it's tempting to conclude as much. In them we find distinguished judges ordering crickets to follow legal instructions, dignified jurists negotiating a settlement between farmers and beetles, and a decorous court granting a horde of rat defendants a continuance on the grounds that some cats prevented them from attending their trial.

One gets the sense from these records that history is playing a bizarre joke or that perhaps Alice's Wonderland was a real place after all. But history isn't playing a joke. And while Wonderland's talking, pipe-puffing caterpillar is fictitious, legal systems that treated caterpillars as if they could talk and might occasionally enjoy a good pipe are very real.

The golden age of ecclesiastical vermin trials was the fifteenth through seventeenth centuries.[2] During this era, people who confronted pest control problems sued pests in class action lawsuits.[3] The courts conducted vermin trials under bishops' authority and jurisdiction. The members of a distressed community were the plaintiffs, the members of a species of insect or rodent, the defendants.

Vermin trials were based on an early modern superstition: if ecclesiastics invoked the appropriate conjurations against animals pestering people without God's permission, God would thwart the pests supernaturally.

The idea of divine pesticide seems patently absurd—until you compare it to other Renaissance-era pest control methods, which included: sprinkling weasel ashes or water in which a cat was bathed over fields to drive away mice; capturing a rodent, castrating it, and releasing it among others to deter them; putting castor-oil plants in afflicted fields to drive away moles; and hanging garlic around flock leaders' necks to protect sheep from wolves.[4]

These remedies were handed down from the ancients. And "apparently the man of the Renaissance was all too ready to accept without question and to recommend to others the remedies he found in the classical authors," for "there is little mention of experimentation" or innovation.[5] With the notable exception of divine pesticide: "When all of these remedies are unsuccessful," an early modern pest control manual instructed, "one must turn to the ban of the Church."[6]

Citizens prosecuted vermin for violating their property rights. In the sixteenth century, for instance, the inhabitants of Autun, France, charged some rats with "having feloniously eaten up and wantonly destroyed the barley-crop of that province."[7] In 1478 the inhabitants of

Berne, Switzerland, sued some "ingers," a species of beetle, for "creeping secretly in the earth devastat[ing] the fields, meadows and all other kinds of grain."[8] And in 1659, the Italian communes of Chiavenna, Mese, Gordona, Prada, and Samolico banded together to prosecute caterpillars they charged with trespassing on and damaging their fields.

Plaintiffs initiated legal action against vermin by addressing their concern to their bishop, their bishop's local representative, or local officials charged with legally representing the community in its dealings with other local governments and the crown. Ultimately plaintiffs' complaints came to the latter's attention. These officials, called procurators, were comparable to modern-day district attorneys.

Following the plaintiffs' appeal, the procurator produced a formal statement of their complaint, which he delivered before the ecclesiastic court exercising the bishop's jurisdiction over the community in question. This statement identified the property crime his clients' alleged and the species of insect or rodent accused of committing it. He then asked the court to order the offending vermin to immediately cease violating his clients' rights, compelling them to if they refused.

Consider the prosecuting attorney's statement to the court in a case aptly dubbed The People v. Locusts. The citizens of Lombardy, Italy, launched this lawsuit against the locusts in 1541:

> Gentlemen, these poor people on their knees and with tearful eyes, appeal to your sense of justice. . . . In the power of excommunication you have a weapon more effective than any wielded by that emperor [Augustus Caesar] to save these poor supplicants from impending famine produced by the ravages of little beasts, which spare neither the corn nor the vines. . . . It remains, therefore, after complying with the usual forms, only to adjudicate upon the case in accordance with the facts stated in the Petition of the Plaintiffs, which is right and reasonable, and, to this effect, to enjoin these animals from continuing their devastations, ordering them to quit the aforesaid fields and to withdraw to the place assigned them, pronouncing the necessary anathemas and

execrations prescribed by our Holy Mother, the Church, for which your petitioners do ever pray.[9]

If the court saw merit in the plaintiffs' petition, it might exhort them to pray publicly for the departure of the vermin, hold processions for this purpose, and direct the plaintiffs to display extra religiosity and repent of their sins. If the vermin remained, it might try them to determine their guilt. Alternatively, judges dispensed with the pious prelude and tried the vermin immediately.

Ecclesiastic courts appointed accused insects and rodents defense attorneys to represent them and went to great lengths to ensure that their representation was adequate. Thus in 1519, when the inhabitants of Glurns, Italy, sued some field mice for property damage, the court appointed the mice legal counsel "to the end that they may have nothing to complain of in these proceedings."[10] Later that century, when the inhabitants of Saint-Jean-de-Maurienne, France, sued some weevils, it appointed the creatures two legal representatives, a procurator and an advocate, "lest the animals against whom the action lies should remain defenseless."[11]

Some court-appointed vermin defense counselors were more than adequate. One of them, Bartholomé Chassenée, was a leading jurist of his era. In 1540 Chassenée became president of the Parlement de Provence, having earned an enviable reputation defending a horde of rats—my distinguished colleague, Baron Baldesmere, among them.

Lawyers for vermin argued strenuously for their clients at trial. A common defense was that the defendants were God's creations and therefore had as much right to enjoy the fruit of his earth as the plaintiffs. Another common defense was that the case was invalid; thus the plaintiffs should be nonsuited.

One argument that vermin defense attorneys made toward this end was that their clients *were vermin*. Consider how the locusts' lawyer argued before the court in The People v. Locusts:

Gentlemen, inasmuch as you have chosen me to defend these little beasts, I shall, an it please you, endeavor to right them and to show

the manner of proceeding against them is invalid and void. I confess
that I am greatly astonished at the treatment they have been subjected
to and at the charges brought against them, as they had committed
some crime. Thus information has been procured touching the damage
said to have been done by them; they have been summoned to appear
before this court to answer for their conduct, and, since they are notoriously dumb, the judge, wishing that they should not suffer wrong
on account of this defect, has appointed an advocate to speak on their
behalf and to set forth in conformity with right and justice the reasons,
which they themselves are unable to allege. . . .

I will state, in the first place, that the summons served on them
is null and void, having been issued against beasts, which cannot and
ought not to be cited before this judgment seat, inasmuch as such a
procedure implies that the parties summoned are endowed with reason and volition and are therefore capable of committing crime.[12]

This would've been an excellent argument against treating vermin
as legal persons were it not offered by way of elaborate judicial proceedings that presumed the legitimacy of treating grasshoppers and moles
as legal persons ipso facto.

There was another legal maneuver that vermin defense attorneys
could resort to. According to a book Chassenée published in 1531,
they could argue that their clients were clerics, entitling them to the
benefit of clergy. This would have permitted insects and rodents to
have an ecclesiastic judge decide their case when the bishop granted
jurisdiction to a secular magistrate.[13] No vermin defense counselor ever
used this argument. Still, the possibility that caterpillars or field mice
might be men of the cloth was an argument the courts were willing to
entertain.

Vermin trials involved much legal wrangling, and judges showed
impressive fairness toward vermin at their trials. Consider, for example,
a fourteenth-century lawsuit that the inhabitants of one community
brought against some flies. To the court's consternation, the flies refused
to appear before the bench after being summonsed. "In consideration of

their small size and the fact that they had not yet reached their majority," the judge decided that he would overlook the flies' failure to appear and appoint them defense counsel to prevent it from happening again.[14]

Occasionally courts exonerated prosecuted vermin, or at least failed to convict them, which amounted to the same. Usually, however, they convicted prosecuted pests, who often lost their case by default. Judges summonsed vermin to appear in court to answer the charges against them three times. "The summonses were . . . served in the usual way by an officer of the court, reading them at the places most frequented by the animals."[15] If the vermin failed to respond the third time, the court could convict them.

To ensure that all members of a convicted species were aware of their conviction, judges announced their verdict publicly and nailed broadsheets declaring it to trees in the affected area. Alternatively, the court might bring some specimens before the bench to inform them of its decision, remitting the creatures to the afflicted region to share the sobering news with their colleagues.[16]

Judges also notified convicted vermin of the penalty they would suffer should they prove contumacious: excommunication from the Holy Church and anathema. Consider the court's decision in The People v. Locusts:

> In the name and by virtue of God, the omnipotent, Father, Son and Holy Spirit, and of Mary, the most blessed Mother of our Lord Jesus Christ, and by the authority of the holy apostles Peter and Paul, as well as by that which has made us functionary in this case, we admonish by these presents the aforesaid locusts and grasshoppers and other animals by whatsoever name they may be called, under pain of malediction and anathema to depart from the vineyards and fields of this district within six days from the publication of this sentence and to do no further damage there or elsewhere.[17]

Vermin trials ended ironically: insects and rodents damned figuratively by beleaguered plaintiffs were damned literally by courts of law.

I see a question. You ma'am, with the clown-like eye shadow . . .

[*The woman points at her face and mutters "jerk" under her breath.*]

"I get how these vermin trials are related to the Lord of the Squirrels. But I don't see what they've got to do with internal costs and all that."

I'm not sure I caught the first part of what you said, but I'm getting to internal costs now. In early modern Europe, the Catholic Church levied tithes (*la dîme ecclésiastique*), a form of taxes, on the lay population.[18] In principle, citizens owed tithes on all agricultural output, livestock, and the proceeds of fishing, hunting, and trade. In practice, churchmen demanded tithes on crops and livestock. Tithes were a central source of Church revenue in the early modern era. According to one estimate, they constituted two-thirds of it on the eve of the French Revolution.[19]

The Church assessed tithes "on the natural yield," as a percentage of physical produce. Rates varied by time, place, and product. Ecclesiastics levied "major tithes" (*grosses dîmes*) on, for example, wheat, oats, barley, rye, and wine and "minor tithes" (*menues dîmes*) on, for instance, vegetables, milk, and wool. But a levy of about 10 percent was typical.[20] Ecclesiastics collected tithes directly or leased the right to collect them to "tithe farmers," who paid their lessors for the privilege up front.[21]

Enforcing tithe payments was difficult—just as tax oversight or policing drug use is today. Government recognized the Church's right to collect them, and churchmen could, and sometimes did, use the state's coercive power to enforce tithe payment. But state enforcement had limited usefulness. It was most useful for preventing blatant refusal to pay, which was easy to detect and thus prosecute. In contrast, state enforcement was often useless for preventing surreptitious, partial underpayment. Tithe evasion was extremely hard, often impossible, to detect.

Citizens developed "1,001 ruses" to evade their tithes.[22] Some were simple: citizens opened new plots and didn't declare them. Similarly, they hid portions of their harvests from tithe collectors before collectors came to assess them.

A more elaborate ruse was crop switching: citizens substituted sowing crops tithable at higher rates with crops tithable at lower rates or crops that weren't tithable at all. Alternatively, they interplanted higher- and lower- (or non-) tithable crops in the same field, permitting them to pay the lower rate on the entire thing.

Citizens also exploited loopholes in the tithe system. Personal gardens were often tithe exempt, so people expanded their gardens' size. The sheaves that formed the bases of crop stacks were tithe exempt, and collectors couldn't inspect stack bases without tearing stacks apart, so people enlarged their stack bases.

Another loophole was the *rompu*: the harvest portion not divisible by the tithe rate. If the tithe rate was, say, one-twelfth and a farmer harvested seventeen sheaves of wheat, the five-sheave remainder was the *rompu*. According to custom, it wasn't tithable. So citizens manipulated their sheaves' size.

Natural variation in agricultural output from plot to plot, farmer to farmer, facilitated even the coarsest of evasive strategies tremendously. It thwarted tithe collectors' ability to discern whether the small harvest someone "declared" reflected a genuinely poor crop or evasion.

Tithe collectors did their best to monitor harvests and prevent such abuses. They weren't totally clueless. They would've had an idea about what the weather was like that year and what a certain-sized plot was capable of producing, which could help them develop lower-bound estimates for individual plots even if they couldn't determine the actual tithable harvests they confronted in particular cases. Still, the fact that the Church levied tithes on products whose nature was so amenable to manipulation presented "almost insurmountable obstacles to tithe collectors, who had only so many carts, so many assistants, and so much time."[23]

Insurmountable obstacles to enforcing tithe compliance through external detection and punishment required the Church to find a way to enforce tithe compliance through internal detection and punishment—like D.A.R.E. for the Renaissance age. But given that it was the Church, it resorted to the supernatural for this purpose instead of education. Supernatural sanctions, as you learned earlier when we discussed Gypsies, execute "automatically." God's omniscience and omnipotence ensure perfect detection and punishment of proscribed behaviors, so the Church supernaturally sanctioned people who defied its orders by claiming to estrange them from God.

Divine estrangement lay on a spectrum. At one end was the simple sinner. The Church claimed that a person who violated its orders sinned, distancing himself from the Lord. Unabsolved sin subtracted from the sinner's time with God in the afterlife and added to his time in purgatory.

At the other end of the spectrum was the excommunicant. In excommunicating someone, the Church separated him from God and God's community, the ordinary channel to salvation.[24] As I mentioned at our stop on cursing monks, excommunication came in several degrees of severity: minor, major, and anathema. A minor excommunication severed the excommunicant from the sacraments, a major one from God and the Church completely. Anathema, recall, was a kind of aggravated major excommunication. It involved a dramatic ceremony, cursing the excommunicant in the name of God and a host of other holy figures, making the delivery of his soul to Satan explicit.

Most of the sinner's punishments were to be manifested in the next world—purgatory and hell. But people estranged from God might feel part of those punishments in this world too. Accursed persons were outside the Church's protection and Lord's grace, hence susceptible to Satan's evils and potential godly punishment in their corporeal lives. That included illness, plagues, and potentially much worse.[25]

The Church deployed these supernatural sanctions to drive parishioners to pay.[26] It declared tithe evasion a sin and tithe evaders excommunicated and anathematized.[27] The Church went as far as to include citizens' moral obligation to pay their tithes in the Church commandments.[28] And it reminded citizens of this incessantly.[29]

Ecclesiastics built up the sin of evading tithes by rendering payment an obligation not merely to God's Church but to God.[30] "The Lord," the Fourth Lateran Council decreed, "has reserved tithes unto himself as a sign of his universal lordship."[31] They "are indeed to be paid of necessity, inasmuch as they are owed in virtue of divine law."[32]

To evade tithes was therefore to deny God what was his—to directly countermand his will. Thirteenth-century French theologian Alexander of Hales put the message to citizens this way: "Christians are bound to give" a tenth of their harvests "or more, if they will enter the kingdom of heaven."[33]

[*The lady wearing heavy eye makeup looks frustrated and interrupts.*]

"Now I see how what you're telling us about is connected to moral costs and tax evasion. But what happened to the vermin? What do the vermin trials have to do with it?"

Patience, Mimi. I'm coming to that now.

The Church's supernatural sanctions had the potential to prevent tithe evasion. But there was a problem: people had to believe in those sanctions for them to work. Similar to the case of the cursing monks, maledictions against tithe evaders could affect citizens' incentives such that in the absence of enforceable external punishments for taking Church property, citizens would find it in their interest to pay their tithes nonetheless. But unlike clerics in the tenth through twelfth centuries, who enjoyed a monopoly on citizens' religious beliefs, clerics in the early modern period didn't.

[*The lady wearing heavy eye makeup:*]

"Why not?"

Because of heretics.

"Heretics? You mean, like, devil worshipers?"

[Another patron shouts:]

"HAIL SATAN!!!! The Dark Lord . . ."

[The priest shrieks like a ten-year-old girl and faints.]

No, not devil worshipers really. But thank you, sir, for that strange and inappropriate outburst.

Leading up to the Protestant Reformation and during the Reformation's heyday in Europe, various sects of citizens who challenged the Catholic Church's proclaimed monopoly on the path to salvation flourished: heretics. A particularly important sect of proto-Reformation heretics was called the Vaudois, or the Waldenses (sometimes the Waldensians).

The Vaudois emerged in Lyon, France, in the late twelfth century. Over the next hundred years, they spread to Languedoc in southern France and to Austria, Bohemia, and eastern Germany. The challenge that the early Vaudois posed to the Church was short-lived. Some of these Vaudois held only marginally unorthodox views, and inquisitorial pressure suppressed them or led them to reintegrate with fully orthodox Catholics comparatively quickly and easily.

However, a more virulent and, as time would tell, resistant strain of Vaudois that descended from those in Lombardy persisted. These Vaudois grew significantly in the fourteenth and fifteenth centuries and were likely strongest at precisely the time vermin trials came into significant use.

Initially, the Vaudois' "heresy" was nothing more than preaching without papal permission. Doctrinally, they were ordinary Catholics. In the thirteenth and fourteenth centuries, however, their views developed into truly heretical ones, albeit of an unusual brand.

Unlike their Reformed Church successors, the Vaudois straddled traditional Catholicism and anti-Catholic thinking. They observed Lent, were baptized in the Church, attended mass, received last rites, and embraced the Church's position on the importance of "good works." They "were not 'radical' heretics, if by that one means heretics who questioned any fundamentals of religion."[34]

But the Vaudois posed a powerful threat to citizens' belief in ecclesiastic authority. In fact, their core beliefs challenged that authority directly. The Vaudois were Donatists: according to their thinking, a person's power in relation to the divine, in particular to administer sacraments, didn't depend on whether he was an official of the Church. It depended on his personal righteousness.

This view attacked ecclesiastic authority on two fronts. First, it suggested that ecclesiastics didn't have the monopoly they claimed on the power to influence one's distance from God. Second, since the Vaudois commonly pointed to what they perceived as ecclesiastics' corruption, their Donatism suggested that many, if not most, ecclesiastics couldn't wield divine authority after all.

These views had important implications for tithing, for if the priests demanding payment didn't have any special line to God and, due to their corruption, may in fact be disconnected from him, it was really up to each person to decide whether he thought he should pay. As early sixteenth-century Provence preacher Pierre Griot observed, the Vaudois believed "there is no sin in withholding tithes when the priests do not behave as they should." Or as a Vaudois put it more bluntly, "God never commanded us to pay tithes."[35]

Equally important, the Vaudois rejected clerics' power to excommunicate and anathematize. In doing so, they denied the validity of ecclesiastics' supernatural sanctions explicitly. As a Vaudois excommunicated in 1486 remarked, "They had been taught that the censures of the church could harm no one and should be ignored."[36] According to another, "he had been taught to take no heed of censures, bulls, or indulgences, as these had been invented to extort money."[37] In the words of inquisitor Bernard Gui, "The sect accepts neither canonical sanctions, nor the decrees and constitutions of the sovereign pontiff."[38] Its members "had contempt for ecclesiastical censure."[39] Among them, "excommunication and anathema . . . were declared to be worthless."[40]

The Vaudois also denied the existence of purgatory. According to one of their proverbs, "In the other world there are only two ways, that is to say Paradise and Hell, and there is no such thing as purgatory."[41] Similar to denying the Church's power to wield divine authority, "Denying the existence of purgatory had . . . dramatic consequences," for once a belief in purgatory's existence "had been firmly established in the hearts of people who were distressed about their chances of life everlasting, it gave rise to a whole host of practices to which the clergy were partial, since they were expressed in money and represented not inconsiderable incomes."[42] Such as tithing.

Most serious, early modern ecclesiastics equated Vaudois with witches, an association "justified by theologians on the grounds that the Waldensians, though originally devoted to poverty and asceticism, had gradually become committed to witchcraft."[43] The Vaudois often held their meetings in secret at night. It was therefore only reasonable to suppose that they engaged in the most outrageous activities imaginable—orgies, sex with demons, and all other manner of ludicrous licentiousness.

"By the fifteenth century, witchcraft had not only been firmly defined as heresy but also identified with . . . the Waldensians, whose name became almost a synonym for witchcraft."[44] In the Jura mountain region, "The identification was so firmly fixed that vauderie came to be a synonym for the sabbat"—a midnight meeting of witches.[45]

Confronted with the threat the Vaudois posed, ecclesiastics sought a way to bolster citizens' faith in the Church's supernatural sanctions—to beef up citizens' weakening internal costs of tithe evasion. Their way: vermin trials.

The ecclesiastics who administered these trials connected the pest infestations that citizens asked them to assist with to citizens' tithe compliance directly. Consider the court's sentence of some bugs convicted of property destruction in Troyes, France, in 1516:

In the name and in virtue of the omnipotence of God, of the Father, the Son, and the Holy Ghost; of the blessed Mary, mother of our Lord Jesus Christ; of the authority of the holy apostles Peter and Paul; and of that with which we ourselves are invested in this affair; we charge by this act the above-named animals—bruches, éruches, or of any other name by which they may be called to return (under penalty of malediction and anathema, within the six days which follow this warning and in accordance with our sentence) from the vines of the said locality of Villenauxe, and never more to cause, in time to come, any damage, either in this spot or in any other part of the diocese of Troyes; that if, the six days passed, the said animals have not fully obeyed our command, the seventh day, in virtue of the power and authority above mentioned, we pronounce against them by this writing anathema and malediction! Ordering, however, and formally directing the said inhabitants of Villenauxe, no matter of what rank, class, or condition they may be, so as to merit the better from God, all-powerful dispensator of all good and deliverer from all evil, to be released from such a great plague; ordering and directing them to deliver themselves up in concert to good works and pious prayers; to pay, moreover, the tithe without fraud and according to the custom recognised in the locality.[46]

A couple things stand out from this sentence. First, the court's sanctions against the bugs are the same supernatural ones that clerics used against tithe evaders: anathema, excommunication, and damnation. The court even uses the same formula to imprecate the bugs, invoking the Trinity, Mary, and the apostles. By leveling the same conjurations at vermin that they leveled at tithe evaders, ecclesiastics set up vermin trials in such a way as to supply evidence for the legitimacy of their supernatural sanctions—and to put everyone, disobedient critters and parishioners alike, on the same playing field.

Second, the court's sentence admonishes citizens to cease evading their tithes explicitly. In doing so, it suggests to the plaintiffs that their tithe evasion is responsible for the insect plague, that tithe compliance will stop the plague, and it offers a thinly veiled threat of continued plague if citizens continue to evade their tithes.

Exhorting citizens to pay their tithes fully was a central feature of many vermin trials. Recall the case of The People v. Locusts. First, the Italian court convicted the defendants under the threat of anathema for disobeying its decision; then it admonished the plaintiffs to observe special devoutness, especially "the payment of tithes without fraud according to the approved custom of the parish."[47]

[*The Satan worshiper:*]

"So, the Church could use the trials as another way to preach. But how could they use them to strengthen citizens' belief in supernatural sanctions?"

Quite simply, it turns out. Vermin trials had two possible outcomes: prosecuted vermin could flee or die, ceasing to plague the plaintiffs' property, or they could remain on the plaintiffs' property, continuing to plague it.

Trials that led to the first outcome evidenced the validity of ecclesiastics' supernatural sanctions. Prosecuted vermin that fled or died during or shortly after their trials did so under ecclesiastic conjurors' imprecations or their threat. Thus, ecclesiastics could claim credit for the pests' departure.

Trials that led to the second outcome evidenced the bogusness of the Church's supernatural sanctions. Prosecuted vermin that remained on plaintiffs' property did so despite ecclesiastic conjurors' imprecations. Thus, they cast doubt on the validity of ecclesiastics' conjurations.

A crucial feature of trying insects and rodents for crimes is that the court conducting such a trial can influence which of these outcomes the trial yields. Insects and rodents are itinerant: a pack of rats that ravages some fields is likely to depart them when feeding prospects begin to look better elsewhere; a swarm of locusts may move on for similar reasons. Alternatively, the pests may be killed or driven away by predators, or flee or die naturally for other unobserved reasons. Over even short periods of time, then, vermin under an ecclesiastic court's imprecations could "miraculously" cease to harass the persons they formerly plagued.

The odds that a vermin problem will remedy itself in one of these ways rise as the period of time in question lengthens. So by protracting the vermin's trial, an ecclesiastic court could improve the chances that the pests would depart under its imprecations or their threat.

And courts had many ways of protracting trials. Indeed, since they determined which legal plays vermin trials consisted of, courts could ensure any trial durations they desired. Consider, for instance, the trial of some weevils prosecuted in 1587 for "depredations and . . . doing incalculable injury" to a community's vines.[48] It lasted eight months. And this trial wasn't exceptional.

"Delays were frequent and long" in vermin trials.[49] "The courts would . . . by every reason for delay, evade" concluding them.[50] One court granted the pregnant members of a convicted species "free and safe-conduct and an additional respite of fourteen days" from predators when it ordered them to depart an afflicted area.[51] Others, such as the court that presided over The People v. Locusts, gave vermin six days to vacate the premises before imprecating them.

Judges granted vermin repeated continuances throughout their trials. Furthermore, they "conducted [them] with solemnity, and with a most solicitous attention to the fine points of the judicial process such as was never afforded . . . to human prisoners brought before the courts."[52] As one court remarked, "The arguments offered by the counsel for the defence against the proceedings instituted by the inhabitants as complainants are worthy of careful consideration and deserve to be examined soberly and maturely."[53] Careful, sober, and mature deliberations were undoubtedly slow ones.

No excuse for protracting a vermin trial seems to have been too specious to permit. Chassenée, for example, argued that his rat clients couldn't attend their trial because the court's summons was too local— officials needed to pronounce it over a wider region for the rats to hear. Still, the rats didn't come. On his second turn before the bench, he argued that the rats were absent because some members of the species were old and feeble—they required more time. Again, the rats didn't come. His third time before the bench he argued that his clients were absent because some cats prevented them from attending. The court countenanced each of these claims.

Or consider the weevil case I mentioned a few minutes ago. Having tired of the trial's length, the plaintiffs proposed settling with the insects. Their lawyer drew up a contract for the court's and weevils' consideration, suggesting a nearby ground, La Grand Feisse, to which the bugs could retire in peace. The court happily agreed to consider this request. Then it happily heard the weevils' lawyer's answer: La Grand Feisse was wholly unacceptable to his clients—it lacked the basic necessities for their sustenance. The court responded to this argument by sending some experts to survey the land, prolonging the trial even further.

This case's outcome is unknown; some vermin destroyed the final page of the corresponding record. But when all the courtroom drama was over, the better part of a year had passed. "Such trials, argued in exhaustive detail, could drag on for months."[54]

[*The Satan worshiper looks eager to speak.*]

You wanted to say something, Ozzy?

"*I get it!*"

Go ahead . . .

"*Bugs and rodents are bound to die naturally at some point. So by drawing out their trials long enough, clerics could make it look like the vermin died because of their sentences, which convinced*

people that those punishments were real, which made people pay
their tithes! All the clerics had to do was keep the trial going until
the vermin kicked it!"

You're getting there—but not quite. As our friend points out, a sufficiently long trial guaranteed that vermin would depart under ecclesiastics' imprecations or their threat. In the limit, winter arrived, killing the pests. The problem for courts was that the positive relationship between the amount of time that passed because of a prolonged trial and a vermin infestation remedying itself was surely understood. Even ill-informed farmers recognize that insects and rodents must die or move on eventually. A vermin trial that was long enough to coincide with the departure of vermin for certain was therefore one that did nothing to increase citizens' belief in ecclesiastics' supernatural sanctions. More generally, the longer a trial lasted, the less convincing was the evidence it supplied for the Church's power to imprecate if the vermin departed.

Conversely, the shorter a trial's duration, the more convincing was the evidence for the Church's power it provided if the vermin departed, hence the greater boost such an outcome offered to give to citizens' belief. The most convincing evidence, and thus greatest boost to belief, was produced by the shortest trial that succeeded—that in which the court immediately declared vermin guilty and the pests quickly departed. But the shorter a trial was, the less likely it was to succeed.

Ecclesiastics, then, confronted a trade-off: a potentially more convincing trial, which was shorter but carried with it a greater chance of backfiring, or a longer trial, which was more likely to provide the outcome ecclesiastics sought but was less convincing when this outcome occurred.

If you're interested in the details of how ecclesiastics negotiated this trade-off optimally, meet me after the tour in the appendix. The intuition, however, is straightforward. By prolonging vermin trials somewhat but not until the vermin were certain to die from natural causes, ecclesiastics could produce false positives—cases where the vermin departed and, because they did so amid trials short enough to preclude Mother Nature as the certain cause, their departure provided persuasive evidence for the validity of ecclesiastics' supernatural sanctions. That evidence in turn boosted citizens' belief in the legitimacy of clerics' sanctions, leading tithe-evading doubters to relinquish some of their doubt and thus more of the tithes they owed.

Of course, ecclesiastics conducted vermin trials only on an as-needed basis—when and where it was profitable for them to try and prop up people's beliefs. Where citizens already had sufficiently strong faith in the legitimacy of ecclesiastics' supernatural sanctions, and thus paid their tithes, conducting a vermin trial was all cost and no benefit. Under these conditions, when citizens came asking for a trial, ecclesiastics would direct them to simply pray on the matter instead.

In contrast, where citizens' faith in the legitimacy of ecclesiastics' supernatural sanctions was weaker, and thus they evaded their tithes, ecclesiastics expected to gain from conducting a vermin trial of the proper duration. Under these conditions, if citizens came asking for a trial, ecclesiastics would give them one.

In other words, ecclesiastics would read their crowd, look at the strength of their beliefs, open their coffers, and decide what made sense.

[*The economist interrupts:*]

"*What about where belief was zero?*"

Well, if citizens didn't believe at all in the Church's power to imprecate, ecclesiastics wouldn't be able to conduct vermin trials.

"*Why not?*"

Because citizens who reposed no faith in the legitimacy of ecclesiastics' supernatural sanctions didn't believe that ecclesiastics could use those sanctions to help them with vermin infestations. Such communities would never bring lawsuits against vermin in the first place.

Since conducting vermin trials where citizens had sufficiently strong belief in the Church's power to imprecate didn't pay, and conducting them where citizens had sufficiently weak belief wasn't possible, ecclesiastics could profitably conduct vermin trials only in communities where citizens' belief in their supernatural sanctions was strong enough that they brought lawsuits against vermin but weak enough that they didn't pay all their tithes already.

[*The economist raises his hand.*]

Another question?

"Another fanciful story. But where's the evid . . . ?"

What kind of evidence would convince you that my "fanciful story" might be true?

"Tithe revenues. If your story is right, tithe revenues should be falling in communities under heretical influence, which is also where we should see vermin trials being conducted. And then, once a trial is conducted, we should see tithe revenues going back up."

You're right. But I don't have tithe revenues by community in early modern France, Italy, and Switzerland, let alone data refined enough to tell me what happened to them before and after vermin trials were conducted. In many cases, I don't even know the exact year a vermin trial was conducted. I know what half-century it falls into, but . . .

"Ha! So you admit it! You have no evidence and . . ."

Slow down, Dr. Spock. You pride yourself on being a clever scientist. Surely you can think of some other way to test my argument—one that isn't precluded by the data.

"Okay. How about this? Vermin trials should be concentrated in those parts of France, Italy, and Switzerland populated by tithe-threatening heretics—your Where's Waldos or whatever they're called."

Perfect! That test I have conducted. Will everyone please take a look at the map on the wall behind you?

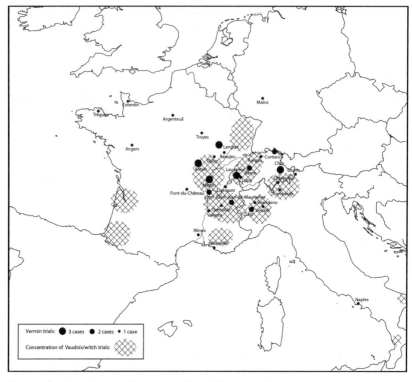

Geographic distribution of vermin trials and heretics, 1450–1700.

[*Ania:*]

"*What's that?*"

That, Ania, is a map that depicts vermin trial hot spots and heretic hot spots in early modern continental Europe.

[*A portly, mustachioed patron shouts:*]

"*It looks like they overlap!*"

It sure does, Tuskernini. Let me tell you a bit more about the map. It reflects forty-six cases of bug and rodent trials for which records survive between 1451, when citizens in Berne, Switzerland, sued some rats, and c.1680, when citizens in Chur, Switzerland, and Constance, Germany, sued some worms.[55] It excludes one trial of rats in an unknown location in Spain. I suspect this trial was conducted in northern Spain near the border of southwestern France, but I can't be sure. I collected these data from the register of ecclesiastical vermin trials that Edward Payson Evans compiled in his book *The Criminal Prosecution and Capital Punishment of Animals.*[56]

Each circle on the map plots the location of one or more early modern vermin trials. The largest circles reflect locations where ecclesiastics conducted three vermin trials, the second-largest circles where they conducted two, and the smallest circles where they conducted one.

The cross-hatched areas reflect approximate regions of known Vaudois concentrations and concentrations of witch trials between 1450 and 1700.[57] The former include Dauphiné and Provence, France, and Piedmont, Apulia, and Calabria, Italy.[58] The latter include areas in which a dozen or more witch trials were conducted during these years. These are, in France, southern Burgundy, most of Rhône-Alpes, eastern Lorraine, and northwestern and southern Aquitaine; in Italy, Lombardy; and in Switzerland, the cantons of Berne, Vaud, Lucerne, and Neuchâtel. I collected my data on witch trials in France, Italy, and Switzerland from the register of such trials that a fellow named Marc Carlson assembled.[59]

[*The economist interrupts:*]

"*What's with the witch trial hot spots? I thought we were looking at Waldaises.*"

Dr. Spock was undoubtedly tuned out again when I was telling everyone about the history of this "WTF?!"-worthy practice. Who can tell him why witch trial hot spots would be a reasonable proxy for heretical—in particular, Waldensian—presence?

[*Ania raises her hand.*]

"*The Waldenses were equated with witches!*"

That's right. The fact that "witches were often equated explicitly with the Waldensians" was unfortunate for the Vaudois.[60] But it's fortunate for me. "The insistence upon the witches' heretical nature often caused witches and heretics to be put on trial together."[61] Thus, together with areas known to be under strong Waldensian influence, I can use areas of intense witch trials to proxy areas of intense heretical, and in pre-Reformation years, in particular Waldensian, influence.

The test my map provides is unavoidably crude. My samples of both kinds of trials are small—surely smaller than the actual number in each case. And the witch trial hot spots depicted in my map are based only on trials whose location is known.[62] They necessarily exclude witch trials whose date and country are known but whose location within the country isn't. Thus, as with any analysis relying on historical data of this nature, my map must be interpreted with caution.

Furthermore, although ecclesiastics in France, Italy, and Switzerland commonly associated Vaudois with witches and viewed witches as heretics, it doesn't follow that most, or even a significant portion of, persons tried for witchcraft were actual Vaudois. The Vaudois weren't the only heretics in early modern Europe, even if they were an especially important group. "Witches" could be Vaudois, other defined heretics, generic people suspected of practicing witchcraft, or merely people distrusted by authorities. The important concern for my test is that the trials of such individuals correlate in an informative way with ecclesiastics' perceptions of heretical activity—activity that weakened belief in their spiritual authority. Since "Witchcraft thrived best . . . wherever and whenever . . . heresy flourished," we can be reasonably confident that this is the case even if witch trials capture such threats only broadly and imprecisely.[63]

As Tuskernini pointed out a minute ago, it's clear that vermin trials and the trials of heretics "exhibit a correlation of time and space."[64] The map displays a pattern: ecclesiastics conducted vermin trials in locations where heretics were busy eroding citizens' faith in the supernatural sanctions supporting tithe compliance. Vermin trials are concentrated in three major areas: eastern France (along the

Saône-Rhône River axis), northern Italy (the Piedmont region), and western Switzerland (the Jura region, which spills over into eastern France). Each of these areas is also a known Waldensian or witch trial hot spot.

The pattern is imperfect. The western coast of Aquitaine in southwestern France saw a large number of witch trials, yet no vermin trials appear near them. If we could precisely locate the case of the Spanish rats, we might find a connection here. But as I mentioned earlier, there's no way to do so. There are also a few cases of "floating" vermin trials in northwestern France. These areas saw witch trials but not in sufficient number to merit cross-hatching.

Still, even accounting for these exceptions, if Waldensian and witch trial hot spots are a reasonable proxy for areas in which ecclesiastics had special concern for belief-eroding heretics, it appears that a good deal of vermin trial activity can be explained by their response to such concern. Considering the crudeness of my exercise, that's pretty . . .

[The burly man with the piercings snarls:]

"What's with that big swath stretching across the southwestern part of France where there aren't any vermin trials?"

The area I think you're pointing to, Karnov, is what was called the Protestant crescent, which extended from La Rochelle on the Atlantic seaboard to Grenoble in the east. It constituted a region of Protestant stronghold from about 1550 to the end of France's Wars of Religion. This crescent included Languedoc and other locations where "tithe strikes"—citizens flatly refusing to pay the Church—began to occur in the 1560s.[65] Among the vermin trials conducted in France in the second half of the sixteenth century and later, none occurred in a location clearly within the Protestant crescent's orbit. Only two vermin trials occur on the eastern edges of this crescent—one in Valence in 1585, the other in Saint-Jean-de-Maurienne in 1587—and here the Huguenots were much weaker.[66]

The Protestant crescent corresponds to a region where belief in ecclesiastics' supernatural sanctions was too weak to lead citizens to seek
ecclesiastics' help to rid them of unwanted pests. Indeed, it's in this region that the United Provinces of the Midi, a kind of Huguenot state
within a state, formed in the second half of the sixteenth century. The
outbreak of tithe strikes further evidences the weakness of citizens' belief
in the Church's authority in this region. Citizens who reposed so little
faith in that authority that they were already flatly refusing to pay their
tithes were beyond ecclesiastics' reach. Their unwillingness to bring suits
precluded ecclesiastics from conducting vermin trials in this area.[67]

The distribution of vermin trials in my map—a distribution consistent with my "fanciful story," as Dr. Spock called it—also explains the
peculiar fact that these trials appear in the most advanced places on the
globe in the early modern era, not the most backward ones. The country that saw the most vermin trials, France, was, in the words of one
historian, "the wealthiest and most populous state in Europe, and the
one with the most coherent political geography."[68] It was also "easily
the most powerful nation in Europe" during the golden age of vermin
trials.[69] Primitivism doesn't explain the locations of those trials. But
heretical activity, and thus tithe-revenue erosion, appears to.

Similarly, the distribution of vermin trials suggested by my reasoning explains why, even within France, they appeared in the more urban
half of the country. "Large towns and cities were a feature of eastern
France," but so were heretics.[70] Thus, we find ecclesiastics there conducting vermin trials more frequently.

And so it is for the vermin trial–afflicted areas of Italy and Switzerland. Ecclesiastics here weren't crazier than elsewhere in Europe. Their
citizens were more exposed to tithe-eroding heretics.

[*The economist:*]

*"Not too shabby. But if you have data on the periods in which
vermin trials and witch trials happened, and the latter meaning-
fully correspond to heretical influence, as you claim, we should also*

*see some correspondence between the occurrence of vermin trials
and witch trials over time. I mean, if ecclesiastics are using vermin
trials when heretical influence is stronger, and witches measure
that influence, we should see vermin trials flourishing at the same
times that witch trials do. What do the time-series data show?"*

Everyone please move to the far end of the room. There you'll find another picture hanging on the wall—a chart.

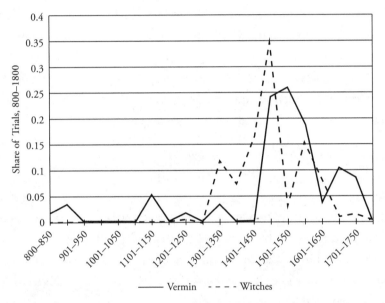

Temporal distribution of vermin trials and heretics, 800–1800.

This chart depicts vermin and witch trials over time: 62 cases of the
former and 572 cases of the latter, spanning the years between 800 and
1800 at fifty-year intervals. It plots the number of vermin and witch
trials in each half-century as a share of their respective kind of trial for
the entire thousand-year period.

For reasons similar to those in the case of my map, my chart is also
crude. I have imprecise dates for several vermin trials: I'm able to place
these trials in a century, but I don't know in which part of the century
they belong.[71]

The witch trial data in my chart consider France, Italy, and Switzerland. And while most vermin trial cases for which I have data were conducted in these countries, several weren't. Two of these cases occurred in Germany—in Constance, on the border with Switzerland. It's reasonable to treat these as Swiss cases, but three cases included in my vermin trial data fall completely outside the France-Italy-Switzerland region. One trial occurred in Mainz, Germany, which isn't a border area. The second, which I mentioned earlier, occurred in Spain. The third, in Als, Denmark. Overlap between the regions my vermin trial data cover and those my witch trial data cover is therefore high but imperfect.

Nevertheless, the data are sufficient to paint a general picture of the relationship between vermin trials and witch trials, and thus ecclesiastics' perceptions of heretical activity, over time.

[*The portly, mustachioed man shouts:*]

"Those lines move together!"

Right again! In time periods with more witch trials, ecclesiastics conducted more vermin trials. Between 1400 and 1550, 50 percent of all vermin trials for the thousand-year period between 800 and 1800 occur. And over the same century and a half, 54 percent of all witch trials for that period occur.

Neither vermin nor witch trials come into significant use until the first half of the fifteenth century, when Waldensian growth was likely highest. Between 1400 and 1450, no vermin trials are conducted, and 17 percent of witch trials occur. In the second half of the fifteenth century, the second-largest share of vermin trials and largest share of witch trials occur: 24 percent and 35 percent, respectively.

In the next half-century, the share of vermin trials reaches its highest level—25 percent—but only a tiny share of witch trials occurs. Together with the pattern I just mentioned, this suggests that vermin trials may be a "lagging indicator" of heresy—the former moving in the same direction as the latter but with a delay. This is consistent with the idea that ecclesiastics used vermin trials to bolster citizens' belief in the years following heretical activity and prosecution.

Between 1550 and 1600, 19 percent of vermin trials and 15 percent of witch trials occur, and at the end of this period, the shares of both types of trials go into decline. Vermin trials rise again in the second half of the seventeenth century, but nowhere near their height from the period 1450 to 1550. And by the second half of the seventeenth century, both sorts of trials become exceptional.

The Vaudois merged with the Calvinist Reformers in the second half of the sixteenth century, but they existed as a distinct group located predominantly in Piedmont until the end of the seventeenth. It's therefore unsurprising that five of the nine vermin trials we're aware of that ecclesiastics conducted in the seventeenth century occurred in Italy.

The close of that century is when Vittorio Amedeo II, duke of Savoy and prince of Piedmont, officially granted the Vaudois the right to practice their religion. This decision, made in 1690, followed on the heels of Amedeo's attempt to rid his territories of Vaudois permanently. Thus, predictably, the end of the seventeenth century also sees the virtual end of vermin trials.

The timing of vermin trials in my chart—timing consistent with my argument—explains why, unexpectedly, these trials appear most frequently in what one historian calls a "period of sustained prosperity" in France, not in one of poverty, devastation, and chaos, such as the mid-fourteenth-century plague.[72] Vermin trials don't reflect economic turmoil or Renaissance backsliding. They reflect an ecclesiastic response to a Renaissance-era threat to citizens' belief in the supernatural sanctions supporting tithe compliance.

You've already seen how, by institutionalizing superstition, seemingly senseless practices—from ordeals to oracles—can incentivize desired, and often socially desirable, behavior. Now you can add vermin trials to that list. You've also seen how seemingly senseless institutions that leverage supernatural sanctions—from *Romaniya* to monastic maledictions—can be used for that purpose. So it goes with vermin trials too. But vermin trials are also unique: they demonstrate how seemingly senseless institutions can be used to *create* additional belief in supernatural sanctions so that those sanctions work better. Seeming senselessness on top of seeming senselessness = pretty damn sensible.

That's it for vermin trials. But I've got one last "WTF?!"-worthy practice to share with you. At our final stop, we'll return to the Dark Ages and go from the continent to the island.

[*The woman who looks like Janeane Garofalo shouts excitedly:*]

"*We're going to Hawaii?! I'm a huge fan of ecotourism. Nature, untouched by the military-industrial complex . . .*"

Wrong island. We're headed to Great Britain—England, to be exact. Follow me.

8

Fighting Solves Everything

When I was in elementary school, Pizza Hut—that great, greasy philanthropist—joined forces with Siebert Elementary, my alma mater, to bribe students . . . to read.

The setup was simple. The school would hold a Pizza Hut–sponsored contest for students in each grade.[1] Within in each grade, teachers divided us into groups of kids at similar reading levels. Whoever in each group could demonstrate that he had read the most pages over the course of the year won a free, Pizza Hut "personal-pan pizza."

I don't know if you've ever seen Pizza Hut's personal-pan pizza, but its circumference can't be much bigger than a DVD. The perfect complement to the shot glass–sized cups of water that restaurants in Europe serve.

I don't know if you've ever been to Midland, Michigan, where I grew up, but I can assure you that nearly all of us ate pizza with great regularity. Pizza Hut pizza was about as exotic as a ride in a minivan.

Finally, I don't know if you've ever eaten Pizza Hut pizza, but it's not exactly the finest fare. It seems to have two ingredients: grease and some kind of salty glue that holds the grease together.

You'd be forgiven, then, if you expected this competition to have little impact on Siebert Elementary students. But, boy, would you be wrong.

When our principal presented the Pizza Hut challenge, it was as if he had announced that anyone who won the reading contest would have the length of their summer vacation doubled and never have to do homework again.

Suddenly kids who hated reading were reading at recess, at home, and on the bus. There were runs on the library. Mrs. Trailor, the school librarian, went from everyone's least favorite school administrator to virtual rock-star status. I got my first paper cut in a frenzied read-fest. It was literacy bedlam. And all for the sweet specter of three-and-a-half bites of crappy pizza.

The winning student in my group turned out to be a girl named Eve. She read some ungodly number of pages. I don't remember how many, but far more than anyone else.

I was, of course, disappointed that I lost the "reading fight." But even then, I recall feeling it was right that Eve had won. Eve was a pizza fanatic; her favorite was the Hut. If anybody wanted that free personal pan more than me, it was her. This was reflected in Eve's reading effort relative to mine and the other students'. Everyone wanted the pizza, and everyone read a lot. But Eve wanted the pizza more, so she spent more time reading to win it. The reading fight produced an economically sound outcome: it allocated the pizza to the student who valued it most.

The reason it did so was that this fight was like an auction. Students "bid" on the free pizza with their time and effort spent reading, a reasonable proxy for money, which none of us had. Whoever bid the most won.

Many kinds of fights are auctions of one sort or another, and vice versa. When you go to an art auction and bid on a painting, for instance, you're engaged in a "fight" with the other bidders. The fight's winner—the high bidder—gets the prize. But it comes at a cost, so there's a good chance that the winner is the bidder who appreciates the painting the most. Given that, it's "efficient" for it to go to her.

[*The muscular patron with the piercings pipes up.*]

"I love fights! I'll throw down with anybody on this tour right now!"

[*scanning the crowd and spotting the gentleman with the glass eye:*]

"Glass-eyed man? You wanna go?!"

We're not going to have any fighting during the tour, sir.

[*the gentleman with the glass eye, visibly relieved:*]

"Thank you! I should hope not! I can't . . ."

Better to save your assault for *after* the tour, when you can use the parking lot in back. There's plenty of space, good light, and sundry objects for you to use as weapons.

[*the gentleman with the glass eye:*]

"What?! No! I'm not fighting anyb . . ."

[*the large patron with the piercings, pointing menacingly:*]

"Parking lot. Done. See you there."

It's settled then. Karnov v. The Tapper. One hour. Now, where was I . . . Ah, yes, I was just about to tell you about our final "WTF?!"-worthy practice. Some of you may have heard of something similar thanks to *Game of Thrones*.

What you see here is a *baculus cornutus*:

It sounds like a virus, but as you can see it's a wooden club. Legal representatives in England used to beat each other with these to resolve property disputes. Hence the name of the practice—trial by battle—or as *Game of Thrones* refers to it, "trial by combat."[2]

Modern legal battles are antagonistic and acrimonious, but they aren't literally battles. Disputants don't resolve conflicts with quarterstaffs; their lawyers don't fight to the death. Yet this wasn't always so. For over a century, England's judicial system decided land disputes by ordering disputants' legal representatives, fittingly dubbed "champions," to bludgeon one another before an arena of spectating citizens. The victorious champion won the property right for his principal. The vanquished lost his cause and, if he were unlucky, his life.

The Norman Conquest introduced trial by battle to England.[3] It was the primary way of litigating land disputes there until 1179, afterward applied more sparingly up to the end of the thirteenth century.[4] During this period, one person challenged another's claim to a piece of land by bringing a legal action called a "writ of right."[5] The plaintiff was called the "demandant," the defendant, the "tenant." The plaintiff initiated his challenge by requesting the crown to issue an order compelling the defendant to appear before a court to defend his property.[6]

A colorable claim was necessary for the plaintiff's challenge to make it to trial; there was no guarantee the crown would fulfill his request for a writ. It therefore behooved him to supply some evidence of his claim's plausibility, such as a charter documenting his connection to the contested property. Supplying a witness who would swear to his connection to the disputed land was helpful too. In fact, the court required such a witness of the plaintiff and could reject his claim if he couldn't produce one. These "screens" helped prevent bogus property challenges from making it to trial, but they did so imperfectly.

Ideally, the legal system would have liked to assign disputed property rights to their true owners. Unfortunately, evidence that might help judges do that was in short supply. The evidence they actually had often amounted to disputants' and their witnesses' (and perhaps charters') competing claims—not very helpful at all.

Faced with this dilemma, Anglo-Norman judges did what any respectable judicial officials would do: pretend to divine the identity of a disputed parcel's true owner through judicial combat. God favored the rightful disputant's cause, they reasoned, so he would favor his cause in a physical fight.

The plaintiff pled before the court by offering to prove his right to the disputed land on his champion's body.[7] Consider the plaintiff's plea in a case from 1198:

> Matthew, the son of William, sought against Ralph of Wicherle and Beatrice, his wife, a wood and other land at Ellenthorpe as the right and dowry of his wife, Emma, whereof the said Matthew was seised [took rightful possession] as of right and dowry in the time of King Henry by taking the issues thereof from wood, timber and pasturing pigs to the value of 5/4d; and this he offered to prove against him by his freeman Utling, who offered to prove this against him as the court should adjudge as of his sight, or by another if any ill should befall him.[8]

The defendant pled by denying the plaintiff's claim, offering his own champion as proof:

> Ralph and Beatrice came and denied the right and seisin [rightful possession] of the said Matthew by a certain freeman of theirs, Hugh of Floketon, who offered to deny this by his body, or by another.[9]

If the court couldn't establish the rightful disputant's identity, it "adjudged that there should be a battle" between their champions:

> The pledges of Hugh (defending) were Ralph his lord and Robert, the son of Payn. The pledges of Utling were Matthew, the son of William, and Robert of Cove. A day was given to them on the coming of the justices into those parts.[10]

In theory, the law required the plaintiff's champion to be a witness to his right to the disputed land. He had to claim that he observed the plaintiff's ancestor's seisin. Alternatively he could claim that his deceased father observed it and instructed him to defend the plaintiff's right.

In practice, however, the law permitted plaintiffs to hire champions, just as it permitted defendants to do.[11] A defendant could object to the plaintiff's champion on the grounds that he had been bought, but "professional champions were so frequently used that the courts paid no attention to this particular objection."[12]

On the appointed day, the champions came to the designated arena and swore oaths affirming their principal's rightness in his cause.[13] Eleventh- and twelfth-century arenas were makeshift; later ones were specially constructed for the purpose. Sixteenth-century records describe the "lists" as "an even and level piece of ground, set out square, 60 feet on each side due east, west, north and south, and a place or seat for the justices of the bench was made without and above the lists, and covered with furniture of the same bench in Westminster Hall, and a bar made there for serjeants-at-law."[14]

Before battle began, the presiding justices made an announcement forbidding spectator interference. Their injunction before one combat conjures images of a deadly tennis match:

> The justices command, in the Queen Majesty's name, that no person of what estate, degree, or condition that he be, being present, be so hardy to give any token or sign, by countenance, speech, or language, either to the prover or to the defender, whereby the one of them may take advantage of the other; and no person remove, but will keep his place; and that every person or persons keep their staves and their weapons to themselves; and suffer neither the said prover nor defender to take any of their weapons or any other thing, that may stand either to the said prover or defender any avail, upon pain of forfeiture of lands, tenements, goods, chattels, and imprisonment of their bodies, and making fine and ransom at the Queen's pleasure.[15]

The plaintiff's champion could win trial by battle in two ways: killing his adversary or forcing him to cry "craven"—an act of submission. The defendant's champion could win in a third way: pushing a stalemate until nightfall. But battle began before noon, so that would be a long haul.

The victorious champion won the contested property right for his principal. The court concluded the trial by ordering the disputed land to his principal's possession and announcing its good title publicly:

> The King to the sheriff, greetings. I command you that, without delay, you give possession to X of [description of land], concerning which there was a suit between him and Y in my court; because such land is adjudged to him in my court by battle.[16]

The defeated champion was less fortunate. If he survived, he paid a £3 fine for perjury and "lost his law": he could never again bear witness in another's legal dispute.[17]

[*The economist raises his hand.*]

Dr. Spock! You're paying attention! I'm very glad that . . .

"I don't buy it."

You don't buy what? I haven't described anything other than historical fact yet. That's why I'm surprised you were listen . . .

"I know what you're going to say. And it doesn't make sense."

What am I going to say, that I haven't said, that you already disagree with?

"You started by telling us about how auctions are like fights. So you're going to tell us that these trial by battle fights were really just auctions that judges used to assign disputed land to the disputant who valued it more when they weren't sure who the land really belonged to."

You're right. That is what I'm going to tell you. When inadequate evidence prevented Anglo-Norman judges from assigning a disputed property right to its true owner, they attempted to do the next-best thing: allocate the right to the litigant who valued it more. But . . .

"But that doesn't make sense—because of the Coase theorem."

Does everyone remember what the Coase theorem is? We talked about it when our economist friend brought it up the first time, back at our stop on wife sales. Dr. Spock, will you remind us?

"The Coase theorem says that if the cost of trading is low, trade between people will move property rights into the hands of those who value them most. It tells us that judges shouldn't have needed to assign disputed land to the disputant who valued it more. If judges assigned the land to the disputant who valued it less, the other would just buy it from him after the fact. Either way, the person who valued the land more would end up with it. The result would be efficient. Your story fails."

Who remembers what happened the last time Dr. Spock claimed that my story failed because of the Coase theorem?

[The priest raises his hand.]

Speak it, Padre.

[grinning devilishly]

"He looked like a damn fool!"

And history repeats itself.

Dr. Spock is correct that judges don't need to worry about allocating a contested property right to the disputant who values it more *if the cost of trading is low.* But sometimes it's not. Negotiating trades takes time, energy, and resources; it can get very expensive. And when it gets expensive enough, property rights become sticky—prone to remain in whoever's hands they first land, since high trading costs prevent them from being traded later to someone else.

In that case, if judges allocate a contested property right "incorrectly"—in other words, to the person who values it less—the right is likely to get stuck in his possession. The higher the trading costs are, the more important it therefore becomes to allocate the right "correctly" from the get-go. And since the cost of trading land in Norman England was very high, that's what Anglo-Norman legal institutions aimed to do—leading to trial by battle.[18]

[*The priest raises his hand.*]

Padre?

"Why was it so hard to trade land in Norman England? Why were property rights in land, as you say, sticky?"

Because of feudalism.[19] The feudal system was one of tenants—people in possession of land that somebody else granted them—and lords—the somebody elses who granted tenants land. In exchange for grants of land, tenants owed their lords service—military, agricultural, or otherwise. Except for the king (who was only a lord) and the lowliest tenants (who were only tenants), everyone in this system was both a tenant of some lord and a lord some tenant(s), connecting them in an elaborate web of land-service relations.

This was a cozy arrangement, but it presented some difficulties. Chief among them: what one person did with his land could have major repercussions for others connected to him in the feudal web. Particularly problematic was land alienation—its sale.

Land sales could take two forms: "substitution," which replaced a strand of the feudal web, and "subinfeudation," which created a new strand.[20] A tenant who substituted his land sold his spot in the feudal web—both its benefits, such as occupancy of the land, and its obligations, such as whatever services the lord had coming. This was sort of like selling a condo with respect to the homeowners' association.

The lord lost one tenant, the seller, who was replaced with a new one, the buyer.

In contrast, a tenant who subinfeudated his land sold some (or all) of it to a buyer but remained a tenant of his lord. This was sort of like subleasing an apartment. The seller became the buyer's lord and the buyer his lord's subtenant.

Both forms of alienation threatened the interests of two feudal associates of would-be land sellers: their heirs and their lords. Heirs' concern was usually simple enough. Subinfeudation threatened to disinherit them in part, substitution in full. Lords' concern, however, had multiple dimensions. For example, if the buyer was less competent or reliable than the seller, the lord was less likely to receive the services he was owed—indirectly in the case of subinfeudation, directly in the case of substitution.

There was also the matter of escheat: lords' right, under certain circumstances, to their dead or legally indisposed tenants' land. Suppose an heirless tenant sold his land to a buyer via subinfeudation for a few peanuts each year. When the tenant died, his lord might end up with a handful of peanuts instead of getting his land. Or suppose an old tenant, nearing his end, sold his land by substitution to a healthy young buck. Instead of getting the tenant's land in a few months, his lord might now have to wait a few decades.

A still bigger concern for lords was the possibility that a tenant might grant his land to a religious house, such as a church or monastery. Churches and monasteries usually held land "in alms." The only services they were obligated to provide were spiritual ones, typically benedictions for whoever made them the grant. The material services the lord used to collect on that land? Gone. If he was lucky, he might get a prayer.

To prevent such injuries from befalling property sellers' heirs and lords, norms developed in Norman England, bolstered in some areas by the law, requiring or making it very desirable for tenants to get their heirs' and lords' consent to alienate land.[21]

Alienation restrictions were flexible. If a would-be seller's interests aligned with those of his lord and heirs, explicit consent to alienate was usually unnecessary. But if, say, a tenant sought to grant his land to the Church, consent was mandatory—his lord could veto the proposed alienation.[22] I mentioned this particular consent requirement, you might remember, when I told you about the gifts of land that laypersons made to monasteries in Francia, protected by monks who put curse clauses in their land charters.

Consent rules governing land sales protected heirs and lords, but they had an unfortunate side effect: they dramatically increased the cost of trading land, stifling its movement. A tenant who wanted to sell his property might have to negotiate with and secure the permission of numerous others: his heirs, his lord, perhaps even his lord's lord. "Multiple consents required from people with diverse standards and concerns retarded the use of land as an economic asset."[23] They made Anglo-Norman land rights sticky.

Sticky land rights meant that it was important for judges to assign disputed property whose true owner remained undiscoverable to the disputant who valued it more. But there was a problem: How could they know which disputant that was?

The solution to this problem was trial by battle. In essence, these trials were "violent auctions" for contested land. Litigants "bid" on contested parcels by spending on champions who literally fought for property rights on their employer's behalf. The disputant who valued the contested land more bid more, and he was more likely to get the land, since his higher bid bought him a better champion.

The best champions developed reputations for their skill in the arena. William of Copeland, for instance, was known far and wide, from Yorkshire to Somerset. "The mere sight of him was enough to scare any tenant who might have considered countering his challenge."[24] Or consider Robert of Clopton, a contemporary of Copeland, who "was [also] in great demand as a champion" in the early thirteenth century.[25]

Because they were in higher demand, better champions commanded higher prices. The abbot of Glastonbury, for example, paid thirteenth-century champion Henry of Fernberg £20 to battle on his behalf in a property dispute. The terms of Fernberg's contract stipulated partial payment when he wagered battle, another part before he fought, and the rest if he struck his opponent but once in the arena. An evidently inferior thirteenth-century champion, John of Smerill, commanded less than half as much for agreeing to battle for William Heynton.[26]

In contrast to the medieval land market, the market for champions was fluid. Selling land could require the consent of many, but hiring a champion required the consent of none. Champions were therefore happy to "desert to the other side if the inducement was sufficiently great," reshuffling themselves easily into the service of the highest bidder.[27]

Hiring a superior champion wasn't the only way for disputants to bid on contested land. They could also hire more champions. Only one actually fought, but purchasing several champions, especially the better ones, shrank the other litigant's choices, leaving him fewer and inferior options.

In 1220, for example, a plaintiff named Cliveden contested the right to a parcel of land then in possession of a fellow named Ken. Ken responded by hiring four champions—one of them the redoubtable William of Copeland. Similarly, in a case of contested fishing rights between the abbot of Meaux and the abbot of St. Mary's of York, Meaux hired seven champions "at great cost."[28] His goal: to "monopolise the market" for professional battlers, "compel[ling] the other Abbot to employ a second-rate champion."[29]

Captain America has his hand up. If you promise that your mouth is chaw-free, sir, you may ask your question.

"I dun gets how this ere lawyerly fightin' was spose to give the land to the plain'iff who wanted the land more. Splain that ag'n."

Maybe an example will help. Consider two medieval Englishmen, Eustace and Osbert. Eustace goes before the king's court and claims that the farmland Osbert occupies is his. Osbert denies Eustace's claim. Both offer to prove their right on their champion's body. Property rights in land are sticky; the cost of trading them is prohibitive. Thus, whomever the legal system awards the farmland to will be its permanent possessor. The court doesn't know who the land truly belongs to, so it orders trial by battle.

Two champions are available for hire: Fernberg and Smerill. Fernberg has a reputation as a great fighter. Smerill doesn't. Both champions sell their services to the highest bidder.

Eustace is a more productive farmer than Osbert; he can make more money from the land, so he values it more. Eustace is therefore willing to pay more for Fernberg's services. He hires Fernberg, leaving Osbert with Smerill. The combat's probable outcome is Fernberg's victory, making Eustace the probable winner of the land.

Trial by battle's violent auction identifies the disputant who values the contested property more and allocates it to him. It substitutes for the Coase theorem where sticky property rights prevent trade from achieving this outcome.

[*the tobacco-chewing patron:*]

"I gets it! It's like when ma got that dog bite and we threaten to sue that scoundr'l whose dog it was. Ma din wanna threaten him. But I told her, 'Ma, we's gonna spend more money to win that case if it comes to. So we's more likely to win it!' I was preparin' to sell all me best firearms if need be."

Yeah . . . I guess it's kind of like that . . . in a weird Jed Clampett sort of way . . .

Captain America's comment about selling his firearms reminds me: the bidders in an auction may have different endowments—sums of money in their pockets and bank accounts—which in some cases could potentially prevent their relative bids from accurately reflecting their relative valuations. You see a lock of Justin Bieber's hair for sale on eBay. You're a Belieber and value the lock at $10,000. Alas, you've only got $50. That might be okay, except some half-Belieber, who only values the lock at $5,000, is going to outbid you. You value the lock more, but he gets it anyway—unbeliebable.

Credit markets, which allow bidders to make bids using others' funds, can help mitigate this problem. Medieval credit markets were far less developed than modern ones, and it's unclear whether they made loans to legal contestants seeking champions. Still, at least in principle, a higher-valuing but cash-short disputant could borrow for this purpose if he needed to—and probably easier than you could borrow $4,950 to buy some of Justin Bieber's hair.[30]

A second factor may have also helped prevent differences in people's endowments, and even differences in their access to credit, from unduly affecting their bids in the violent auctions of trial by battle. Under Norman England's legal system, "Battle seems to have been barred between people of widely differing status."[31] People of similar status likely had similar wealth and abilities to borrow funds.

[*Ania raises her hand.*]

Yes, Ania?

"I see why the legal system had to use a kind of auction to make sure that contested land went to the people who valued it most: Feudalism prevented disputants from freely exchanging property, so judges needed to figure out who valued disputed land more, and trial by battle's violent auctions, as you call them, allowed judges to do that. But I'm having trouble seeing why the legal system would use *violent auctions for that purpose. I mean, why not just auction the contested property off between the disputants in the regular way—you know, like the way they auctioned the wives at wife sales or something? Wouldn't that be better?"*

Another excellent question. I bet Dr. Spock is kicking himself for not thinking of that one. To answer it, it's useful to think about fraudulent lawsuits—legal disputes initiated not to protect property a plaintiff thinks belongs to him but to extort the owner of property he knows does not.[32]

Fraudulent lawsuits are a potentially big problem: people who live in fear of being extorted by bogus legal claims won't invest in their property, which would only make them more attractive targets of extortion. Instead, they'll grow fewer crops on their land, forgo building a house on it, and so on, making the property less useful to everyone.

A central source of fraudulent lawsuits in an auction that allocates disputed property rights is the bids that litigants pay. Somebody gets those bids. In trial by battle's violent auctions, champions got them. In a regular auction, they could go to the legal system—judges or the king—or to the auction's loser as a kind of consolation prize. Since the parties who collect disputants' bid payments get paid whenever there are land disputes, they have an incentive to initiate, or participate in, bogus claims.

In trial by battle, for example, the better champions might encourage unscrupulous plaintiffs to initiate fraudulent claims in the hope that defendants will pay them off—settle. In a regular auction, if the bid collectors are judges, they might ignore the absence of basic evidence required to render a claim colorable, permitting it to go forward to auction. Or if the bid collectors are the losing litigants, anyone who can produce a witness and forge a charter might threaten landowners with baseless claims—heads they win land, tails they win money.

Clearly, whoever the bid collectors are, the more they stand to collect, the stronger their incentive to pursue fraudulent property claims, and thus the more bogus claims there will be. An important feature of trial by battle was that its violent auctions could reduce the number of bogus claims relative to a regular auction by being less generous to bid collectors.[33]

You see, not all auctions are created equal. In the regular kind, or what Dr. Spock would call a "first-price, ascending-bid auction," two contestants bid on a prize until one of them, reaching his limit, drops out of the hunt. The prize is awarded to the contestant who remains—the winner—who values the prize more and thus makes the highest bid (we'll suppose that both contestants are equally wealthy and have equal access to credit). The winner alone pays his bid, which is what the bid collector will get.

How much is that? Just a penny more than the highest amount the loser was willing to pay. If the winner offered any less, he wouldn't win the prize; any more and he'd be throwing his money away.

Trial by battle's violent auction is different. It's what Dr. Spock would call an "imperfectly discriminating all-pay auction."[34] That's fancy talk for an auction in which two contestants bid on a prize, *both* have to pay whatever they bid, and the winner, rather than always being the person who bids more, can sometimes be the person who bids less. This latter bit is similar to the situation with sports teams. The better team is likely to defeat the worse team. But the better team can have a bad day or the worse one a good day, resulting in the worse team's victory.

These features describe trial by battle. To hire champions, both disputants had to pay champions—their bids—and they didn't get their money back if their champion lost. The disputant who paid more to hire a better champion—made a higher bid—had a higher probability of winning, but it was possible that the other litigant's cheaper, inferior champion might upset him.

How much will the bid collector collect in this kind of auction? Less than he collects in the regular kind. At first blush, this might seem strange. After all, in a regular auction, *only* the winner has to pay his bid, whereas in the kind of auction that trial by battle reflected, both the winner *and* loser have to pay.

But this ignores two important facts. First, since he won't have to actually pay his bid, in a regular auction, the contestant who values the prize less has no incentive to bid lower than the maximum he's willing to pay for it. Because of this, the contestant who values the prize more, who *will* have to pay his bid, is forced to bid a bit higher than that in order to win.

In contrast, when both contestants know they're going to have to pay what they bid, the contestant who values the prize less has an incentive to bid lower than his maximum. What's the point of bidding, and thus ultimately paying, his maximum if he's probably going to lose the prize anyway? This in turn allows the contestant who values the prize more to bid less too.

Second, unlike in a regular auction, where the higher bidder wins the prize with certainty, the higher bidder in the kind of auction that trial by battle reflected only wins the prize probabilistically. Despite his higher bid, there's a chance he might lose. This uncertainty reduces the benefit of making higher bids, which encourages contestants to bid less.

If you're interested in the details, see me in the appendix after the tour. But that's the basic idea behind why trial by battle's violent auction was less generous to bid collectors than a regular auction would've been, which meant fewer fraudulent lawsuits.[35]

Fewer, of course, isn't the same as none. And without data on medieval disputants' champion expenditures, it's impossible to measure how common bogus land claims might've been under trial by battle. But indirect evidence suggests they weren't rampant.

It was uncommon, for example, to hire champions on retainer. If illegitimate land disputes had been rampant, hiring champions on retainer probably would've been too. Perpetually threatened by the specter of fraudulent plaintiffs and eager to perpetrate fraudulent claims of their own, many people would've found it worthwhile to keep their thug of choice at his ready in their permanent employment. The fact that "most people" came "to terms with an available champion only when litigation was imminent" is therefore reassuring.[36]

[*The economist interrupts:*]

"*That makes some sense, actually. I see why trial by battle would induce fewer fraudulent lawsuits than a first-price, ascending-bid auction. But that doesn't make trial by battle's auction format superior. There's a trade-off. Trial by battle induces less fraud. But because the higher bidder doesn't always win the auction, trial by battle also allocates the disputed property right to the wrong disputant sometimes. A first-price, ascending-bid auction induces more fraud. But the higher bidder always wins, so the disputed property right always goes to the correct disputant. What do you have to say about that?"*

I say you're right. But that doesn't mean trial by battle was an inferior auction mechanism overall. To determine that, we have to consider the allocative *and* fraud-inducing features of both kinds of auctions. You're probably the only one who cares to see the formalities behind that consideration, Dr. Spock. So I'll reserve the details for our meeting in the appendix. But the upshot of the comparison turns out to be this: as long as the disputant who values the contested property less values it at least half as much as the disputant who values it more, trial by battle's violent auction is superior to a regular auction overall—accounting for both features, it's a better deal for society.

[*The tobacco-chewing man raises his hand.*]

Sir?

"I dun gets it ag'n. Like I was sayin' afore, when Ma got bit, threatn'n with a fancy lawman was anuf to git him to a settlem'nt. When he saw our fancy lawyerin' fella, he knew he was gonna lose. So he paid us that $10 we was askin' fur right there. We never saw no courtroom. So how's it that these here champ-eens, as you call 'em, had to brawl? Why din the worse un's boss settle?"

Great question! And you're spot-on. If you think about the incentives of the litigants under trial by battle, there was no reason they would normally end up with their champions pounding each other in the arena. Once both disputants knew who their adversary had hired, and thus had a good idea about what he had spent, battle was unnecessary. At this point, both parties knew the trial's likely outcome. They could save time and expense by settling their dispute instead.

And in most cases, that's exactly what they did. In fact, even when disputants failed to settle before their champions squared off in the arena, they might still do so midfight. The course of combat reopened the possibility of settlement by clarifying the likely winner's identity. A litigant who stubbornly clung to an unrealistic settlement price before battle could become less stubborn when the unfolding fight showed that his champion was significantly less likely to win than he once thought. As long as the victorious champion's identity wasn't a forgone conclusion, a mutually beneficial settlement existed.

Thus, "Determination of the issue by battle actually fought out . . . was . . . a rare exception, in the writ of right."[37] The usual course of events instead involved each disputant "mak[ing] the best compromise he could at the last moment before the judicial combat."[38] Consider the settlement two litigants made in the reign of Henry II—after their champions entered the arena but before combat began:

> This is the concord by fine [agreement] of combat before Thomas Noel, Sheriff in the county of Stafford, between Godfrey de Shobnall and Juliana de Shobnall concerning the half hide of land which Juliana claimed by writ of the lord king to hold from the abbot of Burton. The aforesaid Juliana received one acre of the land in seisin and the rest of half a bovate of land remains to Godfrey for the rest of his life for the service due Juliana, and for the foresaid Juliana's concession the foresaid Godfrey gave her twenty shillings. After the foresaid Godfrey's death Juliana shall have that land in fee and heredity for herself and her heirs. And the aforesaid Godfrey swore in the county court of Stafford that he would invent no trick or wicked contrivance through which Juliana herself or her heirs could lose this inheritance. Witnesses of this business are: Robert, the priest of Stapenhill, Ralph fitz Ernald, David de Caldwell, Philip

de Burgh, Hugh Bagot, William de Samford and several others and the whole court.[39]

In another twelfth-century case, battle began, but the exhausted champions stopped fighting. When they did, their principals settled. This battle was fought in the earl of Leicester's court. The plaintiff was a churchman, Prior Robert, the defendant a knight named Edward:

> After many blows between the champions . . . they both sat down [and] as neither dared attack the other peace was established as follows: the said Edward did homage for [the land] to the said prior and should hold it by hereditary right against yearly payment of 19s.[40]

The prior got the worse end of this deal. It turns out that "the champion of Edward had lost his sight in the fight," but this "was unknown to the prior and his men."[41] Surely they could've driven a better bargain if they'd known.

[winks at the burly fellow with the piercings]

Historian M. J. Russell collected 598 English cases of trial by battle between 1200 and 1250.[42] Disputants actually wagered battle in only 226 of these cases, and champions only fought in 123 of them.[43] If these data are right, that means nearly 80 percent of disputants settled.[44] Russell suggests that if more data were available, the actual proportion of cases settled might be more like between two-thirds and three-quarters. But this doesn't account for the fact that disputants settled some cases midfight, and accounting for these might actually deliver a higher proportion of settlements.

Even if we take Russell's lower bound, however, "it is abundantly clear that trial by battle in civil cases did from an early time tend to become little more than a picturesque setting for an ultimate compromise."[45] As Russell put it, "battles were often pledged but seldom fought."[46]

[The economist interrupts:]

"I want to go back to this violent auction business. I understand now why an auction was necessary to allocate disputed property rights to the disputant who valued them more. And I get why an imperfectly discriminating all-pay auction may have made sense to use instead of a single-price, ascending-bid auction. But I'm still troubled by your story. It doesn't explain why a violent auction was used instead of a nonviolent one. I mean, why not have disputants hire runners who race, and the race winner's employer gets the right? Or why not have them hire archers who have an archery contest, and whoever's archer gets closest to the bull's-eye wins the right? Any nonviolent contest would be better than trial by battle's violent one. People wouldn't get killed!"

[The woman who looks like Janeane Garofalo yells:]

"Yeah, what Spock said! Give peace a chance!"

That's a good question. Not as good as Ania's question or the one Captain America asked. Still, very good. Let me answer you in two parts.

In the first place, you're greatly exaggerating the human cost of trial by battle. Precisely to keep that cost down, the Anglo-Norman legal system had rules that protected champions from getting maimed or murdered in judicial combats—rules regulating how violent the violent auctions could become. Champions didn't fight with lances on horseback. They didn't even fight with swords. The law required combat with far less lethal weapons, an example of which, recall, you're standing right next too.

[The economist looks over at the baculus cornutus.*]*

Baculi were short clubs. Sometimes they were horn tipped, but the basic variety was no more than a wooden stick. The law also instructed champions to carry bucklers: small shields. When judges ordered trial by battle, they didn't order champions to slay one another.[47] They ordered them to don protective gear and cudgel one another.[48]

Trial by battle's "submission rule" limited combat-sustained damage further still. Recall that one way a champion could lose was by acquiescing to his opponent—crying "craven." Trial by battle needn't come to a bloody end. Because of the submission rule, there was no reason it would in the vast majority of cases. And the evidence suggests it rarely did: "Death very seldom ensued from these civil combats."[49] Russell was able to find only a single case in which a champion died in a land dispute tried by battle.[50]

[*the economist:*]

"But one death is more than zero! In a footrace or archery contest . . ."

Somebody might die of a heart attack or an errant arrow. But I get your point, which brings me to the second part of my answer to your question.

Even though most cases were settled and even though the law required less lethal weapons, protective gear, and had a submission rule, it wasn't possible to entirely eliminate the procedural cost of trial by battle. Injuries and even deaths remained possible. Furthermore, like all other trials, trials by battle took something to hold and administer.

To minimize this remaining cost, the legal system converted as much of it as it could into social benefit. Medieval Englishmen enjoyed watching champions fight for property rights, so the judicial system made trials by battle public events.[51] In later judicial combats, stands surrounded the lists so eager spectators could enjoy the justice system in action. Evidently these were popular enough and well enough attended events to require rules prohibiting the crowd from becoming unruly. Recall the presiding justices' public pronouncements against spectator noise and interference I told you about before. Footraces and archery contests might've provided some entertainment too, but not as much as thugs duking it out.

[*the economist:*]

"But you said that most trials by battle were settled—some just before the champions were to fight! What, then, did judicial officials do with the throngs of anxious spectators eagerly anticipating a brawl?"

They gave 'em a show brawl instead. As one historian put it, when "the parties agree at the last moment" before battle, "the judges call on the champions to strike a blow or two, 'the King's stroke,' for sport . . . and the public, we hope, think the show was good enough without any slaying."[52] The people still got their entertainment.

That concludes the *WTF?!* tour. Thank you for coming, and I . . .

[*the woman who looks like Janeane Garofalo:*]

"Wait!!!"

Janeane???

"How does it end? I mean, why did trial by battle end?"

I'm pleasantly surprised you want to hear more. We had that tiff about wife sales. And I keep calling you Janeane. And . . .

"I was kind of getting into it."

[*catching herself*]

"I mean, how typical that a capitalist pig would try to defraud us by failing to give us our money's worth! We follow you all this way and . . ."

Relax, Janeane. I'll tell you how trial by battle ended.

When the cost of trading land is high, land rights become sticky.

If judges assign contested land "incorrectly," trade won't move it into the "correct" person's possession, so the land gets stuck in the hands of someone who values it less. Trial by battle enabled judges faced with this situation to do what the Coase theorem couldn't: get the land into the hands of the person who valued it more.

In contrast, when the cost of trading land is low, so land rights are fluid, things are different. In this situation, trade will move contested land into the "correct" person's hands even if judges initially assign it "incorrectly." Trial by battle isn't necessary to allocate contested land to the person who values it more because the Coase theorem does this already. So . . .

[*The woman who looks like Janeane Garofalo shouts excitedly:*]

"So England's legal system should've abandoned trial by battle for deciding land disputes when the cost of trading land fell significantly!"

You've got it, comrade. In the second half of the twelfth century, Henry II introduced important legal changes in England: the so-called Angevin reforms.[53] These changes mark the birth of English common law and the beginning of feudalism's end in England.[54] During this period, traditional feudal property arrangements declined significantly. With them, so did the cost of trading land, hence trial by battle.

In the years leading up to 1175, a feudal tenant wasn't a proper owner of the land he occupied. He was a kind of part owner of it, but his lord and heirs had ownership interests in it too—the reason their consent was needed for alienation.

Between 1175 and 1200, tenants became much closer to true owners of their land—owners in the modern sense. Their ownership interest grew substantially, while their heirs' and lords' interests shrank, undermining the justification for alienation restrictions in the process. If heirs and lords no longer had substantial ownership interests in tenants' property requiring protection, there was no reason for requiring their consent. As tenants became truer owners of their land, alienation restrictions therefore withered.

Historians have suggested a variety of reasons for this ownership shift—from the establishment of primogeniture to the introduction of new actions for recovering property to the evolving legal treatment of feudal obligations—and they disagree about which is most important for explaining the disappearance of heir and lord consent requirements for land sales.[55] But they agree that "between 1176 and 1220," tenants gained the "rights . . . to sell securely without the participation of anyone but . . . himself and the purchaser."[56]

This substantially lowered the cost of trading land. Thus, over the same period, "land . . . changed from a relatively frozen asset to a relatively liquid asset."[57] And that, in turn, precipitated a movement away from trial by battle in land disputes.

In 1179, the Council of Windsor introduced an alternative to trial by battle in real property cases: the grand assize, a jury trial by twelve knights of the shire. This option proved immensely popular. Judges continued to order trial by battle in land disputes in the thirteenth century, but it became increasingly rare as litigants opted for trial by jury.

In 1290 a new statute was introduced that prohibited subinfeudation and abolished what vestiges remained of alienation consent restrictions: *Quia emptores terrarum*—"Because they are buyers of lands." After this, judicial combats became antiquated curiosities, leading contemporaries to record them in great detail when they occurred.[58] Land was unstuck, and trial by battle in land disputes dead.[59]

Fighting seems like the resort of barbarians who've given up on reasoning through a solution to their disagreement. Institutionalized fighting, organized and implemented by the law to assign land rights, seems like the mark of a legal system run by barbarians who've given up on reason altogether. Trial by battle in Norman England illustrates why that's not so.

Judicial combat used incentives to solve a social problem: how to allocate contested property to the person who valued it most when judges couldn't know who it truly belonged to and sticky land rights prevented trade from doing the job for them. In solving this problem, trial by battle made society more economically productive, its members better off.

This seemingly senseless social practice is therefore similar to the others you've learned about, each of whose stunningly stupid surfaces belied not only good reason but also a reason that was good—in other words, good sense. And that makes seemingly senseless practices similar not only to each other but also to obviously reasonable ones—the kind that wear the sense in them on their sleeves.

Still don't see it? Ask yourself: Was Norman England's judicial system, which decided property disputes by having litigants hire legal representatives to fight one another physically, less sensible than contemporary England's judicial system, which decides property disputes by having litigants hire legal representatives to fight one another verbally?

Is contemporary Liberia's criminal justice system, which sometimes uses evidence based on a defendant's reaction to imbibing a magical potion, less sensible than contemporary California's criminal justice system, which sometimes uses evidence based on a defendant's reaction to being hooked up to a magical machine that makes squiggly lines when her pulse races?

How about Renaissance-era ecclesiastics' tithe compliance program, which used rats and crickets to persuade citizens to pay their tithes? Any less sensible than World War II-era US Treasury Department officials' tax compliance program, which used Donald Duck to persuade citizens to pay their taxes?

Let's see . . . No, no . . . and—wait a minute—never mind, another no. Each of these practices, and all the others you've learned about, exhibited astonishing ingenuity in harnessing incentives to achieve desired, and desirable, goals. There's as much sense in them as in obviously reasonable practices; you just have to look a bit harder to see it.

When you stop to think about it, this should hardly come as a surprise. Social practices, seemingly senseless and obvious alike, are the products of *people*. And, fundamentally, people themselves aren't so different from one another.

Despite being located everywhere from Europe to Africa, in centuries from the ninth to the twentieth, the people you learned about on this tour confronted similar problems: how to resolve conflict, realize gains from trade, protect property rights, and in general encourage those around them to behave in decent ways. These are the same problems that Guadalajarans faced in 1927, that the ancient Romans faced, that the Japanese faced during the Cold War, that people face everywhere, at any time, in any society—including yours. Moreover, all the people you learned about on this tour approached their problems similarly: in search of the best solutions they could find. The same way, in other words, that everyone approaches their problems.

Which presents a final puzzle: If people themselves aren't so different from one another across time or place, and, at the root, their social practices aren't either, then why do different people's social practices often look so distinct?

If you've been paying attention, you already know: it's because of differences in people's constraints.

Clerics in historical Francia, for instance, faced a constraint in protecting their property rights that clerics in contemporary France don't: the absence of government. Clerics in contemporary France, however, face a different constraint that clerics in historical Francia didn't: their potential predators don't believe in maledictions. So in one case, clerics use maledictions to protect their property rights, in the other, government.

Judges in medieval Germany faced a constraint in finding fact in criminal cases that judges in contemporary Germany don't: the absence of DNA evidence. Judges in contemporary Germany face a different constraint, which judges in medieval Germany didn't: their defendants don't believe in *iudicium Dei*. So in one case, judges use trial by boiling water to find fact in criminal cases, in the other, genetic code.

Unhappy wives in historical England faced a constraint in directly buying their husbands' permission to exit their marriages that unhappy wives in contemporary England (where, under certain circumstances, their spouses' permission is also required to obtain a divorce) don't: the absence of legal property rights. So in one case, unhappy wives use wife sales to buy their husbands' permission indirectly, in the other, their own property to buy it directly.

The same people, facing the same problem, but different constraints, develop solutions with different features.

Suppose you find yourself stranded in a treetop. Your problem: how to get down. You decide to shimmy down the trunk, cutting yourself badly along the way. Now suppose you find yourself in the same situation with one difference: you can fly. You decide to do that and land airily on your feet, not a scratch on you. Was your solution in the first case any less sensible than your solution in the second? Different, surely. But less sensible, surely not. After all, both get you down from a treetop and work within your constraints.

When you exit this museum to go back to your life, you'll leave the weirdness you found here behind for the weirdness of everyday living. But having finished this tour, you'll have a leg up. You'll know that incentives shape people's behavior, that rules shape people's incentives, and that constraints shape people's rules. You'll also have a better idea about how to find the incentives, rules, and constraints in your own and other people's practices. Your "WTF?!" moments will subside faster, and you'll be able to find the sense in what to others seems utterly senseless. When this happens for the first time, I want you to do something for me: pull out that tool I gave you back when we started, the one you've been carrying around all this time—rational choice theory—and give it a big kiss.

Before we say good-bye, three final items: First, don't forget that in fifteen minutes, Karnov and The Tapper are going to bang it out for your entertainment in the parking lot behind the museum.

[*The burly, pierced fellow laughs demonically and flexes; the gentleman with the glass eye starts sobbing.*]

Second, those of you who wanted to hear some technical details behind a few of my claims should meet me in the appendix following the fight.

[*The economist begins salivating.*]

Lastly, I hope you'll take a moment to fill out these *WTF?!* tour comment cards.

[begins distributing cards to the crowd]

We take a lot of pride in the quality of our tour and want to make sure our guests are happy and satisfied with the level of service we provide. If you'd just take a minute to jot down what we did well and where we could improve, we'd greatly appreciate it.

[*The patrons begin writing on their cards; one of them raises her hand.*]

Miss?

"Do you actually read these things?"

No. But pretending we do is a nice gesture.

Comment Cards

WTF?! Tour Comment Card

Left by: Ania

Things I liked: Wife sales. I learned that when one spouse wants out of marriage and the law requires them to get their partner's consent to exit, they can just buy it – except in Industrial Revolution England, where wives didn't have the property rights to do that. But even there, unhappy wives could get their existing husbands to sell them to new husbands, which accomplished the same thing indirectly! When you first mentioned wife selling I thought it was crazy. Now, I see why it wasn't!

Areas for Improvement: I wish the tour guide would've asked me out! Call me: 857-631-9818. I ♥ rational choice.

Thank you and "WTF?!"

WTF?! Tour Comment Card

Left by: "The Tapper"

Things I liked: That Gypsy stuff was nuts! But after you explained that Gypsies can't use government most of the time, and how social ostracism needs some extra help to work in their communities, the need for their superstitions made complete sense. I'll never look at a bar of soap, or my groin, the same way again!

Areas for Improvement: The tour guide is surly for no apparent reason. Kind of an ass, really. And he's clearly prejudiced against the visually disabled – management beware.

Thank you and "WTF?!"

WTF?! Tour Comment Card

Left by: "Padre"

Things I liked: I liked the fact that my holy brethren came into the tour at several points – surely God's hand at work. And while I suspect that your commentary about maledictions was inspired by demonic possession, I found the logic you suggested very interesting. As far as I'm concerned, no cleric ever cursed anyone. But I can see now – albeit only in principle – how clerics could use the threat of divine damnation to protect what was theirs when government couldn't help them.

Areas for Improvement: I will pray for your soul, you God-damned heretic. In the name of the Father, Son, and Holy Spirit. Amen.

Thank you and "WTF?!"

WTF?! Tour Comment Card

Left by: "Cell Phone Holster"

Things I liked: The best stop was the one on oracles. When you first told us about people poisoning a chicken to divine how to act toward their neighbors, I thought it was the dumbest thing I'd ever heard. But after I realized how the poisoned chicken actually coordinates bickering neighbors so that they don't end up punching each other's lights out, the whole thing made perfect sense! It's basically the same as when my roommate and I flip a coin to decide who has to do the dishes. We might try the poison chicken next time – higher stakes.

Areas for Improvement: About that: Do you think spraying McNuggets with Windex would work?

Thank you and "WTF?!"

WTF?! Tour Comment Card

Left by: "Dr. Spock"

Things I liked: Not much. Though I guess the part on vermin trials was somewhat compelling. The evidence does look like ecclesiastics used the trials to bolster waning belief in the supernatural sanctions supporting tithe payments where that belief was under attack by heretics. I might be able to buy this one. Still, in the absence of a formal model or contrived identification strategy, I'm unable to certify your story as scientific or deserving of the appellation "economic."

Areas for Improvement: Rigor. The other patrons seemed to be able to follow what you were saying most of the time – perhaps because you used regular language and common sense. This is no good. You need to use much more math. You'll know you're on the right track if your customers have a glazed look in their eyes and no clue what you're saying.

Thank you and "WTF?!"

WTF?! Tour Comment Card

Left by: "Janeane"

Things I liked: Despite its obvious patriarchal leanings, I actually enjoyed the tour! My favorite was trial by battle. It looks silly and barbaric on the surface. But it makes sense why, when land rights were sticky because trading was difficult, judges would've wanted to assign disputed property rights to the person who valued them more and how trial by battle helped them do that. I don't believe in property rights, of course – enslavement of the proletariat and all. But if I did, I could see the reason in what otherwise seems like such a crazy system.

Areas for Improvement: The museum should have recycling bins. Also, the tour guide should not be such a capitalist pig.

Thank you and "WTF?!"

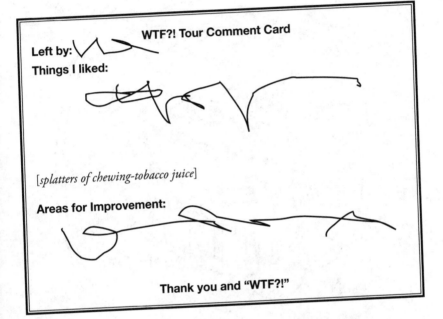

[*splatters of chewing-tobacco juice*]

Tour Sponsors and Supporters

WTF?! is a weird tour: its subject matter, the museum it's housed in, its guide—all weird. When I started work on it, I anticipated that I might encounter some difficulty getting certain kinds of "serious people" to see *WTF?!* as more than just weird. I was right. "Eccentric," it turns out, isn't necessarily a compliment. More often it's a euphemism for, "I think you're fu*king crazy."

First and most important, then, I thank my editor at Stanford University Press, Margo Beth Fleming, who saw madness with method in *WTF?!* where others saw only madness. Because of Margo's support, my museum exists, and because of her help, the tour is worth taking. Margo even let me draw my own illustrations to adorn the museum, which has to make *WTF?!* the only tour created and illustrated by an economist—or at least one who chain-smokes cigars (by the way, feel free to light up; the museum is smoker-friendly). Thank you, Margo.

Michael Munger and Mark White provided excellent and encouraging comments on the tour while it was under construction, as did Pete Boettke, Chris Coyne, and George Souri. Bev Miller put finishing touches on each stop in preparation for the museum's grand opening. I thank each of them for supporting *WTF?!* and helping me improve it.

I make fun of, and relay stories about, numerous people on this tour. All of them are inspired by actual people I've known or still know, though some are more "real" than others. I thank these people for being deserving targets of my fun making.

I thank the Earhart Foundation for generously supporting my development of *WTF?!*

I thank the following journal publishers for permitting me to use my own work in my other own work: Elsevier; Now Publishers; Oxford University Press; Sage Publications; Springer Science+Business Media; and The University of Chicago Press.[1]

I thank my wife and favorite tour patron, Ania, who for a variety of reasons makes me say "WTF?!" every day.

Finally, I thank all the eccentrics out there—past, present, and future—for not being so goddamn boring.

Appendix (for Nerds)

Burn, Baby, Burn

Karnov wanted to me to formally demonstrate my claim that by convicting a positive proportion of probands, it's possible for priests to accurately sort guilty and innocent defendants using ordeals as long as defendants repose even the faintest faith in their legitimacy. Here you go, big boy.

Consider a defendant, j, ordered to an ordeal. $j \in \{j_g, j_i\}$. When j is guilty of the crime he's been accused of, $j = j_g$. When j is innocent of the crime he's been accused of, $j = j_i$.[1]

j can undergo the ordeal or decline it. If j undergoes the ordeal and it finds him guilty, he earns β. If j undergoes the ordeal and it finds him innocent, he earns 0. If j declines the ordeal, he earns θ, where $0 > \theta > \beta$.[2]

j is a skeptic. He believes ordeals may be *iudicia Dei* but also believes they may be a sham perpetrated by crafty priests. $\rho \in (0, 1)$ measures the strength of j's belief that ordeals are *iudicia Dei*.[3]

ρ is the probability j assigns to God revealing his guilt through the ordeal if $j = j_g$ or the probability he assigns to God revealing his innocence through the ordeal if $j = j_i$. j's priest condemns a proportion of defendants who undergo ordeals equal to $\gamma \in (0, 1)$. j knows probands' historical success rate.

From j_g's perspective, if ordeals are *iudicia Dei*, γ reflects guilty persons who underwent ordeals and God condemned, which would happen to him if he underwent the ordeal since he's guilty. If ordeals are a sham, γ reflects priestly condemnations of defendants who underwent ordeals, hence the probability that he'd be condemned if he underwent the ordeal. j_g therefore declines the ordeal if $\rho\beta + (1 - \rho)\beta\gamma < \theta$. This is true for any $\gamma > (\theta - \rho\beta)/(\beta - \rho\beta)$.

From j_i's perspective, if ordeals are *iudicia Dei*, γ reflects guilty persons who underwent ordeals and God condemned, which wouldn't happen to him if he underwent the ordeal since he's innocent. If ordeals are a sham, γ reflects priestly condemnations of defendants who underwent ordeals, hence the probability that he'd be condemned if he underwent the ordeal. j_i therefore undergoes the ordeal if $\rho 0 + (1 - \rho)\beta\gamma > \theta$. This is true for any $\gamma < \theta/(\beta - \beta\gamma)$.

To ensure sorting, the priest must condemn enough probands to deter guilty skeptics from wanting to undergo ordeals but not so many probands as to also deter innocent skeptics from wanting to do so. He must therefore condemn $\theta/(\beta - \rho\beta) > \gamma > (\theta - \rho\beta)/(\beta - \rho\beta)$.

Since, where $\rho \in (0, 1)$ and $0 > \theta > \beta$, $\forall\rho: \theta/(\beta - \rho\beta) > (\theta - \rho\beta)/(\beta - \rho\beta)$ $\Rightarrow \exists\gamma: \theta/(\beta - \rho\beta) > \gamma > (\theta - \rho\beta)/(\beta - \rho\beta)$. Thus, by adjusting the proportion of probands he condemns, the priest can use ordeals to correctly sort criminal defendants by their guilt or innocence for any positive level of belief that ordeals are *iudicia Dei*.

Since the priest prefers not to condemn any innocent persons (recall that the more innocent persons he condemns, the greater the risk he runs of undermining faith in the legitimacy of ordeals), he sets $\gamma = \gamma^* \equiv (\theta - \rho\beta)/(\beta - \rho\beta) + \varepsilon$. This minimizes the number of innocent probands he must condemn to ensure sorting given the strength of individuals' belief that ordeals are *iudicia Dei*. From γ^* it's clear that the optimal proportion of probands the priest condemns falls as individuals' belief that ordeals are *iudicia Dei* rises. As ρ approaches θ/β, the lowest level of belief that prevents a situation in which both guilty and innocent persons choose to undergo ordeals without the priest condemning any innocent probands, γ^* approaches 0. As ρ approaches 0, γ^* approaches θ/β, which is the highest proportion of innocent probands the priest can condemn without inducing both guilty and innocent persons to choose to decline ordeals.

Chicken, Please; Hold the Poison

Some of you wondered why mixing behaviors—choosing to go through the intersection sometimes and to yield at other times in my traffic example, or choosing to stand tall sometimes and to back down at other times in my example of feuding neighbors—was a possible (in fact, likely) outcome for the drivers or neighbors when they lacked a coordination device, such as a traffic light or an oracle. Here's why.

What I called "possible outcomes" are what economists call "Nash equilibria" (named after the economist who pioneered the concept, John Nash). A Nash equilibrium is a situation in which, given what someone else is doing, what you're doing is the best you can do and, given what you're doing, what the other person is doing is the best she can do. When we have such a situation, neither person has an incentive to change their behavior. So neither does. That's why we call this outcome an "equilibrium."

To find the equilibria in some context that two people confront, we want to find combinations of each person's behavior—"strategy pairs"—in which both people are doing the best they can for themselves given what the other is doing. To do that for the drivers or feuding neighbors I told you about, it helps to first restate each party's choices and their payoffs for each choice given what the other party is choosing. I'll use the feuding-neighbors example to do this, but things look the same for the drivers.

The table shown here summarizes the context, or "game," that Myrtle and Mabel confront. Myrtle's choices, or "strategies," are on the left side of the box. She can stand tall or back down. Mabel's choices, or strategies, are on the top of the box. They're the same as Myrtle's. The neighbors choose their strategies simultaneously, and their strategy options and the payoffs that correspond to those options are known to both women.

	Stand tall	Back down
Stand tall	x, x	$y, 0$
Back down	$0, y$	$y/2, y/2$

If Myrtle backs down and Mabel stands tall, Myrtle earns 0 and Mabel earns $y > 0$. This is the lower-left rectangle of the box, inside of which are the neighbors' payoffs as just described: 0 for Myrtle and y for Mabel (in all of the rectangles, Myrtle's payoff comes first, followed by Mabel's). If Mabel backs down and Myrtle stands tall, Myrtle earns y and Mabel earns 0. This is the upper-right rectangle of the box. If both neighbors back down, we have the lower-right rectangle of the box, where each woman earns $y/2$. Finally, if both neighbors stand tall, we have the upper-left rectangle, where each woman earns $x < 0$.

To find the equilibria in this game, we simply check each rectangle of the box to see whether either neighbor in the situation that rectangle describes would want to move to another rectangle—choose a different strategy—given the strategy her neighbor is following in the rectangle we started in. Make sense? Don't worry if it doesn't; it will once we start doing it. It's very simple.

Let's start with the upper-left rectangle, where Myrtle and Mabel stand tall and each earns x. If Myrtle stands tall, Mabel can earn more by changing her strategy to back down, where she earns 0 instead of x (remember, $x < 0$). And if Mabel stands tall, Myrtle can earn more by changing her strategy to back down, where she earns 0 instead of x. Both neighbors therefore want to back down if the other neighbor stands tall. So the situation described in the upper-left rectangle—mutual standing tall—can't be an equilibrium. It's not a possible outcome of Myrtle's and Mabel's interaction.

Next let's check the lower-right rectangle, where both neighbors back down. If Myrtle backs down, Mabel can earn more by changing her strategy to stand tall, where she earns y instead of $y/2$. And if Mabel backs down, Myrtle can earn more by changing her strategy to stand tall, where she earns y instead of $y/2$. Both neighbors therefore want to stand tall if the other neighbor backs down. So the situation described in the lower-right rectangle—mutual backing down—can't be an equilibrium of Myrtle's and Mabel's interaction either.

The two rectangles that remain are the lower-left one, where Myrtle backs down and Mabel stands tall, and the upper-right one, where Mabel backs down and Myrtle stands tall. Let's see if the lower-left rectangle is an equilibrium.

If Myrtle backs down, Mabel earns y if she stays in the lower-left rectangle, where she stands tall. But she earns only $y/2$ if she changes her behavior to back down too. So Mabel wants to stay in the lower-left rectangle, where she stands tall when Myrtle backs down.

What about Myrtle? If Mabel stands tall, Myrtle earns 0 by remaining in the lower-left rectangle, where she backs down. But Myrtle earns only x if she changes her behavior to stand tall too. So Myrtle wants to stay in the lower left-rectangle, where she backs down when Mabel stands tall.

In the lower-left rectangle, neither Myrtle nor Mabel wants to change her strategy given the strategy her neighbor is following. We've found our first equilibrium! One possible outcome of the neighbors' interaction is therefore for Myrtle to back down and Mabel to stand tall.

The last rectangle to check is the upper-right one, where Mabel backs down and Myrtle stands tall. Here we have the exact reverse situation that we had in the lower-left rectangle we just considered. As you've probably figured out, the strategies represented by this rectangle are therefore also an equilibrium of the neighbors' interaction. So the second possible outcome of the neighbors' interaction is for Mabel to back down and Myrtle to stand tall.

What about the equilibrium that involves both Myrtle and Mabel mixing their strategies—each sometimes standing tall and sometimes backing down? That's the one I promised to show to you. Where is it?

Recall that a Nash equilibrium refers to a situation in which, given the strategy her neighbor is following, neither Myrtle nor Mabel wants to change the strategy she's following. For there to be an equilibrium that involves each neighbor mixing her strategies, then, it must involve each woman standing tall and backing down in some combination—following each strategy with some probability—that yields the same expected payoff for her neighbor no matter what her neighbor does.

Think of it this way. If, say, Myrtle mixed her strategies with some probabilities that yielded unequal payoffs for Mabel depending on what Mabel does, Mabel would want to follow the strategy that yielded her the higher payoff all the time. But if Mabel always followed that strategy, Myrtle would want to change her strategy. If Mabel always backs down, Myrtle wants to always stand tall; if Mabel always stands tall, Myrtle wants to always back down. If Myrtle wanted to change her strategy in this way, her initial mixture of strategies couldn't be part of an equilibrium, since an equilibrium requires that Myrtle not want to change her strategy given the strategy Mabel is following. The same is true on the other side of things for Mabel. An equilibrium that involves Myrtle mixing stand tall and back down must therefore involve her doing so with probabilities that yield the same expected payoff for Mabel no matter what Mabel does.

So to find the equilibrium that involves both women mixing their strategies, we need to find the strategy mixtures—the probabilities of stand tall and back down—each woman could use that would yield her neighbor the same expected payoff regardless of what her neighbor does.

Here's how we do that. Suppose Myrtle mixes her strategies by standing tall with probability p and backing down with probability $1 - p$. If Mabel stands tall, she therefore earns: $px + (1 - p)y$. If instead Mabel backs down, she earns: $p0 + (1 - p)y/2$. Mabel's expected payoff is the same no matter what she does when: $px + (1 - p)y = p0 + (1 - p)y/2$. So the p that makes this equality true is the probability with which Myrtle will stand tall in equilibrium. Solving for p, we get $p = y/(y - 2x)$. An equilibrium that involves Myrtle mixing strategies therefore requires her to stand tall with probability $p = y/(y - 2x)$ and to back down with probability $1 - p$.

The situation Mabel faces is symmetric to her neighbor's, so she does the same. Given that Myrtle is mixing her behavior by standing tall with probability $p = y/(y - 2x)$ and backing down with probability $1 - p$, Mabel does the best for herself by mixing her behavior in the same way, and vice versa. We've found an equilibrium in which both neighbors mix their strategies by standing tall sometimes and backing down at other times in the same proportion.

Jiminy Cricket's Journey to Hell

At the vermin trials stop on our tour I promised to show those who were interested how, exactly, ecclesiastics optimally negotiated the trade-off they confronted between prolonging vermin trials, which improved their chances of a successful trial—the departure of the vermin—but provided less-convincing evidence for ecclesiastics' power to imprecate when they got this result, and conducting shorter trials, which increased ecclesiastics' chances of an unsuccessful trial—the persistence of vermin—but provided more-convincing evidence for their power to imprecate when the trial was a success. Here I do that, and along the way I also show explicitly how ecclesiastics could use vermin trials to bolster rational citizens' belief in the validity of their supernatural sanctions and thus tithe revenues.[4]

Before getting down to business, a warning: in addition to being frightfully boring, the discussion that follows assumes familiarity with the concept of Bayesian rationality (and Bayes' rule). Since you're here in the appendix, there's a good chance that you're familiar with this concept—and that people often describe you as "bright but socially awkward." But if you aren't familiar with it, at least some of what I'll say shortly may not make sense to you. You can remedy this situation by reading about Bayesian rationality or, what's more likely, you can skim over the next few pages, perhaps pausing to enjoy the pretty symbols. Here we go.

By choosing how much information to reveal about the state of the world, one person can persuade another to take an action he would prefer over the action that the target of his persuasion originally planned to take. This is true even when both persons are rational Bayesians and even though the target of persuasion knows the persuader makes his choice of how much information to reveal with the goal of manipulating the target's behavior for his own benefit.

The key feature of Bayesian rationality that permits this is the fact that Bayes' rule restricts only the expectation of posterior beliefs. Bayesian rationality requires that an individual's expected posterior belief equals his prior belief but otherwise puts no constraints on the distribution of his posteriors. Thus, as long as a target of persuasion doesn't act linearly in his beliefs, a persuader can influence the target's behavior in his interest. The persuader does so by manipulating the target's distribution of posteriors, which he achieves by controlling the information he conveys to the target.

To understand how ecclesiastics leveraged this logic through vermin trials to convince citizens to pay more tithes, consider an ecclesiastic court and a risk-neutral, fifteenth-century French farmer, Pierre. Pierre's community is plagued by beetles and seeks the court's supernatural assistance to remove the pests. He and the ecclesiastics who compose the court are rational Bayesians.

There are two unknown states of the world $\omega \in \{0, 1\}$: ecclesiastics' supernatural sanctions are real, or they're bogus. $\omega = 1$ denotes the former case, where ecclesiastics have the power to end the beetle plague and thus tithe evasion is costly for Pierre's soul. The court and Pierre share a common prior that $\omega = 1$, $\mu_0 = (0, 1]$.

Upon the appeal of Pierre's community, the court chooses a trial duration $\sigma = [0, 1]$. Its choice of duration affects the trial outcome $s \in \{$depart, not$\}$ conditional on the state. If $\omega = 0$, the beetles flee or die (s = depart) with probability σ. If $\omega = 1$, the beetles are expunged by God, so s = depart with probability 1. The duration σ and the outcome s are publicly observed.

Note that the court's choice of trial duration is a choice of how much information about the state of the world to reveal to Pierre. We may say that σ is the court's "signal" to Pierre about that state. A minimal trial duration, $\sigma = 0$, is a completely informative signal about the world's state. The court declares the beetles' guilt immediately, and the beetles either depart or persist. In this case, Pierre learns about the validity of ecclesiastics' supernatural sanctions definitively.

A maximal trial duration, $\sigma = 1$, is completely uninformative. By protracting the trial to the point at which the beetles reach their natural life spans, the court fully obfuscates the reason for their departure. Indeed, a maximal trial duration is equivalent to not conducting any trial at all or, what's also equivalent, to exonerating the beetles. In this case, Pierre learns nothing about the validity of ecclesiastics' supernatural sanctions.

Ecclesiastics want to maximize tithe revenue from Pierre. Doing so requires optimizing σ. What trial duration maximizes Pierre's expected tithe payment as a function of his prior belief in the validity of ecclesiastics' supernatural sanctions, μ_0? To find out, we need to derive Pierre's optimal tithe payment as a function of his posterior belief in that validity, μ_s, after observing a trial's outcome, s.

Suppose Pierre's total tithable harvest has dollar value $y > 0$, which faces a tithe rate $t \in (0, 1)$. Pierre chooses how much of that value to declare to the tithe collectors, $x \geq \underline{y}$, where $\underline{y} > 0$ is the minimum tithable harvest value he can get away with declaring. The vagaries of agricultural production preclude tithe collectors from observing y, but tithe collectors have a lower-bound estimate of Pierre's tithable harvest value based on factors they can observe, such as the weather and Pierre's plot size.

The Church supernaturally sanctions tithe evaders by claiming to estrange them from God. It declares them sinners, excommunicates them, and/or anathematizes them. These sanctions are divine, so they always and "automatically" execute on evaders who repose any belief in them. The Church's imprecations threaten a (utility) penalty for evaders that scales with the extent of their sin, hence the extent of their tithe evasion, $\varphi(y - x)$, where $\varphi > 0$. Tithe collectors don't observe the extent of a citizen's evasion, but God does.

Pierre maximizes

$$\max_x y - tx - \mu_s \varphi \, (y - x).$$

This maximization problem has simple solution: Pierre declares his actual tithable harvest value, y, and thus pays ty, if and only if $\mu_s \geq t/\varphi$. Otherwise he declares the minimum tithable harvest value he can get away with, $\underline{y}$, and thus pays $t\underline{y}$. Given this behavior, ecclesiastics' expected valuation of Pierre's posterior belief is a step function equal to $t\underline{y}$ when $\mu_s < t/\varphi$ and equal to ty when $\mu_s \geq t/\varphi$.

Since Pierre declares his full tithable harvest value if his prior belief in the validity of ecclesiastics' supernatural sanctions is $\mu_0 \geq t/\varphi$, ecclesiastics stand to gain nothing by conducting a vermin trial when this is the case. Thus, if $\mu_0 \geq t/\varphi$, the court chooses $\varphi = 1$; it doesn't conduct a trial. In contrast, if $\mu_0 < t/\varphi$, there's room for the court to convince Pierre to declare more of his tithable harvest value though a vermin trial; so it conducts one.

Two observations help identify this trial's optimal duration. First, note that when $\mu_0 < t/\varphi$, a trial of any duration whose outcome is unsuccessful ($s = $ not) has the same effect on Pierre's behavior. Any such trial, which reduces Pierre's posterior, leaves his belief too weak to induce tithe compliance: $\mu_s < t/\varphi$. Since a trial duration that induces a lower posterior when an unsuccessful outcome is realized induces a higher posterior when a successful outcome is realized ($s = $ depart), the optimal trial duration if $\mu_0 < t/\varphi$ is one that drives Pierre's posterior to zero when $s = $ not.

Second, note that Pierre's behavior is the same whether his posterior is just equal to t/φ or is greater than this. Since a trial duration that induces a higher posterior when a successful outcome is realized is less likely to produce such an outcome, the optimal trial duration if $\mu_0 < t/\varphi$ is one that increases Pierre's posterior to exactly t/φ when $s = $ depart.

These observations imply that the court's optimal trial duration is one that induces a binary distribution over Pierre's posteriors, generating $\mu_s = 0$ with some probability and $\mu_s = t/\varphi$ the rest of the time. To find these probabilities, simply recall that Bayesian rationality requires Pierre's expected posterior to equal his prior. Where $\tau(\mu_s)$ denotes the probability of $\mu_s = t/\varphi$,

$$\mu_0 = \frac{t}{\varphi}\tau(\mu_s) + 0[1 - \tau(\mu_s)].$$

Solving this equation for τ, the court's optimal trial duration is one that induces $\mu_s = 0$ with probability $1 - \mu_0\varphi/t$ and induces $\mu_s = t/\varphi$ with probability $\mu_0\varphi/t$.

From here, it's easy to compute the court's optimal trial duration. Using Bayes' rule,

$$\mu_s(\omega) = \frac{\sigma(s|\omega)\mu_0(\omega)}{\sigma(s|\omega)\mu_0(\omega) + \sigma(s|\omega')\,\mu_0\,(\omega')}$$

and the fact that

$$\tau(\mu_s) = \sigma(s|\omega)\mu_0(\omega) + \sigma(s|\omega')\mu_0(\omega')$$

produces

$$\mu_s(\omega) = \frac{\sigma(s|\omega)\mu_0(\omega)}{\tau(\mu_s)}.$$

Solving for σ results in

$$\sigma(s|\omega) = \frac{\mu_s(\omega)\tau(\mu_s)}{\mu_0(\omega)}.$$

With this equation, we can use the values for μ_s, τ, and μ_0 from above to find the court's optimal σ. Doing so yields the binary signal

$$\sigma(\text{not}|\omega = 0) = \frac{t - \mu_0\varphi}{t(1 - \mu_0)} \quad \sigma(\text{not}|\omega = 1) = 0$$

$$\sigma(\text{depart}|\omega = 0) = \frac{\mu_0(\varphi - t)}{t(1 - \mu_0)} \quad \sigma(\text{depart}|\omega = 1) = 1.$$

When $\mu_0 \geq t/\varphi$, the court conducts no trial, and ecclesiastics collect tithe revenue from Pierre equal to ty. When $\mu_0 < t/\varphi$, the court conducts a trial, and ecclesiastics expect to collect tithe revenue from Pierre equal to $\mu_0\varphi(y - \underline{y}) + ty$. This is more than what they collect from Pierre without the trial, ty. Although Pierre is a rational Bayesian and is aware that the court manipulates the length of vermin trials to manipulate his belief, the court is able to use vermin trials to improve Pierre's tithe compliance.

Fighting Solves Everything

Dr. Spock wanted to me to formally demonstrate my claim that trial by battle's violent auction is less generous to bid collectors than a regular (first-price, ascending-bid) auction and that a violent auction is a superior (lower-cost) method of assigning disputed property rights overall as long as the disputant who values the contested property less values it at least half as much as the disputant who values it more. To render my demonstration as persuasive as possible to you, Dr. Spock, I've used plenty of unnecessary mathematics.

Consider two risk-neutral litigants, a tenant, T (remember, that's the defendant in an Anglo-Norman land dispute), and a demandant, D (the plaintiff in such a dispute), who contest ownership to a piece of land. T values the disputed land v_T. D values it $v_D > v_T > 0$. Disputants know their own and each other's values.

Recall that in a regular auction, only the winning disputant must pay his bid, and his payment, collected by the bid collector, equals the contested property's value to the disputant who values it less: v_T.

Recall that in trial by battle's violent auction, both disputants must pay their bids. T and D bid on the disputed property by spending $t > 0$ and $d > 0$, respectively, on champions who fight in the arena for their employers' right. The disputants make their expenditures simultaneously and independently. Expenditures on champions and the land's value are in the same units.

To calculate t and d, we use Gordon Tullock's contest success function, which describes each disputant's probability of winning the violent auction given his and his adversary's expenditures on champions.[5] D's probability of winning the contested land under trial by battle is

$$\rho_D (d,t) = \frac{d^\alpha}{d^\alpha + t^\alpha}.$$

(1.1)

T's probability of winning is

$$\rho_T (d,t) = 1 - \rho_D(d,t) = \frac{t^\alpha}{d^\alpha + t^\alpha}.$$

(1.2)

$\alpha > 0$ is the mass effect (decisiveness) parameter. The return to spending on champions is constant: $\alpha = 1$.

T's expected profit of trial by battle is

$$\pi_T(d,t) = \frac{v_T t}{d + t} - t.$$

(2.1)

D maximizes

$$\pi_D(d,t) = \frac{v_D d}{d + t} - d.$$

(2.2)

T's first-order condition, which describes his profit-maximizing level of spending on champions, is

$$\frac{\partial \pi_T}{\partial t} = \frac{v_T d}{(d + t)^2} = 1.$$

(3.1)

D's first-order condition is

$$\frac{\partial \pi_D}{\partial d} = \frac{v_D t}{(d + t)^2} = 1.$$

(3.2)

T's second-order sufficiency condition, which guarantees an interior maximum, is

$$\frac{\partial^2 \pi_T}{\partial t^2} = \frac{-2v_T d}{(d + t)^3} < 0.$$

(4.1)

This is satisfied since $v_T > 0$, $d > 0$, and $t > 0$. D's second-order sufficiency condition is

$$\frac{\partial^2 \pi_D}{\partial d^2} = \frac{-2v_D t}{(d + t)^3} < 0.$$

(4.2)

This is satisfied since $v_D > 0$, $d > 0$, and $t > 0$.

Taking the ratio of equations 3.1 and 3.2 gives

$$\frac{t}{v_T} = \frac{d}{v_D}.$$

(5)

Solving for d and substituting into equation 3.1 gives T's optimal spending on champions:

$$t^* = \frac{v_T^2 \, v_D}{(v_D + v_T)^2}.$$

(6.1)

Solving for t and substituting into equation 3.2 gives D's optimal spending on champions:

$$d^* = \frac{v_D^2 \, v_T}{(v_D + v_T)^2}.$$

(6.2)

With equations 6.1 and 6.2, we can calculate total spending on champions—the sum of the bids paid by disputants in trial by battle's violent auction:

$$t^* + d^* = \frac{v_T \, v_D}{v_D + v_T}.$$

(7)

Since $v_D > v_T > 0$ and $\forall v_T > 0$: $\frac{v_T v_D}{v_D + v_T} < v_T$, the sum of disputants' bid payments in a violent auction, hence the payment collected by bid collectors in such an auction, is less than the bid payment the winner makes in a regular auction, hence the payment collected by bid collectors in that kind of auction.

Next, to find when a violent auction is superior to a regular one overall—when it's cheaper *including* the former's allocative-inefficiency cost, which for the latter, you'll recall, is zero—we need to calculate the allocative-inefficiency cost of a violent auction.

That cost is the probability that trial by battle assigns the contested property to the disputant who values it less, $\rho_T = \frac{t^*}{d^* + t^*}$, times the social value lost when this happens, $v_D - v_T$. Substituting disputants' equilibrium expenditures on champions, this is

$$\frac{v_T^2 v_D}{v_D^2 v_T + v_T^2 v_D} (v_D - v_T).$$

(8)

Now we can find the total cost of a violent auction. From equation 7, we know that the fraud-inducing cost of a violent auction is $\frac{v_T v_D}{v_D + v_T}$. So its total cost is

$$\frac{v_T v_D}{v_D + v_T} + \frac{v_T^2 v_D}{v_D^2 v_T + v_T^2 v_D} (v_D - v_T).$$

(9)

The allocative-inefficiency cost of a regular auction is zero. From above, we know that its fraud-inducing cost is v_T. So the total cost of a regular auction is v_T.

A violent auction is therefore less expensive than a regular one overall when

$$\frac{v_T v_D}{v_D + v_T} + \frac{v_T^2 v_D}{v_D^2 v_T + v_T^2 v_D} (v_D - v_T) < v_T \Rightarrow v_T > \frac{v_D}{2}.$$

(10)

There you have it, Dr. Spock.[6]

Notes (for Naysayers)

Waiting in the Lobby

1. For a discussion of weird markets in particular, in historical Japan, see Ramseyer, J. Mark. 2008. *Odd Markets in Japanese History: Law and Economic Growth.* Cambridge: Cambridge University Press. Regarding people's tendency to find the commodification of certain things revolting (hence, to react to the suggestion that they be commodified with a "WTF?!") and why that tendency may be counterproductive, see Block, Walter. 1976. *Defending the Undefendable: The Pimp, Prostitute, Scab, Slumlord, Libeler, Moneylender, and Other Scapegoats in the Rogue's Gallery of American Society.* New York: Fleet Press; and Brennan, Jason, and Peter M. Jaworski. 2015. *Markets without Limits: Moral Virtues and Commercial Interests.* New York: Routledge. See also Miller, William Ian. 1997. *The Anatomy of Disgust.* Cambridge, MA: Harvard University Press; Nussbaum, Martha C. 2003. *Hiding from Humanity: Disgust, Shame, and the Law.* Princeton: Princeton University Press; Rossman, Gabriel. 2014. "Obfuscatory Relational Work and Disreputable Exchange." *Sociological Theory* 32:43–69.

Tour Stop 2

1. Reliance on judicial ordeals appears in the earliest of legal codes the world over. On the ubiquity and varieties of ordeals, see Gilchrist, James 1821. *A Brief Display of the Origin and History of Ordeals* . . . London: Printed for the author by W. Bulmer and W. Nicol; Groitein, H. 1923. *Primitive Ordeal and Modern Law.* London: George Allen and Unwin; and Lea, Henry C. 1866. *Superstition and Force: Essays on the Wager of Law, the Wager of Battle, the Ordeal, Torture.* Philadelphia: Collins.

2. The hot water and hot iron ordeals sometimes came in "strengths," corresponding to the severity of the alleged crime or extent of the defendant's disrepute. In the "single" hot water ordeal, the proband put his arm into boiling

water up to his wrist; in the hot iron ordeal, he carried a piece of hot iron that weighed a pound. In the "triple" hot water ordeal, the proband put his arm in boiling water up to the elbow; in the hot iron ordeal, he carried a piece of iron that weighed three pounds.

3. Hot water ordeals are older. They first appear in the *Lex Salica* circa 507–511. Cold water ordeals were a ninth-century invention.

4. The particulars of ordeals varied by time and place, but their basics were similar. Throughout the existence of ordeals, individuals invoked them for a variety of purposes, ranging from political ("Who is the rightful heir to this office?") to religious ("Is this relic genuine?"). I consider only unilateral ordeals invoked for judicial purposes.

5. Usually the proband was the defendant, though occasionally the plaintiff.

6. Howland, Arthur C., ed. and trans. 1901. *Ordeals, Compurgation, Excommunications and Interdict*. Philadelphia: Department of History, University of Pennsylvania, 7–9.

7. Continental justice systems sometimes used another variety of hot ordeal: trial by plowshares. The idea was the same as in the other hot ordeals, but the proband walked across burning plowshares instead of thrusting his arm into boiling water or carrying burning iron. See, for instance, King Athelstan's 928 doom. Howland, *Ordeals*, 12–13.

8. Howland, *Ordeals*, 11.

9. In England there are a few post–Norman Conquest instances of ordeals being used in civil cases, but they're rare.

10. In pre-eleventh-century England, for instance, criminal punishment was financial. Klerman, Daniel. 2001. "Settlement and the Decline of Private Prosecution in Thirteenth-Century England." *Law and History Review* 19:1–5. Under the Assize of Clarendon, criminal punishment was mutilation and under the Assize of Northampton, death. The Assizes of Clarendon and Northampton required probands who passed the ordeal but whose communities considered them to be of "very bad repute" and who had been "evilly defamed by the testimony of many legal men" to "abjure the realm" nonetheless. Howland, *Ordeals*, 16.

11. See Bartlett, Robert. 1986. *Trial by Fire and Water: The Medieval Judicial Ordeal*. Cambridge: Cambridge University Press; Bloomfield, Morton W. 1969. "Beowulf, Byrhtnoth, and the Judgment of God: Trial by Combat in Anglo-Saxon England." *Speculum* 44:545–559; Davies, Wendy, and Paul Fouracre, eds. 1986. *The Settlement of Disputes in Early Medieval Europe*. Cambridge: Cambridge University Press; Groitein, *Primitive Ordeal and Modern Law*; Lea, *Superstition and Force*; McAuley, Finbarr. 2006. "Canon Law and the End of the Ordeal." *Oxford*

Journal of Legal Studies 26:473–513; Miller, William Ian. 1988. "Ordeal in Iceland." *Scandinavian Studies* 60:189–218; and Thayer, James Bradley. 1898. *A Preliminary Treatise on Evidence at the Common Law.* Boston: Little, Brown. A panel of judges, or "court presidents," usually heard criminal cases. Depending on the court, these could be royal justices, clerics, counts, or local landowners. Judges decided whether an ordeal was required in a particular case and, in most instances, if so, which one. A cleric administered and officiated the ordeal itself.

12. See Bartlett, *Trial by Fire and Water*, 26; see also 28, 135. According to James Whitman, witnesses or others with factual knowledge of defendants' guilt often existed but were unwilling to come forward because they didn't want blood on their hands if the people they testified against were convicted and executed. Whitman, James Q. 2008. *The Origins of Reasonable Doubt: Theological Roots of the Criminal Trial.* New Haven: Yale University Press. Maybe so, but from the perspective of the legal system, this situation is no different than if such people didn't exist: either way, no conclusive "ordinary" evidence was available to judges.

13. In theory, the Assizes of Clarendon and Northampton required ordeals in all cases involving accusations of serious crimes. But in practice, even under these assizes, courts didn't order people to ordeals if there was clear evidence of their guilt. Groot, Roger D. 1982. "The Jury of Presentment before 1215." *American Journal of Legal History* 26:1–24. For a summary of some basic features of Anglo-Saxon law, see Pollock, Frederick. 1898. "English Law before the Norman Conquest." *Law Quarterly Review* 14:291–306; Pollock, Frederick, and Frederic William Maitland. 1959. *The History of English Law.* 2 vols. Washington, DC: Lawyers' Literary Club.

14. On the role of oath helpers in England, see, for instance, Beckerman, John S. 1992. "Procedural Innovation and Institutional Change in Medieval English Manorial Courts." *Law and History Review* 10:197–252.

15. Other kinds of "ordinary" evidence might also be possible in certain situations. Although it wasn't particularly useful in criminal cases, medieval courts might consider written evidence, for instance, when it was available, especially after the eleventh century.

16. Since ordinary evidence was hard to come by for alleged crimes involving unobservable acts or states of mind, ordeals were also sometimes used to try accusations of magic, idolatry, and heresy, as well as for accusations of incest and adultery.

17. Another reason a court might order an ordeal: the law prescribed judicial combat for the case at hand but one of the would-be combatants couldn't fight because, for instance, she was a woman and was unable to find a champion as a

replacement, or if the defendant had no specific accuser to combat because he had been accused on public suspicion.

18. In this sense, an ordeal's judgment and citizens' perceptions of its justice were joint products of the ordeal. On humans' fascination with justice proceedings and the interaction between judicial procedures' judgments and popular perceptions of their justice, see Robinson, Paul H., and Sarah M. Robinson. 2015. *Pirates, Prisoners, and Lepers: Lessons from Life outside the Law.* Lincoln, NE: Potomac Books.

19. Lea, *Superstition and Force,* 176.

20. Henry, Robert. 1789. *The History of Great Britain, From the First Invasion of it by the Romans . . .* vol. 2. Dublin: Printed for Byrne, 272.

21. The *Regestrum* actually contains 308 cases of ordeal outcomes, but in 100 of them, the ordeal was aborted before it produced a final result. Seventy-five of these cases were settled; in the other 25, the plaintiff withdrew his complaint. Some of these withdrawals came after the proband had already carried the hot iron but before his arm was unwrapped. It's very likely that these probands were innocent—or at least that their plaintiffs thought the ordeal would find them so. This is the only reason the plaintiffs would've withdrawn their complaints: to avoid a possible perjury charge, which could result if the ordeal exonerated the proband.

22. This is a conservative estimate. See n. 21.

23. The English pipe rolls contain references to a similar number of ordeal outcomes. But since they recorded only ordeal failures, this being the only instance in which ordeal outcomes had implications for the royal exchequer, we can't use data from them to illuminate the proportion of probands who passed ordeals. Kerr, Margaret H., Richard D. Forsyth, and Michael J. Plyley. 1992. "Cold Water and Hot Iron: Trial by Ordeal in England." *Journal of Interdisciplinary History* 22:573–595, 579; see also Klerman, "Settlement and the Decline of Private Prosecution," 12.

24. As legal historian Frederic Maitland put it, "success at the ordeal" was "far commoner than failure." Maitland, Frederic, ed. 1887. *Select Pleas of the Crown,* vol. 1: *A.D. 1200–1225.* London: B. Quaritch, xxiv.

25. Nor does the idea that ordeals were really just criminal punishments. Efficient criminal punishment imposes a high penalty on criminals with a low probability. Becker, Gary S. 1968. "Crime and Punishment: An Economic Approach." *Journal of Political Economy* 76:169–217. In the context of ordeals, that would mean one of two things. If the ordeal itself was supposed to be the punishment, it would mean using ordeals infrequently and boiling or burning everyone to whom

they were applied. But ordeals were used in exactly the opposite way: frequently and boiling or burning only a small percentage of those to whom they were applied. If, instead, the boiling or burning was supposed to be the punishment, it would mean boiling or burning only a small percentage of accused persons, not going through the costly process of pretending to boil or burn every accused person, which is what ordeals did. Closely related, if boiling or burning was supposed to be the punishment, ordeals were a highly inefficient way to administer it. Ordeals were multiday undertakings that involved masses, endless rituals, and so on. It's much cheaper to just boil or burn somebody instead. A third reason ordeals don't make sense as punishments is that they were applied "indiscriminately"— without regard to the accused's guilt or innocence, since this hadn't been determined yet. The theory of efficient punishment says something like, "Boil every tenth criminal." But ordeals boiled every tenth *accused person*, which is very different. Finally, while punishments have the same expected cost for both the guilty and the innocent, ordeals didn't; the innocent person's was much lower. The features of ordeals are consistent with ordeals as fact-finding procedures, not punishments.

26. He can also avoid the ordeal by fleeing his town. But for this example, I suppose that fleeing is more costly to Frithogar than confessing or settling, so he never considers this option.

27. Courts considered a person's refusal to undergo an ordeal to be evidence of his guilt. See, for instance, White, Stephen D. 1995. "Proposing the Ordeal and Avoiding It: Strategy and Power in Western French Litigation, 1050–1110." In Thomas N. Bisson, ed. *Cultures of Power: Lordship, Status, and Process in Twelfth-Century Europe*. Philadelphia: University of Pennsylvania Press, 115–116.

28. Howland, *Ordeals*, 12–13.

29. Henry, *History of Great Britain*, 273.

30. Howland, *Ordeals*, 12.

31. Thorpe, Benjamin. 2003. *Ancient Laws and Institutes of England*. Clark, NJ: Lawbook Exchange, 96. See also Howland, *Ordeals*, 7–9.

32. See, for instance, Colman, Rebecca V. 1974. "Reason and Unreason in Early Medieval Law." *Journal of Interdisciplinary History* 4:571–591; Brown, Peter. 1975. "Society and the Supernatural: A Medieval Change." *Daedalus* 104:133–151; and Ho, H. L. 2003–2004. "The Legitimacy of Medieval Proof." *Journal of Law and Religion* 19:259–298.

33. Howland, *Ordeals*, 12–13.

34. Under West Frisian Synod Law, in certain cases it was possible to appeal to the community to decide ordeal outcomes. Colman, "Reason and Unreason," 590. At least here, this also limited priests' power to find the outcomes they desired.

35. Rollason, D. W. 1988. *Two Anglo-Saxon Rituals: Church Dedication and the Judicial Ordeal.* Vaughan Paper No. 33, University of Leicester, 13.

36. Lea, Henry Charles. 1973. *The Ordeal.* Philadelphia: University of Pennsylvania Press, 72–73.

37. Some legal systems gave the plaintiff the right to choose the kind of ordeal the defendant would undergo, others the defendant. Typically, though, the court chose. Lea, *The Ordeal,* 45–46.

38. Kerr et al., "Cold Water and Hot Iron," 581.

39. Maitland, *Select Pleas,* nos. 12, 119.

40. Ibid., no. 101. Twelfth-century Icelandic law required men to undergo cold water ordeals and women to undergo hot water ordeals. In twelfth- and thirteenth-century England, where the data considered here come from, the law didn't make any provision for differential treatment of men and women in terms of hot or cold ordeals. Lea, *The Ordeal,* 46; and Kerr et al., "Cold Water and Hot Iron," 581.

41. Pilarczyk, Ian C. 1996. "Between a Rock and a Hot Place: Issues of Subjectivity and Rationality in the Medieval Ordeal by Hot Iron." *Anglo-American Law Review* 25:87–112, 101.

42. People with complete faith that ordeals are *iudicia Dei* entirely discount the possibility that ordeal outcomes are anything other than God's work. They interpret a 100 percent acquittal rate as evidence that 100 percent of probands were innocent, hence saved by God.

43. Before undergoing their ordeals, probands spent several days with the priests who officiated them, partaking in mass and prayer. This likely permitted priests to glean additional information about probands' guilt or innocence. Pilarczyk, "Between a Rock and a Hot Place," 98; Henry, *History of Great Britain,* 273. Such information supplemented that which priests received from observing defendants' willingness to undergo ordeals, facilitating their ability to identify and thus condemn a guilty defendant who took his chances with the ordeal because priests condemned too few probands, because he had figured out that ordeals were a sham, or because some other obstacle prevented perfect sorting.

44. Bartlett, *Trial by Fire and Water,* 160.

45. Ibid.

46. Lea, *The Ordeal,* 33.

47. Howland, *Ordeals,* 7–9.

48. Lea, *The Ordeal,* 34. See also, Bartlett, *Trial by Fire and Water,* 1.

49. Howland, *Ordeals,* 8.

50. Lea, *The Ordeal,* 36.

51. Howland, *Ordeals*, 11.

52. Ibid., 8. Also, note the biblical references again.

53. Lea, *Superstition and Force*, 257. See also Hyams, Paul R. 1981. "Trial by Ordeal: The Key to Proof in the Early Common Law." In Morris S. Arnold, Thomas A. Green, Sally A. Scully, and Stephen D. White, eds., *On the Laws and Customs of England*. Chapel Hill: University of North Carolina Press, 111.

54. Some high-ranking ecclesiastics questioned ordeals from their inception in Christendom, but their criticisms didn't gain ground until the twelfth century. When they did, ordeals began to disappear in some places toward the end of that century. Caenegem, R. C. van. 1991. *Legal History: A European Perspective*. London: Hambledon Press, 85–86. The widespread disappearance of ordeals didn't occur until the thirteenth century, however, after Pope Innocent III's edict.

55. Bartlett, *Trial by Fire and Water*, 83.

56. Numbers 5:11–31.

57. The next closest thing to a judicial ordeal in the Bible is the casting of lots that a crew of sailors undertakes to decide who offended God and caused a storm. Jonah 1:7.

58. Deuteronomy 6:16; Matthew 4:7.

59. There were other objections to ordeals. The most significant one I don't discuss was the argument that clerics shouldn't participate in activities that potentially involved the shedding of blood. For a detailed discussion of the theological issues driving the Fourth Lateran Council's ordeal prohibition, see Baldwin, John W. 1961. "The Intellectual Preparation for the Canon of 1215 against Ordeals." *Speculum* 36:613–636; and McAuley, "Canon Law and the End of the Ordeal."

60. Howland, *Ordeals*, 16.

61. Caenegem, *Legal History*, 87.

62. Ibid.

63. Bartlett, *Trial by Fire and Water*, 101. See also, Lea, *Superstition and Force*, 267.

64. Plucknett, Theodore F. T. 1956. *A Concise History of the Common Law*. 5th ed. Boston: Little, Brown, 118.

65. The sasswood tree is also called *Erythrophleum guineense*. In eastern and western Africa, animals are sometimes used as proxies for defendants, the former imbibing the poisonous mixture on the latter's behalf. Evans-Pritchard, E. E. 1937. *Witchcraft, Oracles and Magic among the Azande*. Oxford: Oxford University Press, 282; Davies, Louise Sarah. 1973. "The Sasswood Ordeal of the West Atlantic Tribes of Sierra Leone and Liberia: An Ethnohistoriographic Survey."

Master's thesis, Portland State University, 33. In Liberia, however, the defendants themselves imbibe the poisonous concoction.

66. Afzerlius, Adam. 1967. *Sierra Leone Journal 1795–1796*. Uppsala, Sweden: Studia Ethnographica Upsaliensa, 25. This description refers to sassywood in Sierra Leone but also characterizes its basics in Liberia.

67. Hening, E. F. 1850. *History of the African Mission of the Protestant Episcopal Church in the United States with Memoirs of Deceased Missionaries, and Notices of Native Customs*. New York: Stanford and Swords, 45. See also Tonkin, Elizabeth. 2000. "Autonomous Judges: African Ordeals as Dramas of Power." *Ethnos* 65:366–86, 368.

68. In 1961 the US Supreme Court guaranteed oath takers the right to not swear to a deity.

Tour Stop 3

1. Although wife-selling husbands and their wives overwhelmingly came from lower- and middle-class couples, wife buyers could be and, as I discuss later, often were people of more substantial means.

2. According to popular belief, a sold wife needed to be wearing a halter for the transaction to be valid. Pateman, Carole. 1988. *The Sexual Contract*. Stanford: Stanford University Press.

3. See, for instance, *Hampshire Advertiser & Salisbury Guardian*, May 12, 1849.

4. Menefee, Samuel Pyeatt. 1981. *Wives for Sale: An Ethnographic Study of British Popular Divorce*. New York: St. Martin's Press, 77. See also, *Leeds Mercury*, June 7, 1879.

5. Vaessen, Rachel Anne. 2006. *Humour, Halters, and Humiliation: Wife-Sale as Theater and Self-Divorce*. Master's thesis, Simon Fraser University, 26. Wife-selling husbands also used criers and newspaper ads to publicly notify purveyors that their wives' future debts were no longer their concern, since, as I discuss later, after a successful sale, such debts became the responsibility of their wives' purchasers. A wife sold at Tongmoor Gate, Bolton, for example, "On Wednesday was delivered up to the purchaser, according to contract, and on Thursday morning the bellman announced that her husband would not be answerable for any debts which she might in future contract." *Times*, June 15, 1831; see also, *Grub Street Journal*, March 27, 1735. Or consider this notice, which one husband published in the *Ipswich Journal*: "OCT. 29, SAMUEL BALLS sold his wife to ABRAHAM RADE in the parish of Blythburgh in this county for 1s. A halter was put round her, and she was resigned up to this Abraham Rade. No person or persons to

intrust her with my name, Samuel Balls, for she is no longer my right." Menefee, *Wives for Sale*, 97–98; see also *Morning Chronicle*, January 2, 1819.

6. Thompson, E. 1991. *Customs in Common*. London: Merlin Press, 419.

7. Menefee, *Wives for Sale*, 57.

8. *Morning Chronicle*, July 21, 1828.

9. Thompson, *Customs in Common*, 465.

10. *Times*, April 26, 1832.

11. Menefee, *Wives for Sale*, 52.

12. *Times*, September 25, 1822. See also *Examiner*, September 29, 1822.

13. *Morning Post*, September 16, 1803.

14. Menefee, *Wives for Sale*, 96. See also *Sheffield & Rotherham Independent*, January 13, 1877; *Derby Mercury*, January 5, 1881; *Newcastle Courant*, June 17, 1881.

15. Thompson, *Customs in Common*, 425. See also *Sheffield & Rotherham Independent*, October 16, 1880.

16. See, for instance, *Aberdeen Journal*, December 12, 1860; *Blackburn Standard*, January 15, 1868; *Graphic*, October 28, 1871; *Dundee Courier & Argus*, November 10, 1875; *Bristol Mercury*, February 10, 1877; *Pall Mall Gazette*, July 4, 1882; *York Herald*, May 9, 1884; *Nottinghamshire Guardian*, November 26, 1886; *Leeds Mercury*, July 15, 1887; *Birmingham Daily Post*, December 19, 1893; *Morning Chronicle*, June 13, 1797.

17. In our search, we came across a handful of potentially similar cases in Australia, New Zealand, and the American colonies. And a few newspaper reports referred to wife sales in France, Russia, and China. We omitted these cases, however, not only because we were interested in the English practice of wife sales but also because of their extreme rarity and a lack of substantiation for their authenticity.

18. Historians disagree about the total number of wife sales that may have taken place over this period. Lawrence Stone suggests that the number of cases collected by researchers so far is not terribly far from the actual number of wife sales that took place. Stone, Lawrence. 1990. *Road to Divorce*. Oxford: Oxford University Press, 148. In contrast, Thompson suggests that the cases collected thus far may be only the "tip of an iceberg." *Customs in Common*, 412.

19. Thompson, *Customs in Common*, 432. See also Kenny, Courtney. 1929. "Wife-Selling in England." *Law Quarterly Review* 45:494–497.

20. Menefee, *Wives for Sale*, 109.

21. Ibid., 93.

22. Thompson, *Customs in Common*, 433.

23. Ibid., 430.

24. *Chambers Journal of Popular Literature, Science and Arts* 1861, 240.

25. *Hampshire Telegraph and Sussex Chronicle etc.*, June 15, 1812.

26. *Public Advertiser*, June 25, 1791.

27. *World*, November 12, 1790. See also *Times*, April 26, 1832.

28. Of course, not every sold wife expressed happiness at her sale. Being auctioned like cattle, even if the result was to improve one's marital situation, was surely traumatic. Moreover, while wives' veto power ensured that they were sold only when they preferred their buyers to their existing spouses, this doesn't mean that a sold wife couldn't be saddened by the failure of her existing marriage or disappointed that joining her buyer, while the best of her available options, and thus desirable in a relative sense, was nevertheless undesirable in an absolute sense.

29. *Liverpool Mercury etc.*, April 20, 1821.

30. *Standard*, August 10, 1864.

31. *York Herald*, May 5, 1876.

32. Menefee, *Wives for Sale*, 50.

33. Ibid., 55.

34. Technically, husbands didn't acquire wives' real property per se but rather were "seised" of such property and enjoyed exclusive rights to revenues flowing from it. Baker, J. H. 2007. *An Introduction to English Legal History*. Oxford: Oxford University Press, 485. In practice this distinction meant simply that if husbands alienated their wives' land inheritances against their wives' will, their wives (or their heirs) could get them back after their husbands' death (though wives married after 1833 lost the ability to recover; see Crane, F. R. 1960. "Family Provision on Death in English Law." *New York University Law Review* 35:984–1000, 985). Wives, however, couldn't sell, rent, or mortgage their real property without their husbands' consent. Since both control rights and cash-flow rights to wives' real property devolved exclusively to their husbands upon marriage, for nearly all intents and purposes, wives lost, and husbands gained, ownership in the former's real property when they got married.

35. Hill, Bridget. 1994. *Women, Work, and Sexual Politics in Eighteenth-Century England*. Montreal and Kingston: McGill-Queen's University Press, 199.

36. Menefee, *Wives for Sale*, 61–62.

37. At least outside the nobility, the dominant pattern of family formation in eighteenth- and nineteenth-century England was for individuals to choose whom they wished to marry. The freely given consent of both parties had been considered a core tenet of marriage in England since the thirteenth century. The Hardwicke Act of 1753 mandated that minors secure parental consent prior to marriage, but

marriages without the consent of both parties wouldn't have been solemnized or considered valid by the courts. Stone, *Road to Divorce*, 50, 122–124. Even parental pressure in marriage choices had ebbed by the eighteenth century. Largely as a result of industrialization, English youths were earning wages earlier and were less susceptible to parental influence. Gillis, John R. 1985. *For Better, for Worse: British Marriages, 1600 to the Present*. New York: Oxford University Press, 119. Moreover, a relatively low life expectancy and high average age at first marriage meant that many young people had already been living away from home and may have even lost one or both of their parents by the time came to marry. Adair, Richard. 1996. *Courtship, Illegitimacy and Marriage in Early Modern England*. New York: Manchester University Press, 129–148; Hill, *Work, Women, and Sexual Politics*, 185. Stone notes that while it wasn't uncommon for lower-middle-class parents to seek out potential spouses for their children for the sake of financial betterment, children in poor and middle-class families nevertheless tended to enjoy substantial autonomy in their marital decisions. Stone, Lawrence. 1977. *The Family, Sex and Marriage in England 1500–1800*. New York: Harper and Row, 325–340.

38. However, if an ecclesiastic court determined that a marriage supposed to have taken place had not actually taken place because of the parties' ages, mental incompetence, sexual impotence, or fraud, the marriage-that-never-was was declared as much officially and the parties were free to remarry.

39. Criminal conversation was a trespass action arising from adultery. A person who slept with another man's wife encroached on the latter's property rights by depriving him of his wife's "comfort, fellowship and society." Baker, *An Introduction to English Legal History*, 456–457. This entitled such a husband to financial damages from his wife's lover.

40. Gibson, Colin S. 1994. *Dissolving Wedlock*. London: Routledge, 67. This wage is for the year 1871.

41. Stone, *Road to Divorce*, 432.

42. In 1857, when jurisdiction over actions granting judicial separation was moved to secular courts, the grounds for seeking such a separation were expanded to include desertion for over two years "without cause."

43. Stone 1990, *Road to Divorce*, 53.

44. Gibson, *Dissolving Wedlock*, 17. However, if after trying excommunication, an ecclesiastic court remained unable to compel payment, it could hand the matter over to secular authorities, who could imprison the deserter. Moreover, if a wife became a burden on her parish as the result of her husband's failure to provide her support, her husband could be "prosecuted by the Overseers of the Poor for criminal neglect." Stone, *Road to Divorce*, 195.

45. Menefee, *Wives for Sale*, 61–62.

46. Peaslee, R. J. 1902. "Separation Agreements under the English Law." *Harvard Law Review* 15:638–656. Although secular courts began reliably enforcing such contracts in the 1840s, ecclesiastic courts continued to deny their validity right up until the end of such courts' involvement in legal actions relating to marriage in 1857.

47. See Coase, R. H. 1960. "The Problem of Social Cost." *Journal of Law and Economics* 3:1–44.

48. Actually, Dr. Spock is more right here than I let on. The absence of legal property rights needn't in all cases preclude an individual from exercising some property rights, and thus bargaining power, in practice. For example, wives deprived of legal property rights might still have wielded bargaining power in their marriages by performing household services less diligently, shirking in employment, being less effective lovers, and more generally behaving in ways that made their husbands miserable. Of course, countering this was husbands' ability, in part legally supported, to make their wives miserable by physically or otherwise abusing them, confining them, and so on. In such cases, wife sales provided spouses "at war" with one another a means of exiting this situation to their mutual benefit.

49. Menefee, *Wives for Sale*, 78.

50. Of course, husband philandering also could lead to the conditions motivating couples to use wife sales. When a husband's affections were devoted elsewhere, his wife's valuation of him as husband was likely to drop significantly, making the wife more likely to want to exit. Thus, as one scholar notes, adultery appears to be the "most common . . . cause for sales . . . often, but not exclusively, by the wife." Menefee, *Wives for Sale*, 63.

51. *Illustrated Police News*, November 19, 1870.

52. *Times*, February 9, 1837. Explicit or implicit references to sold wives' extramarital relations are common in period sources. See, for instance, *True Briton*, August 11, 1797; *Oracle and Public Advertiser*, July 20, 1797; *Leeds Mercury*, April 7, 1827; *Times*, September 23, 1834; *Times*, February 3, 1837; *Times*, July 15, 1837; *Standard*, December 29, 1843; *Times*, December 30, 1843; *Manchester Times and Gazette*, June 20, 1848; *Blackburn Standard*, December 15, 1852; *Huddersfield Daily Chronicle*, January 3, 1873; *Sheffield & Rotherham Independent*, May 2, 1882; *Illustrated Police News etc.*, April 18, 1885; *Blackburn Standard: Darwen Observer, and North-East Lancashire Advertiser*, May 7, 1887.

53. *Illustrated Police News*, November 19, 1870. See also, Menefee, *Wives for Sale*, 2.

54. Menefee, *Wives for Sale*, 92.

55. See, for instance, *Liverpool Mercury etc.*, July 26, 1833; *Liverpool Mercury etc.*, April 6, 1849; *Lancaster Gazette and General Advertiser, for Lancashire, Westmorland, &c.*, December 6, 1806.

56. Menefee, *Wives for Sale*, 1.

57. Religious authorities' attitudes toward wife sales were equally confused. Some of them condemned wife selling as illegitimate. But other religious authorities seemed to legitimize wife selling, if not in word, in practice. By attaching relief-dependent wives to new husbands, wife sales eased the burden on welfare doles that religious authorities were charged with financing. Thus, far from aiding the prosecution of wife sales, several religious authorities encouraged them. See, for instance, Menefee, *Wives for Sale*, 56; Stone, *Road to Divorce*, 51; Thompson, *Customs in Common*, 437.

58. Indeed, one early nineteenth-century newspaper concluded "from the frequency of such occurrences" that England's magistrates "must either be ignorant or negligent of their duty." *Times*, February, 25, 1832.

59. Menefee, *Wives for Sale*, 146. As one scholar points out, in 1814–1815 "the legitimacy of ritual wife sale went unquestioned in the parishes of Effingham and Dorking," for instance. Thompson, *Customs in Common*, 438.

60. See, for instance, *Illustrated Police News*, November 24, 1883.

61. Shanley, Mary Lyndon. 1982. "'One Must Ride Behind': Married Women's Rights and the Divorce Act of 1857." *Victorian Studies* 25:355–376, 370.

62. Furthermore, this act expanded the grounds on which wives could seek a de jure divorce. Those grounds included their husbands' adultery aggravated by incest, bigamy, vicious cruelty, or desertion for a period of two years or more without "reasonable excuse," or rape, sodomy, or bestiality.

63. Rubenstein, Joseph Samuel. 1882. *The Married Women's Property Act, 1882* . . . London: Waterlow Bros. and Layton, 89–93.

64. Menefee, *Wives for Sale*.

65. See, for instance, ibid., 47.

66. See, for instance, Clark, Simon. 1999. "Law, Property, and Marital Dissolution." *Economic Journal* 109:C41–54.

Tour Stop 4

1. "Gypsy" may also refer to a few, ethnically non-Romani who "converted" by adopting Gypsy beliefs and were accepted by Gypsies into their community.

2. Supposedly the Roma were dubbed "Gypsies" because early Roma migrants claimed to hail from "Little Egypt."

3. Gypsies have been persecuted since this time, and in some countries, they

continue to suffer persecution today. For an account of the history of Gypsy persecution, see Hancock, Ian. 1987. *The Pariah Syndrome*. Ann Arbor, MI: Karoma.

4. Other prominent subgroups include the Finnish Kaale, located in northern Europe, whom I discuss later; the Iberian Kaale, located in Spain and neighboring countries; the Sinti, located in German-speaking Europe; and the Romanichal, located in the United Kingdom.

5. Sutherland, Anne Hartley. 2004. "Roma of the United States and Europe." In Carol R. Ember and Melvin Ember, eds., *Encyclopedia of Medical Anthropology: Health and Illness in the World's Cultures*, vol. 1. New York: Springer, 923–929. Gypsy population estimates vary wildly. They're notoriously unreliable because Gypsies don't typically classify themselves as such when asked; similar to other people on the fringe of society, they are among the least likely to be counted in official census measures; and officials commonly confuse Gypsies with various other ethnicities. All such estimates should therefore be taken with a grain of salt. That said, according to one estimate, there are between 3 million and 15 million Gypsies worldwide living in forty countries. Weyrauch, Walter Otto, and Maureen Anne Bell. 1993. "Autonomous Lawmaking: The Case of the 'Gypsies.'" *Yale Law Journal* 103:323–399, 340. An estimated 100,000 to 300,000 Roma live in the United States. Sutherland, "Roma of the United States and Europe."

6. The leadership positions filled by *bare* and *pure* aren't mutually exclusive. For example, an elder *baro* with a reputation for knowledge of *Romaniya*, or Gypsy law, which I discuss later, may also act as a *puro* and serve as a *krisnitori*, or Gypsy judge, which I also discuss later.

7. Gypsies' belief system, which defines ritually pure and impure or moral and immoral things/actions, has religious and spiritual aspects but "is more suggestive of magical emphasis than it is of a religious one." Trigg, Elwood B. 1973. *Gypsy Demons and Divinities*. Secaucus, NJ: Citadel Press, 27. In this sense, Gypsies' belief system might better be described as a folk religion, which may be adhered to alongside an at least professed belief in the dominant religion of the host society in which a Gypsy is located.

8. Though these categories may overlap. Contact with fecal matter, for example, is both physically and, according to *Romaniya*, spiritually polluting.

9. My description of *Romaniya* and Gypsy organization is based on the (largely overlapping) descriptions provided in: Brown, Irving. 1929. "The Gypsies in America." *Journal of the Gypsy Lore Society* 8:145–176; Clébert, Jean-Paul. 1963. *The Gypsies*. Baltimore, MD: Penguin Books; Lee, Ronald. 1967. "The Gypsies in Canada." *Journal of the Gypsy Lore Society* 46:38–51; Yoors, Jan. 1967. *The Gypsies*. Long Grove, IL: Waveland Press; Trigg, *Gypsy Demons*; Gropper, Rena C. 1975.

Gypsies in the City. Princeton, NJ: Darwin Press; Miller, Carol. 1975. "American Rom and the Ideology of Defilement." In F. Rehfisch, ed. *Gypsies, Tinkers and Other Travellers*. London: Academic Press; Sutherland, Anne. 1975. *Gypsies: The Hidden Americans*. Long Grove, IL: Waveland Press; Liégeois, Jean-Pierre. 1986. *Gypsies: An Illustrated History*. London: Al Saqi Books; Sway, Marlene. 1988. *Familiar Strangers: Gypsy Life in America*. Urbana: University of Illinois Press; Weyrauch and Bell, "Autonomous Lawmaking"; and Lee, Ronald. 1997. "The Rom-Vlach Gypsies and the Kris-Romani." *American Journal of Comparative Law* 45:345–392.

10. See, for instance, Fraser, Angus. 1992. *The Gypsies*. Oxford: Blackwell, 244.

11. There has been considerable debate about how to define "Gypsy" and, given the impossibility of doing so "correctly" (there being no such thing as a "true Gypsy"), some have suggested that no attempt should be made at all. While I appreciate this perspective, for many purposes—or at least my own—offering some definition, or otherwise distinguishing Gypsies from non-Gypsies, is necessary. The most sensible definition or distinction for my purpose is in terms of adherence to the basic ritual-purity/pollution beliefs/rules embodied in *Romaniya*, so that's the definition/distinction I use.

12. Sway, *Familiar Strangers*, 53–54.

13. See, for instance, Okely, Judith. 1983. *The Traveller-Gypsies*. Cambridge: Cambridge University Press, 82. The Gypsies in this case were Romanichal rather than Vlax Rom; however the *Romaniya* principle involved is shared.

14. Thompson, T. W. 1910. "Defilement by a Dog's Tongue." *Journal of the Gypsy Lore Society* 3:320.

15. On Gypsies' economic activities and strategies, see Lauwagie, Beverly Nagel. 1979. "Ethnic Boundaries in Modern States: Romano Lavo-Lil Revisited." *American Journal of Sociology* 85:310–337; Williams, Patrick. 1982. "The Invisibility of the Kalderash of Paris: Some Aspects of the Economic Activity and Settlement Patterns of the Kalderash Rom of the Paris Suburbs." *Urban Anthropology* 11:315–346; and Silverman, Carol. 1982. "Everyday Drama: Impression Management of Urban Gypsies." *Urban Anthropology* 11:377–398.

16. Weyrauch and Bell, "Autonomous Lawmaking," 337.

17. For an odd defense of Gypsy criminality, see Lee, "Gypsies in Canada."

18. Abusing and defrauding government welfare programs is also popular among some modern Roma.

19. Gypsies may lobby public officials to keep fortunetelling illegal in order to restrict entry into this industry. See Tyrner-Stastny, Gabrielle. 1977. *The Gypsy in Northwest America*. Olympia: Washington State American Revolution Bicentennial Commission, 38.

20. Many small, socially homogeneous societies that might rely on social ostracism as a form of governance don't confront this problem. Consider the Maghribi traders. Greif, Avner. 1989. "Reputations and Coalitions in Medieval Trade: Evidence on the Maghribi Traders." *Journal of Economic History* 49:857–882. This group was a commercial one, so here, punishing dishonest coalition agents benefited coalition members rather than costing them. A dishonest agent's debtors benefited directly by cutting him out of the coalition: they got to keep the money they otherwise would have had to repay. A dishonest agent's creditors benefited indirectly by doing so: they stopped sending him goods for which he probably wouldn't have paid anyway. Every group member had an incentive to punish dishonest agents. Gypsies aren't so lucky. Unlike the Maghribi traders, their societies aren't commercial ones. Gypsies don't have open accounts with all other members of their societies. Thus, not every society member, and often only a few, stands to benefit from ostracizing an individual who has had bad dealings with another, particularly when that individual lies outside one of a Gypsy's immediate communities, such as his *kumpania*.

21. Gypsy nomadism is less pronounced today than it was in past. However, nomadism remains an important part of some Gypsies' lifestyles and identities.

22. Brown, "Gypsies in America," 158. In the past, Gypsies arranged debris on roadsides and configured bits of torn cloth in nearby tree branches to communicate messages to passing fellow Roms. But it's doubtful that these messages could've communicated the identity of rule breakers.

23. Historically, Gypsies' societies are different from most other small, socially homogeneous societies in this respect. Consider, again, the Maghribi traders. Greif, Avner. 1993. "Contract Enforceability and Economic Institutions in Early Trade: The Case of the Maghribi Traders." *American Economic Review* 83:525–548. Maghribi traders were dispersed geographically. They therefore had to communicate information about coalition members' misconduct over long distances. But coalition members knew each other's locations and thus how to contact one another. Gypsies often didn't.

24. Trigg, *Gypsy Demons*, 54.

25. See, for instance, Weyrauch, Walter O. 2001. "Oral Legal Traditions of Gypsies and Some American Equivalents." In Walter O. Weyrauch, ed., *Gypsy Law: Romani Legal Traditions and Culture*. Berkeley: University of California Press, 246, 263; Weyrauch and Bell, "Autonomous Lawmaking," 351; Trigg, *Gypsy Demons*, 55, 71.

26. Block, Martin. 1939. *Gypsies: Their Life and Their Customs.* New York: AMS Press, 14.

27. In some cases, Gypsies also permit women to attend and participate.

28. The precise procedures followed by the *kris* differ by the source one considers and likely by Gypsy community. In broad form, however, the operation is similar: judges oversee the interactions of community members at courts convened to resolve stubborn disputes; those interactions yield a consensus about the dispute and how it should be resolved; that consensus is reflected in the judges' decision or verdict.

29. Gropper, *Gypsies in the City*, 90.

30. Weyrauch and Bell, "Autonomous Lawmaking," 385.

31. Clébert, *The Gypsies*, 160–161. See also Thompson, "The Uncleanness of Women," 40.

32. Weyrauch and Bell, "Autonomous Lawmaking," 359.

33. See, for instance, Brown, "Gypsies in America," 165; Gropper, *Gypsies in the City*, 100.

34. Yoors, *The Gypsies*, 177.

35. Brown, "Gypsies in America," 165.

36. Ibid., 166. See also, Lee, "The Rom-Vlach Gypsies," 370.

37. Block, *Gypsies*, 176.

38. Yoors, *The Gypsies*, 6.

39. Grönfors, Martti. 1997. "Institutional Non-Marriage in the Finnish Roma Community and Its Relationship to Rom Traditional Law." *American Journal of Comparative Law* 45:305–327, 317.

40. Grönfors, Martti. 1986. "Social Control and Law in the Finnish Gypsy Community: Blood Feuding as a System of Justice." *Journal of Legal Pluralism* 24:101–125, 103.

41. Kaale Gypsies do in fact "divorce," just as they "marry"—clandestinely and without acknowledgment. However, since, like marriage, divorce officially doesn't exist, the potential conflicts that require adjudication when Vlax marriages end don't, and in fact can't, create conflicts when Kaale (non-)marriages end.

42. Grönfors, "Institutional Non-Marriage," 309. Kaale kin groups tend to pursue economic activities in separate territories, each viewing a territory as its own. However, this "cartelization" is different from the Vlax's. Kaale cartelization is informal and tacit. Vlax cartels are explicit inter-*kumpania* agreements to restrict competition.

43. Grönfors, "Institutional Non-Marriage," 317.

44. Miller, "American Rom," 46.

45. See, for instance, Grönfors, "Social Control and Law"; Acton, Thomas, Susan Caffrey, and Gary Mundy. 1997. "Theorizing Gypsy Law." *American Journal of Comparative Law* 45:237–249.

46. Except that popular thinking about the Hatfield and McCoy feud, which sees it as a bloodbath, is mostly incorrect. In fact, few actually died.

47. Not quite: senior Gypsy women, for instance, play important roles in running extended households and negotiating the terms of family members' marriages, which offer opportunities for misbehavior.

48. Department of Justice and Federal Bureau of Investigation. 2004. *Crime in the United States 2004*. Available at http://www.fbi.gov/ucr/cius_04/persons_arrested/table_38–43.html.

49. Miller, "American Rom," 43.

50. Weyrauch and Bell, "Autonomous Lawmaking," 343.

51. Sutherland, *Gypsies*, 263.

52. Okely, *The Traveller-Gypsies*, 168. See also Sutherland, *Gypsies*, 262.

53. Lee, "The Rom-Vlach Gypsies and the Kris-Romani," 381.

54. Ibid., 384.

55. Ibid., 390.

56. Weyrauch and Bell, "Autonomous Lawmaking," 357.

57. Lee, "The Rom-Vlach Gypsies and the Kris-Romani," 360.

Tour Stop 5

1. Neither "Francia" nor "France," however, precisely describes the territory in question. Little offers a more accurate description: "The territory in question . . . stretches from the valley of Charente, which lies about 120 miles south of the Loire, north and east to the valley of the Rhine." Little, Lester K. 1993. *Benedictine Maledictions: Liturgical Cursing in Romanesque France*. Ithaca, NY: Cornell University Press, xiv.

2. Little, *Benedictine Maledictions*. See also Little, Lester K. 1975. "Formules monastiques de malédiction au IXe et Xe siècles." *Revue Mabillon* 58:377–399; Little, Lester K. 1979. "La morphologie des malédictions monastiques." *Annales* 34:43–60; Little, Lester K. 1998. "Anger in Monastic Curses." In Barbara H. Rosenwein, ed. *Anger's Past: The Social Uses of an Emotion in the Middle Ages*. Ithaca, NY: Cornell University Press; Geary, Patrick J. 1979. "L'humiliation des saints." *Annales* 34:27–42; Geary, Patrick J. 1991. *Furta Sacra: Thefts of Relics in the Central Middle Ages*. Princeton: Princeton University Press; Geary, Patrick J. 1995. *Living with the Dead in the Middle Ages*. Ithaca, NY: Cornell University Press; Rosenwein, Barbara H., Thomas Head, and Sharon Farmer. 1991. "Monks and Their Enemies." *Speculum* 66:764–796; Bitel, Lisa M. 2000. "Saints and Angry Neighbors: The Politics of Cursing in Irish Hagiography." In Sharon Farmer and Barbara H. Rosenwein, eds., *Monks and*

Nuns, Saints and Outcasts: Religion in Medieval Society. Ithaca, NY: Cornell University Press.

3. Little, *Benedictine Maledictions*, 9.

4. Clamors weren't technically curses. But clerics could use them to invoke curse-like effects, sometimes in tandem with proper maledictions.

5. Little, *Benedictine Maledictions*, 28.

6. Ibid., 23.

7. On excommunication in the Middle Ages, see Vodola, Elizabeth. 1986. *Excommunication in the Middle Ages.* Berkeley: University of California Press.

8. Little, *Benedictine Maledictions*, 43.

9. See, for instance, Dunbabin, Jean. 1985. *France in the Making, 843–1180.* Oxford: Oxford University Press; Bisson, Thomas N. 1994. "Feudal Revolution." *Past and Present* 142:6–42.

10. Little, *Benedictine Maledictions*, 53.

11. Rosenwein, Head, and Farmer, "Monks and their Enemies," 771. Maledictions weren't the only means that communities of monks and canons used to improve their property protection, but they were a central one.

12. Little, *Benediction Maledictions*, 9.

13. Ibid., 60.

14. Ibid., 25.

15. Ibid., 56.

16. Just because a strongman believes in the Bible, and thus biblical prohibitions on theft, doesn't mean he might not be willing to appropriate church property. He may see himself as reclaiming property that's legitimately his rather than stealing, or for some other reason view his seizure as justified in God's eyes. Even a strongman who sees his appropriation as theft may be willing to steal if the discounted cost of the punishment he expects God to mete out to him when he dies is lower than the present benefit he expects to enjoy from the stolen property. In both cases, maledictions add to the expected cost of appropriation and shift much of that cost to the present, reducing the likelihood that the strongman will take from the church.

17. The Book of Psalms is another hotbed of biblical cursing. See, for instance, Psalms 35:6, 35:8, 55:15, 69:22, 69:23, 69:25, 69:28, 83:17, 109:8, 109:9, 109:10, 199:11, 109:12, 109:13, 140:10. On Psalm maledictions, see Curraoin, Tomás Ó. 1963. "The Maledictions in the Psalms." *Furrow* 14:421–429.

18. Little, *Benedictine Maledictions*, 60–61.

19. Geary, *Living with the Dead in the Middle Ages*, 96. Since the effectiveness of maledictions depended on people's belief in them, predators may have had an

incentive to develop disbelief in clerical curses in particular and the Bible/Christianity more generally. I've found no evidence that they tried to do so. This isn't to say that self-delusion isn't possible or never occurred. But deliberately changing one's religious beliefs is difficult. A Christian who desires to drop his religious beliefs confronts a time-consistency problem. At the time he considers doing so, he believes that in the future, when his belief is gone, he'll be damned as a consequence. To be willing to deliberately jettison one's belief in Christianity, one must therefore already significantly disbelieve in it.

20. Little, *Benedictine Maledictions*, 56.

21. Some maledictions came closer to being actually specific—the kind that might in principle be falsified. One, for example, fulminates: "May they drain out through their bowels, like the faithless and unhappy Arius." Another declares: "May they be buried with dogs and asses; may rapacious wolves devour their cadavers." Little, *Benedictine Maledictions*, 36, 47. But even these curses remain vague ("When are my bowels supposed to drain out again?") and promise punishments that can't be verified until the target is dead (looking up at one's grave from the depths of hell: "They weren't kidding! Rapacious wolves really are devouring my cadaver!"). Moreover, the same maledictions that offered more specific curses also offered completely nonspecific ones.

Tour Stop 6

1. See Evans-Pritchard, E. E. 1937. *Witchcraft, Oracles and Magic among the Azande*. Oxford: Oxford University Press,. See also Evans-Pritchard, E. E. 1928. "Oracle-Magic of the Azande." *Sudan Notes and Records* 11:1–53; Evans-Pritchard, E. E. 1929. "Witchcraft (*Mangu*) amongst the A-Zande." *Sudan Notes and Records* 12:163–249; Evans-Pritchard, E. E. 1932. "The Zande Corporation of Witchdoctors." *Journal of the Royal Anthropological Institute of Great Britain and Ireland* 62:291–336; Evans-Pritchard, E. E. 1933. "The Zande Corporation of Witchdoctors." *Journal of the Royal Anthropological Institute of Great Britain and Ireland* 63:63–100; Evans-Pritchard, E. E. 1935. "Witchcraft." *Africa* 8:417–422; Evans-Pritchard, E. E. 1960. "A Contribution to the Study of Zande Culture." *Africa* 30:309–324; Evans-Pritchard, E. E. 1960. "The Organization of a Zande Kingdom." *Cahiers d'Études Africaines* 1:5–37; Evans-Pritchard, E. E. 1963. "A Further Contribution to the Study of Zande Culture." *Africa* 33:183–197; Evans-Pritchard, E. E. 1963. "The Zande State." *Journal of the Royal Anthropological Institute of Great Britain and Ireland* 93:134–154; Evans-Pritchard, E. E. 1965. "A Final Contribution to the Study of Zande Culture." *Africa* 35:1–7; Evans-Pritchard, E. E. 1971. *The Azande: History and Political Institutions*. Oxford: Clarendon Press.

2. Of course, this isn't to say that the oracles used in other societies have the same features or function as the Azande's *benge*. Perhaps the most famous oracle in history, for instance, the Oracle of Delphi, had different features and performed a different function. On the economics of the Delphic oracle, see Iannaccone, Laurence R., Colleen E. Haight, and Jared Rubin. 2011. "Lessons from Delphi: Religious Markets and Spiritual Capitals." *Journal of Economic Behavior and Organization* 77:326–338.

3. See, for instance, Santandrea, Fr. S. 1938. "Evil and Witchcraft among the Ndogo Group of Tribes." *Africa* 11:459–481; White, C. M. N. 1948. "Witchcraft Divination and Magic among the Balovale Tribes." *Africa* 18:81–104; Retel-Laurentin, Anne. 1969. *Oracles et Ordalies chez les Nzakara*. Paris: Mouton; Almquist, Alden. 1991. "Divination and the Hunt in Pagibeti Ideology." In Philip M. Peek, ed., *African Divination Systems*. Bloomington: Indiana University Press; Bascom, William R. 1941. "The Sanctions of Ifa Divination." *Journal of the Royal Anthropological Institute of Great Britain and Ireland* 71:43–54; Gray, Natasha. 2001. "Witches, Oracles, and Colonial Law: Evolving Anti-Witchcraft Practices in Ghana, 1927–1932." *International Journal of African Historical Studies* 34:339–363; Zeitlyn, David. 1993. "Spiders In and Out of Court, or, 'The Long Legs of the Law': Styles of Spider Divination in their Sociological Contexts." *Africa* 63:219–240.

4. I consider private oracular usage among the Azande in cases of low-grade conflict. I don't consider others, such as Zande political rulers' use of oracles for "matters of state."

5. Nearly all commoners are accused of witchcraft on occasion. However, individuals who are habitually accused of witchcraft may develop reputations as witches and be viewed differently.

6. Evans-Pritchard, *Witchcraft, Oracles and Magic*, 107.

7. Mair, Lucy. 1974. *African Societies*. Cambridge: Cambridge University Press, 224. There are actually three distinct *benge* consultation roles, in principle performed by three different people: the poison owner; the oracular operator, who prepares the poison and administers it to the fowl; and the questioner, who poses the questions of interest to *benge*. In practice, the owner and questioner are nearly always the same person. To more clearly explain oracular usage, I consider the case where he's also the operator.

8. Evans-Pritchard, "Witchcraft," 421.

9. Evans-Pritchard, *Witchcraft, Oracles and Magic*, 100.

10. Evans-Pritchard, "Witchcraft," 420.

11. As in the case of the drivers, I assume here that the neighbors choose

their behaviors simultaneously or, what's equivalent, without knowing what their counterpart has chosen at the time they make their own choice.

12. Wagner, Günter. 1937. "Witchcraft among the Azande." *Journal of the Royal African Society* 36:469–476, 472.

13. Evans-Pritchard, *Witchcraft, Oracles and Magic*, 330.

14. I say "in principle" with respect to the possibility of manipulation because, as I discuss later, no Zande would ever in fact manipulate *benge* given his belief in, and respect for, the poison oracle. In the words of Evans-Pritchard, "A man would not tamper with the poison because he does not believe it possible to alter the verdict of an oracle once the poison has been administered to a fowl." Ibid., 328.

15. However, variation in poison doses and fowl size may not be as important for deciding the oracle's result as one might think. According to Evans-Pritchard, "It is evident that the number of doses is not the sole determining cause of death. Out of 8 fowls" he observed in oracular consultations, "3 died after a single dose while 5 survived after 2 doses had been administered." Likewise, "it would seem that the size of the fowls is not the deciding factor, since in the tests described above a tiny chicken survived two doses while a very much larger chicken died after a single dose, and the largest fowl of them all, almost a fully developed bird, though it recovered, was very strongly affected by two doses, whereas a tiny chicken showed no discomfort after the same number of doses. I have often seen large fowls die and small fowls recover after the same number of doses." Ibid., 326. The particular poison the Azande use in *benge* may have been selected precisely because of its largely invariant effects on fowls of different sizes and those effects' independence from the dose administered.

16. Ibid., 323.

17. Ibid.

18. Ibid., 336.

19. Ibid., 330.

20. Ibid., 328.

21. Douglas, Mary. 1966. *Purity and Danger*. London: Routledge, 128.

22. Evans-Pritchard, *Witchcraft, Oracles and Magic*, 123.

23. If such a situation does occur, the Azande can appeal to a third oracle, such as a trusted community member's, or their chief's, to deliver a definitive verdict. Political involvement, which is otherwise nearly nonexistent in private *benge* use, can find a role here.

24. Wagner, "Witchcraft among the Azande," 472.

25. Evans-Pritchard, "Oracle-Magic of the Azande," 21, 49. This distin-

guishes the poison oracle from several lesser oracles that the Azande also consult for various purposes, which, according to Zande thinking, may err. When a Zande consults one of these other oracles, he accepts its declaration as definitive only if that declaration is confirmed by *benge*.

26. Evans-Pritchard, *Witchcraft, Oracles and Magic*, 89.

27. Ibid., 96–97.

28. Colonization didn't destroy Zande political organization but rather grafted colonial-created laws and legal institutions onto it. It took several decades for colonial rule to have a noticeable effect on Zande society. In the years of Evans-Pritchard's stay, some changes were apparent, but at the level of ordinary citizens, Zande society operated largely as it had before colonization. Private oracular usage, for example (though not governmental usage), remained essentially unaffected. On the ways in which colonization did affect Zande life and over a longer period, see Reining, Conrad C. 1966. *The Zande Scheme*. Evanston, IL: Northwestern University Press.

29. Evans-Pritchard, *Witchcraft, Oracles and Magic*, 101.

30. Evans-Pritchard, "Witchcraft (*Mangu*) amongst the A-Zande," 201.

31. Ibid., 199.

32. Ibid., 248.

33. Douglas, *Purity and Danger*, 128.

Tour Stop 7

1. Here's the link: http://www.youtube.com/watch?v=HAlnUnw1WSI.

2. I consider only ecclesiastical vermin trials. Most treatments of these trials overlap with, or essentially recount, E. P. Evans's discussion of them: Evans, E. P. 1906. *The Criminal Prosecution and Capital Punishment of Animals*. New York: Dutton. See, for instance, Anonymous. 1880. "Animals as Offenders and as Victims." *Albany Law Journal* 21:265–267; Westermarck, Edward. 1906. *The Origin and Development of the Moral Ideas*, vol. 1. New York: Macmillan; Carson, Hampton L. 1917. "The Trial of Insects: A Little Known Chapter of Medieval Jurisprudence." *Proceedings of the American Philosophical Society* 56:410–415; Mc-Namara, Joseph P. 1927–1928. "Animal Prisoner at the Bar." *Notre Dame Lawyer* 3:30–36; Weiss, Harry B. 1937. "The Criminal Prosecution of Insects." *Journal of the New York Entomological Society* 45:251–258; Beach, Frank A. 1950. "Beasts before the Bar." *Natural History Magazine* 59:356–359; Beirnes, Piers. 1994. "The Law Is an Ass: Reading E. P. Evans' *The Medieval Prosecution and Capital Punishment of Animals*." *Society and Animals* 2:27–46; Humphrey, Nicholas. 2002. *The Mind Made Flesh: Essays from the Frontiers of Psychology and Evolution*. Oxford:

Oxford University Press; Girgen, Jen. 2003. "The Historical and Contemporary Prosecution and Punishment of Animals." *Animal Law* 9:97–133. I don't consider the prosecution of domestic animals, such as dogs and pigs, which took place in secular courts. On these trials, which are often considered alongside those I address, see, for instance, Evans, *Criminal Prosecution of Animals*; Finkelstein, J. J. 1981. "The Ox That Gored." *Transactions of the American Philosophical Society* 71:1–89. On the trial of inanimate objects, which are also occasionally considered alongside vermin trials, see, for instance, Hyde, Walter Woodburn. 1916. "The Prosecution and Punishment of Animals and Lifeless Things in the Middle Ages and Modern Times." *University of Pennsylvania Law Review* 64:696–730; Hyde, Walter Woodburn. 1917. "The Prosecution of Lifeless Things and Animals in Greek Law: Part I." *American Journal of Philology* 38:152–175; Hyde, Walter Woodburn. 1917. The Prosecution of Lifeless Things and Animals in Greek Law: Part II." *American Journal of Philology* 38:285–303; Pietz, William. 1997. "Death of the Deodand: Accursed Objects and the Money Value of Human Life." *ReS: Anthropology and Aesthetics* 31:97–108. On the trial of animals under Roman law, see Jackson, Bernard S. 1978. "Liability for Animals in Roman Law: A Historical Sketch." *Cambridge Law Journal* 37:122–143.

3. On class action lawsuits in fourteenth-century France, see Cheyette, Frederic. 1962. "Procurations by Large-Scale Communities in Fourteenth-Century France." *Speculum* 37:18–31; and Lewis, P. S. 1968. *Later Medieval France*. New York: St. Martin's Press, 279–280.

4. See, for instance, Dannenfeldt, Karl H. 1982. "The Control of Vertebrate Pests in Renaissance Agriculture." *Agricultural History* 56:542–559. A few pest control methods of the day were more effective; mouse traps are one example, poison another. But even these displayed ignorance: one pest control manual suggests using butter to poison rats.

5. Dannenfeldt, "Control of Vertebrate Pests," 558.

6. Ibid., 555. Early modern citizens' pesticide superstition is still less surprising when you consider the beliefs that Europe's intellectual elite held during the same period. These individuals thought, for example, that the continent was infested by witches who had intercourse with demons and stole men's genitals in their sleep. Compared to this, simple farmers' belief that God might be able to exterminate pests is unremarkable.

7. Evans, *Criminal Prosecution of Animals*, 18.

8. Ibid., 117.

9. Ibid., 96–97.

10. Ibid., 112.

11. Cohen, Esther. 1993. *The Crossroads of Justice: Law and Culture in Late Medieval France*. Leiden: E. J. Brill, 120.

12. Evans, *Criminal Prosecution of Animals*, 98–99.

13. Ibid., 32–33.

14. Ibid., 110–111. This vermin trial occurred outside the France-Italy-Switzerland region, in Mainz, Germany.

15. Jamieson, Philip. 1988. "Animal Liability in Early Law." *Cambrian Law Review* 19:45–68, 51.

16. Dinzelbacher, Peter. 2002. "Animal Trials: A Multidisciplinary Approach." *Journal of Interdisciplinary History* 32:405–421, 410.

17. Evans, *Criminal Prosecution of Animals*, 107.

18. On the early history of tithes, in particular in England, see Clarke, Henry W. 1887. *The History of Tithes from Abraham to Queen Victoria*. London: George Redway. On the early history of tithes in Italy, see Boyd, Catherine E. 1946. "The Beginnings of the Ecclesiastical Tithe in Italy." *Speculum* 21:158–172. On the history of tithes and tithe legislation more generally, see Lansdell, Henry. 1906. *The Sacred Tenth, or, Studies in Tithe-Giving, Ancient and Modern*, vol. 1. London: Society for Promoting Christian Knowledge.

19. Scott, James C. 1987. "Resistance without Protest and without Organization: Peasant Opposition to the Islamic *Zakat* and the Christian Tithe." *Comparative Studies in Society and History* 29:417–452, 439.

20. Le Roy Ladurie, Emmanuel, and Joseph Goy. 1982. *Tithe and Agrarian History from the Fourteenth to the Nineteenth Centuries*. Cambridge: Cambridge University Press, 15. See also Le Roy Ladurie, Emmanuel. 1987. *The Royal French State, 1469–1610*. Oxford: Blackwell, 39, 157; Beik, William. 2009. *A Social and Cultural History of Early Modern France*. Cambridge: Cambridge University Press, 49.

21. On the details of the politics of tithing in sixteenth- and seventeenth-century Bresse, see Vester, Matthew. 2004. "The Bresse Clergy Assembly and Tithe Grants, 1560–80." *Sixteenth Century Journal* 35:771–794; Vester, Matthew. 2010. "Who Benefited from Tithe Revenues in Late-Renaissance Bresse?" *Catholic Historical Review* 96:1–26.

22. Le Roy Ladurie and Goy, *Tithe and Agrarian History*, 27. See also Scott, "Resistance without Protest," 444–446; Vester, "Who Benefited from Tithe Revenues," 11.

23. Scott, "Resistance without Protest," 444–445.

24. On the history of excommunication, see Lea, Henry C. 1869. *Studies in Church History: The Rise of Temporal Power, Benefit of Clergy, Excommunication*.

London: Sampson Low, Son, and Marston; and Vodola, *Excommunication in the Middle Ages*.

25. The Church could level its supernatural sanctions at particular individuals, whole communities (interdiction), or generically against all people who engaged in particular proscribed behaviors. Heretics, for instance, became excommunicants when they took up heretical thinking whether the Church identified them individually as heretics or not. Such "excommunication *latae sententiae*," as it was called, excommunicated offenders "in the act." Formal proclamations of excommunication or anathema that might follow merely recognized offenders' pre-existing spiritual state publicly. The pope and his bishops commanded authority to define sins, excommunicate, and anathematize. Lower-level clerics hurled supernatural sanctions under the former's jurisdiction. The pope or bishops granted them permission to do so individually or en masse through synods and councils.

26. In some times and places in the early modern period, the traditional tithe collected on agricultural output wasn't important or didn't exist. In these cases, ecclesiastics relied on the "sacramental tithe" to earn revenue: charging for Easter communion, baptism, funerals, and so on. Torre, Angelo. 1992. "Politics Cloaked in Worship: State, Church and Local Power in Piedmont 1570–1770." *Past and Present* 134:42–92, 54. Of course, weak believers or nonbelievers, who might not seek such sacraments, might not pay these tithes either. Thus, here too, bolstering belief in ecclesiastics' supernatural sanctions was critical to collecting revenue.

27. See, for instance, Baumgartner, Frederic J. 1995. *France in the Sixteenth Century*. New York: St. Martin's Press, 35; Lansdell, *The Sacred Tenth*, 229; Tanner, Norman P., ed. and trans. 1990. *Decrees of the Ecumenical Councils: From Nicea I to Vatican II*. Washington, DC: Georgetown University Press; Tausiet, María. 2003. "Excluded Souls: The Wayward and Excommunicated in Counter-Reformation Spain." *History* 88:437–450, 441; Waterworth, J., trans. 1848. *The Canons and Decrees of the Sacred and Oecumenical Council of Trent*. London: Burns & Oates, 269.

28. Villien, Antonine. 1915. *A History of the Commandments of the Church*. St. Louis: B. Herder, 348–349.

29. Jackson, Samuel Macauley, ed. 1911. *The New Schaff-Herzog Encyclopedia of Religious Knowledge*, vol. 9. New York: Funk and Wagnalls, 454.

30. See, for instance, Lansdell, *The Sacred Tenth*, 191.

31. Tanner, *Decrees of the Ecumenical Councils*, 258.

32. Ibid., 256.

33. Lansdell, *The Sacred Tenth*, 196.

34. Cameron, Euan. 1984. *The Reformation of the Heretics: The Waldenses of the Alps, 1480–1580*. Oxford: Clarendon Press, 94.

35. Audisio, Gabriel. 1999. *The Waldensian Dissent: Persecution and Survival c.1170–c.1570*. Cambridge: Cambridge University Press, 97.

36. Cameron, *Reformation of the Heretics*, 81.

37. Ibid.

38. Audisio, *The Waldensian Dissent*, 55.

39. Cameron, *Reformation of the Heretics*, 82.

40. Audisio, *The Waldensian Dissent*, 55.

41. Cameron, *Reformation of the Heretics*, 73.

42. Audisio, *The Waldensian Dissent*, 58.

43. Russell, Jeffrey Burton. 1972. *Witchcraft in the Middle Ages*. Ithaca, NY: Cornell University Press, 220.

44. Russell, *Witchcraft in the Middle Ages*, 243.

45. Ibid., 220.

46. Vizetelly, Henry. 1882. *A History of Champagne*. London: Henry Sotheran, 24–25.

47. Evans, *Criminal Prosecution of Animals*, 107. See also Dinzelbacher, "Animal Trials," 409.

48. Evans, *Criminal Prosecution of Animals*, 42.

49. Hyde, "Prosecution and Punishment of Animals," 705.

50. Jamieson, "Animal Liability in Early Law," 51.

51. Evans, *Criminal Prosecution of Animals*, 112–113.

52. Finkelstein, "The Ox That Gored," 64.

53. Evans, *Criminal Prosecution of Animals*, 105.

54. Jamieson, "Animal Liability in Early Law," 52.

55. My map considers European vermin trials between 1450 and 1700. But a handful of cases that fall outside this region and time period also exist. These include a late seventeenth-century case in Canada, an early eighteenth-century case in Denmark, an early eighteenth-century case in Brazil, an early nineteenth-century case in Denmark, and two cases in Croatia in the second half of the nineteenth century.

56. Evans' book is an expanded and elaborated version of two articles he published twenty-two years earlier. See Evans, E. P. 1884. "Bugs and Beasts before the Law." *Atlantic Monthly* 54:235–246, and Evans, E. P. 1884. "Medieval and Modern Punishment." *Atlantic Monthly* 54:302–308.

57. On the Vaudois, their concentrations in these areas, and their resistance to persecution, see Cameron, *Reformation of the Heretics*; Cameron, Euan. 2000. *Waldenses: Rejections of the Holy Church in Medieval Europe*. Oxford: Blackwell; Treesh, Susanna K. 1986. "The Waldensian Recourse to Violence." *Church History*

55:294–306; Audisio, Gabriel. 1990. "How to Detect a Clandestine Minority: The Example of the Waldenses." *Sixteenth Century Journal* 21:205–216; Audisio, *The Waldensian Dissent*. See also Tice, Paul. 1829. *History of the Waldenses, from the Earliest Period to the Present Time*. Philadelphia: American Sunday School Union; Beattie, William. 1838. *The Waldenses, or, Protestant Valleys of Piedmont, Dauphiny, and the Ban de la Roche*. London: George Virtue.

58. With the exception of Apulia and Calabria, these areas had long histories as heretic enclaves. Audisio, *The Waldensian Dissent*, 33, 61.

59. Carlson, I. Marc. 2004. "Witchcraft Trials." Available at http://www.personal.utulsa.edu/marc-carlson/carl4.html.

60. Russell, *Witchcraft in the Middle Ages*, 248.

61. Ibid., 219.

62. Furthermore, Catholics didn't monopolize witch trials. After the Reformation, Protestants got in on the act too. I'm unable to identify witch trials that may have been conducted by Protestants rather than Catholics, so my data consider all witch trials.

63. Russell, *Witchcraft in the Middle Ages*, 268.

64. Cohen, Esther. 1986. "Law, Folklore, and Animal Lore." *Past and Present* 110:6–37, 33. See also Jamieson, "Animal Liability in Early Law," 51; Dinzelbacher, "Animal Trials," 410.

65. See, for instance, Le Roy Ladurie, Emmanuel. 1974. *The Peasants of Languedoc*. Urbana: University of Illinois Press.

66. Nicholls, David. 1984. "The Social History of the French Reformation: Ideology, Confession and Culture." *Social History* 9:25–43, 37.

67. In 1529 there was a tithe strike in Lyon. The vermin trials conducted there, however, appeared circa 1500—likely in an attempt to bolster belief, which ecclesiastics may have sensed was waning.

68. Garrisson, Janine. 1995. *A History of Sixteenth-Century France, 1483–1598: Renaissance, Reformation and Rebellion*. London: Macmillan, 4.

69. Ibid., 115.

70. Small, Graeme. 2009. *Late Medieval France*. New York: Palgrave Macmillan, 45.

71. I assigned these cases as follows: a ninth-century trial of serpents in France to the period from 851 to 900; a fourteenth-century trial of flies in Germany to the period from 1301 to 1350; and three fifteenth-century trials (caterpillars, worms, and beetles) in Switzerland and Germany to the period from 1451 to 1500.

72. Garrisson, *A History of Sixteenth-Century France*, 10, 15.

Tour Stop 8

1. If memory serves, this contest was called "Book It!" I think it may have been run nationally, so some of you may remember it too.

2. In medieval documents, trial by battle is commonly called *"duellum"* (or *"bellum"* in Domesday Book). Subsequent commentators on this institution called it "trial by battle" or "judicial combat," both of which terms I use.

3. I consider trial by battle as England's legal system used it to decide real property cases. I don't consider it as that system used it to decide criminal cases. Nor do I consider trial by battle in England's courts of chivalry, where judges used it to decide cases involving affronts to honor, treason, and criminal acts committed abroad. On judicial combat in criminal appeals, see Russell, M. J. 1980. "II Trial by Battle and the Appeals of Felony." *Journal of Legal History* 1:135–164. On judicial combat in courts of chivalry, see Russell, M. J. 2008. "Trial by Battle in the Court of Chivalry." *Journal of Legal History* 29:335–357. For classic treatments of the variety of single combats that have existed and their history in England and elsewhere, see Selden, John. 1610. *The Duello or Single Combat*. London: Printed by G. E. for I. Helme; Gibson, William Sidney. 1848. *On Some Ancient Modes of Trial, Especially the Ordeals of Water, Fire, and Other Judicia Dei*. London: Printed by J. B. Nichols and Son; Nielson, George. 1891. *Trial by Combat*. New York: Macmillan. For examples of judicial duels outside England in cases unrelated to land disputes, see Howland, *Ordeals*.

4. Prior to 1179, in a small minority of cases, unilateral ordeal, witness investigation, testimony of a hundred court, and jury-like arrangements were used to resolve property disputes. See, for instance, Caenegem, R. C. van, ed. 1990–1991. *English Lawsuits from William I to Richard I*. 2 vols. London: Selden Society, 50–51, 82.

5. At some point in the mid-twelfth century, it became impossible to initiate a real property dispute without such a writ. Watkin, Thomas Glyn. 1979. "Feudal Theory, Social Needs and the Rise of the Heritable Fee." *Cambrian Law Review* 10:39–62.

6. The plaintiff purchased the writ, which also ordered a particular court to hear the case. This could be a seignorial, county, or royal court.

7. The detailed descriptions we have of trial by battle in property cases describe judicial combats that took place after the eleventh and twelfth centuries, but their general features are applicable across time.

8. Russell, M. J. 1959. "Hired Champions." *American Journal of Legal History* 3:242–259, 243.

9. Ibid.

10. Ibid.

11. The law never even theoretically restricted who defendants could use as champions. Unlike plaintiffs, defendants could also choose to fight in person, though they almost never did. Later law eliminated this choice, requiring defendants to use champions too.

12. Russell, "Hired Champions," 257. In 1275 judges dropped the charade, abandoning the plaintiff's champion-witness requirement. Russell suggests that the earlier in the period one goes, the more likely it is that plaintiffs' champions were genuine witnesses. "Hired Champions," 243.

13. They also promised that they hadn't concealed charms on their bodies or resorted to sorcery.

14. Russell, M. J. 1983. "Trial by Battle Procedure in Writs of Right and Criminal Appeals." *Law and History Review* 51:123–134, 126.

15. Russell, "Trial by Battle Procedure," 126. This injunction was made at a seventeenth-century judicial combat in a criminal case.

16. Ibid., 127. This announcement concluded a thirteenth-century trial by battle.

17. Russell, M. J. 1980. "I Trial by Battle and the Writ of Right." *Journal of Legal History* 1:111–134, 116, 123. See also Lea, *Superstition and Force*, 122. Since, at least in theory, the plaintiff's champion had to be a witness, also in theory, a champion who lost a battle, hence his law, might be prevented from working again as a champion for a plaintiff (though, it would seem, not for a defendant). In view of courts' unwillingness to uphold the plaintiff champion-witness rule in the first place, however, it's doubtful that they would've, or in some cases could've, enforced this rule.

18. Officially, the Anglo-Norman period closed with the end of Stephen I's reign in 1154. The Angevin period followed it. Thus, trial by battle in the years I'm concerned with (1066–1179) overlapped both periods. Despite this overlap and the resulting technical inaccuracy, for want of a better term, when I refer to "Norman England" or "Anglo-Norman" legal institutions, I'm referring to England during the period between 1066 and 1179.

19. Technically it's incorrect to speak of land ownership in the context of feudal relations. One should speak of land tenure and holding or seisin. As I discuss later, tenant ownership didn't emerge until the late twelfth and early thirteenth centuries. References in my discussion to land "ownership," "buying and selling" land, and so on should therefore be understood to refer to land tenure/holding and the buying and selling of tenures/holdings.

20. For a good summary of substitution, subinfeudation, and the problems that alienation created, see Baker, *An Introduction to English Legal History*.

21. Feudal property arrangements created another problem relating to land alienation: a lord's decision to alienate his property could injure his tenant, whom the alienation would place under a new lord ("attornment"). Some restrictions also developed to regulate this issue. For instance, a tenant couldn't be forced to do homage to a new lord who was his enemy.

22. The Church—itself a large landowner—had its own rules governing land alienations. To alienate Church land, a landholder required the prelate's and chapter's consent. Cheney, Mary. 1985. "Inalienability in Mid-Twelfth-Century England: Enforcement and Consequences." In Stephan Kuttner and Kenneth Pennington, eds. *Proceedings of the Sixth International Congress of Medieval Canon Law*. Vatican City: Biblioteca Apostolica Vaticana.

23. Palmer, Robert C. 1985. "The Economic and Cultural Impact of the Origins of Property: 1188–1220." *Law and History Review* 3: 75–396, 387.

24. Russell, "Hired Champions," 259.

25. Ibid., 246.

26. Ibid., 254. Smerill's contract paid him only £8 if he defeated his opponent and nothing if he failed to land a blow. However, hiring a champion, even under a contract as advantageous to his employer as the one Heynton negotiated, still involved some unrecoverable expense. Heynton, for example, had to collateralize his promise to pay Smerill in the event of Smerill's victory with a parcel of his property. The cost of this collateralization, while probably minimal, was nevertheless positive and couldn't be recovered regardless of Smerill's outcome.

27. Ibid., 254–256.

28. Ibid., 246.

29. Ibid., 255.

30. If he couldn't access credit markets, a tenant might nevertheless be able to get his lord to chip in to help him hire an appropriate champion. If, in his lord's eyes, the tenant was the higher-valuing user of the contested property, the lord would've been happy to do so. In this situation, the lord would've lost revenue if his tenant lost the case, since the challenger was less productive and thus would've produced less for him. If the tenant wasn't the higher-valuing user in his lord's eyes, the lord probably wouldn't have been willing to chip in to help the tenant hire a good champion. Such a tenant would therefore have been more likely to lose his land. But this outcome would still be efficient, as the higher-valuing user would tend to win the contested property. Thus, lords may have had an interest to behave in ways that promoted efficient land allocation under trial by battle.

31. Russell, "I Trial by Battle," 120. The law also limited judicial combat to cases involving land worth at least 50 pence and exempted some towns from battle.

32. This is an example of what economists call "rent seeking." See Tullock, Gordon. 1967. "The Welfare Costs of Tariffs, Monopolies, and Theft." *Western Economic Journal* 5:224–232; Krueger, Anne. 1974. "The Political Economy of the Rent-Seeking Society." *American Economic Review* 64:291–303.

33. One of my favorite economists, David Friedman, makes a point about efficient punishment that's closely related to my point here. See Friedman, David. 1999. "Why Not Hang Them All: The Virtues of Inefficient Punishment." *Journal of Political Economy* 107:S259–S269. As he notes, when punishment is efficient, the cost borne by the punished is captured as a corresponding benefit by someone else. However, this property of efficient punishment is what may actually make it inefficient. When the cost borne by the punished is captured as a corresponding benefit by someone else, the benefit's recipient is given an incentive to seek rents. Using auctions to allocate disputed property rights creates an analogous problem.

34. Technically, it would be an imperfectly discriminating all-pay auction with asymmetric valuations. See, for example, Nti, Kofi O. 1999. "Rent-Seeking with Asymmetric Valuations." *Public Choice* 98:415–430, which models a rent-seeking contest with asymmetric valuations.

35. A sealed, high-bid auction produces the same total spending as a first-price, ascending-bid auction. See Hirshleifer, Jack, and John G. Riley. 1992. *The Analytics of Uncertainty and Information.* Cambridge: Cambridge University Press, 373. Thus, a violent auction's fraud-inducing superiority to a regular auction applies equally to the sealed, high-bid auction, which one might consider an equally obvious alternative to trial by battle's violent auction.

36. Russell, "Hired Champions," 254.

37. Pollock, Frederick. 1898. "The King's Justice in the Early Middle Ages." *Harvard Law Review* 12:227–242, 240.

38. Pollock, "The King's Justice," 240. Disputants paid a fee to the king when they settled.

39. Caenegem, *English Lawsuits*, 639.

40. Ibid., 265.

41. Ibid., 265.

42. Russell, "I Trial by Battle," 129.

43. Eighty-two of these cases were criminal, 38 were civil, and 2 were uncertain. Unfortunately, Russell doesn't provide an analogous breakdown of criminal and civil cases for the 598 total. This would provide a better idea about what was happening in land disputes, which is the case I'm concerned with. Still, the logic behind settling in criminal cases tried by battle is the same. These figures should

therefore provide a reasonable estimate of the frequency with which disputants settled land disputes under judicial combat.

44. Not all of these failures of battle to transpire necessarily reflected settling by the parties, however. A battle may not have transpired for other reasons, such as one party's failure to appear or a disputant's death. Or the records of the battle itself may have been lost.

45. Pollock, Frederick. 1912. "The Genius of the Common Law. II. The Giants and the Gods." *Columbia Law Review* 12:291–300, 295.

46. Russell, "Hired Champions," 245.

47. On the accoutrements of judicial combat, see Russell, M. J. 1983. "Accoutrements of Battle." *Law Quarterly Review* 99:432–442.

48. See, for instance, Truman, Ben C. 1884. *The Field of Honor: Being a Complete and Comprehensive History of Duelling in All Countries*. New York: Fords, Howard, and Hulbert, 33.

49. Gilchrist, James 1821. *A Brief Display of the Origin and History of Ordeals* . . . London: Printed for the author by W. Bulmer and W. Nicol, 32.

50. Russell, "I Trial by Battle," 124.

51. The judicial system doesn't seem to have charged citizens for the pleasure of taking in a trial. This is sensible: charging may have reintroduced legal officials' incentive to rent seek.

52. Pollock, "Genius of the Common Law," 295. See also Pollock, Frederic. 1904. "Expansion of the Common Law. III. The Sword of Justice." *Columbia Law Review* 4:96–115, 105.

53. For a discussion of some of these reforms, see Biancalana, Joseph. 1988. "For Want of Justice: Legal Reforms of Henry II." *Columbia Law Review* 88:433–536.

54. See, for instance, Caenegem, R. C. van. 1973. *The Birth of the English Common Law*. Cambridge: Cambridge University Press; Caenegem, R. C. van, ed. 1958–1959. *Royal Writs in England from the Conquest to Glanvill*. London: Selden Society; Milsom, S. F. C. 1976. *The Legal Framework of English Feudalism*. Cambridge: Cambridge University Press; Palmer, Robert C. 1985. "The Origins of Property in England." *Law and History Review* 3:1–50.

55. See, for instance, Pollock and Maitland, *History of English Law*; Milsom, *Legal Framework of Feudalism*; Thorne, S. E. 1959. "English Feudalism and Estates in Land." *Cambridge Law Journal* 17:193–209.

56. Palmer, "Economic and Cultural Impact of the Origins of Property," 385. See also, Thorne "English Feudalism," 194, 209.

57. Palmer, "Economic and Cultural Impact of the Origins of Property," 385 (also 382).

58. Russell, "I Trial by Battle," 127.

59. However, England didn't formally abolish trial by battle until 1819.

Acknowledgments

1. The following chapters use, with publisher permission, my previous work from the following journal articles: Chapter 2: Leeson, Peter T. 2012. "Ordeals." *Journal of Law and Economics* 55:691–714. © The University of Chicago Press; Leeson, Peter T., and Christopher J. Coyne. "Sassywood." *Journal of Comparative Economics* 40:608–620. © Elsevier. Chapter 3: Leeson, Peter T., Peter J. Boettke, and Jayme S. Lemke. 2014. "Wife Sales." *Review of Behavioral Economics* 1:349–379. © Now Publishers. Chapter 4: Leeson, Peter T. 2013. "Gypsy Law." *Public Choice* 155:273–292. © Springer Science + Business Media. Chapter 5: Leeson, Peter T. 2014. "God Damn: The Law and Economics of Monastic Malediction." *Journal of Law, Economics, and Organization* 30:193–216. © Oxford University Press. Chapter 6: Leeson, Peter T. 2014. "Oracles." *Rationality and Society* 26:149–169. © Sage Publications. Chapter 7: Leeson, Peter T. 2013. "Vermin Trials." *Journal of Law and Economics* 56: 811–836. © The University of Chicago Press. Chapter 8: Leeson, Peter T. 2011. "Trial by Battle." *Journal of Legal Analysis* 3:341–375. © Oxford University Press. Appendix: Leeson, Peter T. 2012. "Ordeals." *Journal of Law and Economics* 55:691–714. © The University of Chicago Press; Leeson, Peter T. 2013. "Vermin Trials." *Journal of Law and Economics* 56:811–836. © The University of Chicago Press; Leeson, Peter T. 2011. "Trial by Battle." *Journal of Legal Analysis* 3:341–375. © Oxford University Press.

Appendix

1. I assume that although the legal system doesn't initially know whether j is guilty or innocent, j knows whether he's guilty or innocent. This is a reasonable assumption in most cases, but it may not always hold. Suppose j's legal system doesn't distinguish between justifiable homicide and ordinary murder. In this case, although j may know that he killed the person he's accused of killing, he may be uncertain about his guilt from God's perspective and hence the ordeal's.

2. I assume that all ordeal alternatives require the defendant to pay the same price, θ.

3. I assume that j and the priest know j's level of belief. Medieval priests knew how often their community members went to church, received communion, confessed, and practiced other religious rituals, so this assumption seems reasonable. Others observe j's level of belief imperfectly.

4. My explanation is an application of Kamenica and Gentzkow's theory of

Bayesian persuasion. Kamenica, Emir, and Matthew Gentzkow. 2011. "Bayesian Persuasion." *American Economic Review* 101:2590–2615.

5. Tullock, Gordon. 1980. "Efficient Rent-Seeking." In James M. Buchanan, Robert D. Tollison, and Gordon Tullock, eds. *Toward a Theory of the Rent-Seeking Society*. College Station: Texas A&M Press.

6. Since lower bid-payment collections under trial by battle make challenging another person's property right cheaper, you may wonder whether trial by battle might actually provide a stronger incentive to fraudulently challenge others' land claims than a regular auction would. For a certain range of disputants' valuations of the contested property, at least, the answer is no. Recall that trial by battle's auction is imperfectly discriminating. In contrast, a regular auction is perfectly discriminating. Because of this, the expected payoff of challenging another person's property claim under trial by battle is often *lower* than it is under a regular auction. Specifically, when $v_T < \frac{v_D\sqrt{5} - v_D}{2}$ the higher-valuing disputant's expected payoff of challenging the lower-valuing disputant's property under trial by battle is less than it is in a regular auction; hence, his incentive to fraudulently challenge that person's property is too.

Index